A Serious Hobby

Hobby

Inside Rock's Greatest Generation

b y

CHARLIE BERMANT

ISBN-10: 1475126603
EAN-13: 9781475126600

"Most rock journalism is people who can't write interviewing people who can't talk for people who can't read."

—F r a n k   Z a p p a

For Lili Bermant, 1927-2011

The Note Stops Here

Lately I've wondered if this whole music thing has gotten out of hand, and whether it has been a tremendous waste of time. It's impossible to calculate the money I've spent on recorded music, concerts, magazines and books along with the energy spent getting there, which I could have expended doing something more useful like writing books about things that matter and raising children who could change the world.

Just kidding.

The songs from the 1960s and 1970s have lived on longer than anyone had ever imagined. The convergence of sound, light and culture created experiences so potent that many of the participants have spent the subsequent years attempting to recreate them. For this you always go back to the well for another viewpoint, a lost witness with additional details recalled, or someone who has decided that it's time to tell the truth.

Sometimes it seems there is no bottom, that the romanticized times represent an infinite multicolored elephant from long ago, and every few months another blind man comes forth to describe how it felt at the time.

This book provides a street-level view of some of the era's best music and those responsible. The pieces are presented in more or less chronological order, with digressions into areas that are best understood outside of a timeline.

They appear here as they were first published, again more or less. The grammar and punctuation has been cleaned up and made more consistent. On a few occasions I added a word or two to clarify what I probably meant to say at the time. Throughout I strove to add clarity without losing authenticity.

When I graduated college I walked into the pre-security *Washington Post* newsroom to claim my job as a rock critic. I received a rude awakening when I was told to go work for a local paper for a few years, work my way up and then give them a call later. I never made it back, at least not as a full-time music critic. While I pursued different areas I'd always come back to music writing.

There would be someone I wanted to meet, or a particularly cool album about which I wanted to provide some insight. It became a serious hobby, and was done for enjoyment's sake. I never had to write any of these pieces or talk to any of these people. I did it because I wanted to. So if I lack the critical insight and access of someone who has done this full time for years, I also lack the jaded cynicism that happens when you've done anything for too long.

`Everything new cycles back to the old, so this collection is bracketed by two pieces about Tom Rush. This 1974 story was the first interview I ever conducted, with anyone. Most professional writers start small with a teacher or someone on the team. I aimed higher. But at the time I had no idea that I was to become a professional writer.

The second piece was conducted backstage at a high school auditorium where Rush was performing 35 years later. He was polite enough to say he remembered the first time we had met. His answers hadn't changed that much, although my confidence level was higher and I had become a better storyteller.

Port Townsend, WA; April 2012

Contents

Early Days: 1974-1977

A *few months out of high school my friend Dave and I went to the Cellar Door in Georgetown to see Jackson Browne, who had released his first album earlier that year. After the show Dave, who was driving, proposed that we go up to the dressing room for a few minutes. I demurred but really had no choice, so Dave told the guy at the door some tale about playing there the day before and forgetting his guitar strap. There wasn't a lot of security in 1972.*

Once upstairs I melted into the background, or as much as I could in that tiny room, Aside from Browne and his guitarist, David Lindley, there were four guys who I recognized as the Eagles, who had just had a hit with Browne's "Take it Easy." I don't remember much, except that I was too scared to say anything and had to call my parents from a pay phone on the wall to tell them I'd be late. I'm pretty sure that neither Browne nor the Eagles heard this conversation; if they did they were too polite to laugh.

Dave's memory is a bit better: "Don Henley and Glenn Frey were very outgoing, especially Frey — boisterous, funny, joking around. Everybody was fairly nice though. I don't remember anyone treating us badly and I don't think we stayed too long, maybe 30-45 minutes."

I remember this as a stressful situation, since I really didn't belong in that dressing room. I would have liked to talk to Jackson and Glenn and Don about their lives and music, and tell them about mine but I didn't have the license to do so.

I returned to the Cellar Door dressing room two years later as a guest of Tom Rush, to conduct my very first interview. I'd learned that being a reporter allowed me to be in the room, and that musicians and actors always need to go to their dressing room and it was the best place to find them in order to make an interview request. This strategy worked a few months later when I used that tactic to approach Diana Rigg.

As with a regular conversation you can always tell when a writer doesn't have much confidence or skill. They provide too much extraneous detail. This changes as time passes. In journalism this is known as getting published. In real life it's called growing up.

You can't take all of the green away, but the early pieces included here are the ones that seemed successful at the time and gave me a reason to continue. I still relied on cliches and was trying to press too many thoughts into too few column inches; laboring under the misconception that the reader cared about these folks half as much as I did and needed to know every detail. It takes a while for young writers to learn how to leave stuff out.

Writers learn by doing, soon enough I learned how to relax. But these early pieces set the stage for a transition from being just a listener to a participant.

Rush Tears Them Up

Tom Rush, Washington DC, September 1974
Interviewed at the Cellar Door, Washington, DC.

Tom Rush is one of the most constant figures in folk (or folk rock) music. His sensitive interpretations and originals have played upon the emotions of national audiences for close to ten years. Although he is an accomplished (but not prolific) composer, he is best known for his renditions of other artists' songs and his uncanny ability to scout out such material by other composers. *The Circle Game*, released in 1967, featured songs by then-unknown Joni Mitchell, Jackson Browne and James Taylor.

"Joni came up and introduced herself in Detroit and did a guest set in a club where I was working," Rush said. "She did a few songs and subsequently sent me the tapes because I kept asking her for them. Jackson I heard on tape. I recorded a couple of his songs before I ever met him. James I met in New York through a producer when I was looking for new material."

Rush was playing the club circuit around the time of the release of *Circle Game*. He is still primarily a club performer, and in recent years his Cellar Door appearances have become somewhat of a Washington Tradition. He plays the Georgetown club at least once a year and attracts much of the same crowd, as well as new converts to the Rush mystique.

Mitchell, Browne and Taylor fans will not soon see their favorites in this small club. They must seek out larger venues to view these artists, the price such excessive fame demands is loss of intimacy in performance. Rush accounts for the situation thusly:

"They (Mitchell, Browne and Taylor) are really good. I thought they were very good and I wasn't surprised they were successful. I make records and it's the company's job to sell them as best they can, I'm more of an interpreter than any of those people, they write 99 percent of their own stuff. I don't write all that much because I'm lazy. I do a lot of other people's stuff, which I think is a worthwhile undertaking."

Rush talks about the songs featured on his latest album.

"Wayne Berry wrote two of the songs. He's just put out an album in RCA and he's a good writer. There's only one of mine—that's "No Regrets," which is a remake. I wanted to do the song again to try and get it better. I hope I succeeded, There are two by Lee Clayton, who is a country-ish writer from Los Angeles. Waylon Jennings has done some of his stuff. In fact, I think Waylon's album is called *Ladies Love Outlaws*, as is mine.

"I am fond of finding writers and songs that people don't know, exposing them to new material. Dylan stuff gets done so much that it doesn't intrigue me from that aspect. I've been thinking of doing a record of a series of tunes that have been famous by various different people. I'd only do them if I had something radically different to say about the tunes than anybody has said so far.

"I haven't written anything lately...actually, I've written a couple of tunes but they really didn't fit the album. One of them, 'Glory Road,' I've been doing onstage."

Rush recently dissolved his partnership with Trevor Veitch, the phenomenal singer/songwriter/guitarist of "no fixed address." Rush worked as a solo for a short time and now plays with Orphan, previously a working band. On the current tour, Orphan does a set of its own material and then returns to back Rush.

"Trevor's a great guitar player. I think we worked pretty well together, but we did it for four years and I think we both felt it was time to do something else for a change. We never did seem to put together the right combination of people. One of the reasons I'm currently working with Orphan is that I didn't feel I had the stamina to put together another band from scratch. It's really hard to find four or five guys who can live together and play together on the road.

"I think I might do a live album with Orphan, although not in the immediate future. The next record will probably be a studio record, and the following one may be live. I'm going to the studio in January. My next record will be out either a year from now or possibly less than that. It'll be out in the early spring or fall."

Tom Rush has proved that in the music business the best aren't always the best-known, and that originality is more than merely composition. His years of recording have yielded some of the best records of his genre. Anyone fortunate enough to have ever seen him perform could not suppress the impulse to dance to "Who Do You Love" or avoid being deeply moved by "Urge for Going" or "Child's Song."

"That one always tears them up."

THE MONTGOMERY COLLEGE SPUR, September 1974

More Than Just a "Peel:" Diana Rigg Speaks

Diana Rigg, Washington, DC March 1975
Interviewed at the Kennedy Center, Washington DC

Where do you like working the best?

I prefer the theater because I like people. I think it is the best barometer of where you are and what you are doing. The reaction to you on the stage, if you play for a laugh and you get it, it's the most wonderful feeling in the world. If you don't get it, then you need to go away, think about it and find out why. In movies you never know. In fact, in movies, the way they cut, they can give you the laugh. Onstage it's up to you. No one else can take the blame. It's much more challenging.

You have a reputation as a sex symbol. When I asked for questions from my friends they all suggested a proposition, or a proposal.

It's not something that I pursue myself. I'll never do pinup photographs. I'm incapable of taking them seriously. One is sexual, and it's quite nice to be regarded as a sex symbol if you don't have to work at it. You know, the boredom of having your boobs jacked up. I don't go for that at all.

For the most part, the parts I've played haven't been very sexual at all. Except for *The Avengers*, which catered to every sexual appetite. Including flagellation, the leather kick, the shoes, bondage, it was all there.

People idolize you for that role.

If one wasn't admired, one wouldn't be where one was in the sense that I wouldn't have a lead in a play. I wouldn't be offered parts and the extension of it is that people buy tickets to see what you are doing. The bad part of that is idolization, because I don't think I'm qualified to be idolized. I know too much about myself, and I know plenty of other people they should be idolizing that are worthy of it. It's a twentieth-century sort of thing that has gathered momentum in the entertainment industry. A lot of people court it, pretend to be what they are not, and swell the ranks of idolaters.

How do you choose your roles?

Sheer perversity, right across the board. I've done a horror movie. I've done crappy bits and pieces of this, that and the rest of it. I've done a total failure of a TV series in California. I follow my appetite, that's all.

The horror movie—"Theater of Blood"—was something else.

It was marvelous. Vincent Price is much underrated, and this film proved exactly what he could do. He could play Shakespeare on his head. Unfortunately, it's the business in America to categorize people, out them in a mold and never let them leave it.

And you played a nun in "In This House of Brede."

It worked. Once we started working in convents and began to chat with the nuns, who were marvelous women. Bright and contemporary, very intelligent. Everyone thinks they are sort of saints, boring and dreary and twirling their beads all the time. It aggravated me once I'd met them and gotten close to them, how badly they've been treated by screenwriters.

How do you react to bad notices?

It doesn't affect you for very long, but the initial effect is one of disappointment because you've failed. They thought your interpretation of the part was wrong. On the other hand it's one of the hazards of this business. Whatever you do you are going to be criticized. Like when you are being interviewed it can be by someone who finds you unsympathetic, who doesn't like you and you come out sounding like a right old shitbag. In the end I've developed for myself an attitude, which says I am what I am. If you don't like it, then it's your preference but I refuse to compromise. I refuse to be ingratiating.

A lot of critics get a following as to exactly how bitchy they can be about performers. It's a bit Roman in a sense, a bit Nero-ish, you know, the thumbs-up or thumbs-down and then you are hacked to pieces. They can do it in a very witty way which makes them readable. Like John Simon, he said I looked like a bridge with insufficient flying buttresses.

What's most important to you right now?

I think its necessary to travel. And I think at your age—I sound like a grandma. I don't mean just see the sights like the Parthenon and St Paul's Cathedral but to really come to terms with another culture .This is absolutely essential in this life. The remote countries fascinate me. I was brought up In India. I've been to Russia, Czechoslovakia, Hungary, Romania, Persia. I travel a lot. I spend all my money on travel. When I'm not working I just go. In a country where you don't speak the language you are very vulnerable. It's a good exercise to be vulnerable, to have to ask people the way, to have to learn the language, Not necessarily fluently, but essential words like "food."

Why did you agree to this interview?

Because you're young, you're beginning and because I'm bored with old jaded journalists asking a lot of fucking stupid questions, if you excuse my language. You've heard it all before.

Unpublished, edited transcript of a March 1975 interview conducted for The Montgomery College Spur

Mick Ronson

When David Bowie and the Spiders from Mars barnstormed America almost two years ago they managed to astound anyone who saw them perform. The Spiders maintained a phenomenal energy level throughout their performance; they were simply the most exciting rock act to tour the States in eons. Almost all the band's material was written by Bowie, and he was responsible for the staging as well as providing the focal point for the futuristic show. But his focus was challenged by Mick Ronson, a guitarist transcending the role of accompanist. Bowie may have been the intended star of the show, but much of the productions dynamism and outrageousness originated from Ronson.

Mick Ronson first teamed with David Bowie in 1970 and was instrumental in the arranging and production of such notable albums as *Hunky Dory*, *Ziggy*

Stardust and *Aladdin Sane*. In performance his white noise style playing was balanced by Trevor Bolder's bass gymnastics, and his recorded work showed he was as skilled in studio technique as he was in live playing. Bowie dissolved the Spiders in 1973 to pursue other ventures, and the always subordinate Ronson began his solo career.

The second Ronson album, *Play Don't Worry* (RCA APL 1-0681), recently released, is far better than his debut, *Slaughter on Tenth Avenue*. The first album was excellent in parts, but Ronson seemed unsure of himself. The result was the inclusion of weak material and poor mixing of the vocals. *Play*, on the other hand, is a more assured and independent effort. Ronson had a hand in writing only four of the album's songs, but he is credited with all guitar and most vocal work and he tries his hand at bass, synthesizer, keyboards and drums. He handles all the material as wholeheartedly as if it were his own, In contrast to *Slaughter*, the production and mixing on the new album is almost faultless. Only on one occasion, a rendition of "The Girl Can't Help It," are the vocals lost in the mix.

The printing of Ronson's pleasantly unsophisticated lyrics emphasizes their awkwardness, but they sound much better than they read.

Ronson's live role with the Spiders was that of lead guitarist; his tonal expertise combined with sheer volume produced some wonderfully frenetic guitar work. For the most part his playing is more subdued on his own records, but at times he releases all inhibition. His guitar wails through "Angel No. 9" and he recalls his live work with "White Light/White Heat." Fast-fingered bassist Trevor Bolder and pianist Mike Garson recreate their Spider roles. Overzealous drummer Aynsley Dunbar sometimes borders on sloppiness, but adequate percussion work is supplied throughout the album by Paul Francis, Richie Dharma and Tony Newman.

The overall tone of the album is gentler than "Slaughter" or any of the work with Bowie. This is felt through two Ronson originals, that lead off side two, "Play Don't Worry" and "Hazy Days." Laurie Heath's "This is for You" is embellished by soothing multi-tracked harmonies, and Sid Sax leads an ample string section through "The Empty Bed."

The original version of "The Empty Bed," "Io Me Ne Andrei" was done by Italian crooner Claudio Baglioni. Ronson's English lyrics are not a literal translation, but the ultra-romantic sentiments are left intact. An Italian music/English lyric fusion, "Music Is Lethal," was attempted on "Slaughter on Tenth Avenue" but it failed because the involved lyrics were unsuited to the frail melody. "The Empty Bed," on the other hand, works perfectly. Ronson has become an assured vocalist, signing in his best saccharine-tinged voice. His vocal proficiency allows him to handle the hard and the soft with equal finesse.

According to his manager, Ronson is planning a large hall tour with Ian Hunter this spring. In the immediate future, Ronson will probably serve Hunter in much the same way he served Bowie. But however he expresses himself, be it solo or with Bowie, Hunter or even Jagger, Mick Ronson is a presence that will be felt and *Play Don't Worry* is an excellent sample of his musical talent.

THE WASHINGTON POST, March 9, 1975

Back on Course With The Bee Gees

Interviewed at the Holiday Inn, downtown Philadelphia, PA

BARRY GIBB IS pleased. It is a good season for the Bee Gees, (Barry and his brothers, Maurice and Robin) whose new *Main Course* album is earning them substantial praise. "Jive Talkin'," the first single from the LP is well on its way to becoming their first significant hit since 1972's 'Run To Me."

"I'm absolutely knocked out," Barry says of the album. "I can't take it off my cassette player." And rightly so. *Main Course* is an unqualified success, one of 1975's best albums, and an artistic and a commercial triumph.

"We're into music now that is better than anything, we've ever done," he continues. "Therefore it's our main course. It also means we're on the right track." If the reaction to their recent American concert tour is any indication, they certainly are on the right track to regaining the powerful commercial hold they had prior to their two-year separation in 1969.

Experimentation

A good deal of *Main Course* draws freely from the current disco influence, but the result is neither derivative of that style or compromising of the Bee Gees own. "Songbird" and "Come On Over" are archetypal Bee Gees songs, not unlike many of their previous melodic successes. Other R&B influenced tracks, such as "Nights On Broadway" and 'Wind Of Change" are results of successful experimentation with the new style.

"Being in America when we recorded helped us," says Barry. "When we wrote the album we were listening to a lot of radio, and we tried to get an idea of what people wanted to hear — from anyone. The main vein at the moment is soul, R&B, disco, so we moved into that area. There's so much of this kind of music going on, around us and we want to do it but we want to do it better if we can."

Innovative

The new ground covered by *Main Course* does not end with the introduction of a new style. The Bee Gees were always known for their vocal proficiency, and the bending harmony of the three brothers are the group's strong point. The trading-off of lead vocals between Barry and Robin (often in mid-verse) is done so well that it gives the impression of one very versatile vocalist.

On the album, they try a few new tricks with their voices. The "screaming" vocal—the piercing voice complementing the regular Bee Gees harmonies on several tracks—is in fact Barry. This has caused some confusion among listeners who were certain that extra vocal help was enlisted.

"Baby, As You Turn Away," the album's closing track, showcases Barry singing an entire verse in falsetto, a feat he did not know he was capable of until last year.

The introduction of the new style, along with vocal and instrumental (synthesizers dominate instead of strings) experimentation, makes this their most innovative offering since *Bee Gees 1st*, a 1967 album partially responsible for the introduction of symphonics into the rock genre.

The previous Bee Gees album was *Mr. Natural*, an uneven masterpiece containing the hit-that-never-was title track along with 'Give A Hand, take A Hand' (recorded by the Staples Singers) and the chorally superb "Had A Lot of Love Last Night.""That was experimental," says Barry. "We just wanted to try as many harmonies as we could there."

Mr. Natural was similar to a many of its predecessors; there were a few outstanding tracks and a few more "good" ones, but on the whole the album didn't work as well as it could have. Maurice Gibb shrugs the album off as "a predecessor to *Main Course*," but Barry has other ideas.

"*Mr. Natural* was an album that we made but never listened to. You know something's wrong when you don't bother to listen to your own albums. If you are not going to bother, other people might not bother either. There are a few nice tracks on it actually, but nothing stands out as a hit."

Self-appraisal

"After we made that album I went home, and I didn't have a good hi-fi set up at the time so I never put it on," Barry continued. "A month went by and I actually forgot to play it. The new album I keep playing all the time, and I've listened to it more that I've listened to anyone before."

Over-inflated ego? It's more like realistic self-appraisal.

Like *Mr. Natural*, *Main Course* was produced by the illustrious Arif Mardin (whose other current chart entry is the Average White Band's *Cut the Cake*). As sound supervisor, Mardin has an at-least-equal voice as to what goes down on tape.

On previous tours, the Bee Gees were a unique performing group because they toured with a full orchestra. The strings provided an added dimension to the performance, and rock-and-rollers fronting an orchestra was indeed a new sight.

The new tour, however, finds the band augmented only by a six-piece brass section. The parts previously performed by the orchestra originate from the synthesized strings of Blue Weaver, a keyboardist who has previously played with the Strawbs, Mott the Hoople and Hunter/Ronson.

The depth of the orchestra is certainly missed; the synthesizers are not as convincing but they do provide a viable alternative. The band plays with infectious enthusiasm, and their concert renditions are much livelier than those on record.

"It's just the band this time, playing for what the band can do," says Barry. " We use string synthesizers and Moogs and all that. We can experiment now, we have room to experiment with Moogs whereas before we didn't. Instruments were instruments and you could only go so far with them. A Moog is capable of doing so many things."

Guitarist Allan Kendall, who has performed and recorded with the brothers for almost five years, is an important part of the Bee Gees lineup. While his solos are often inspired he manages to remain unobtrusive for the most part, for the Bee Gees are not a guitar band. He stays in the background, and Barry Gibb has been known to turn his back on the audience while Kendall solos (a forgivable deception).

Dynamite

A master of "no comment," Kendall says, "I just play" and leaves it at that. Drummer Dennis Bryon rounds out the lineup; he was in Amen Corner with Blue Weaver and has played with the Bee Gees since 1972.

The live show is a combination of old favorites and featured tracks from the new album. Midway though the show, the backing band leaves the brothers to play a medley of their most popular numbers; beginning with "New York Mining Disaster" and moving through "Holiday," "How Can You Mend a Broken Heart" and "Run to Me," among others.

Happily, *Main Course* is on its way to establishing the Bee Gees as a viable musical force. It is selling considerably better than any other of their recent efforts ("Jive Talkin" entered the American singles chart at number 22) but it is also making waves on other levels of the music business.

David English, an actor appearing in Ken Russell's "Lizstomania," signed on as a roadie for the recent tour because "I like the Bee Gees music and they're my friends."

He delights in telling the story about one reaction to *Main Course*: "Jack Bruce sent a telegram to the boys saying he's just heard the record and he had thought it was the best new black band he'd heard. This was before he knew it was the Bee Gees."

Maurice Gibb has his own tale to tell: "There was a party the other night and the Stones were in Robert Stigwood's apartment. He just put the album on and didn't tell them who it was, and Mick Jagger says 'That's fucking dynamite, who's that? Some new group you've signed up?'"

All this excitement indicates that the Bee Gees are shaking their Top 40 Only image and making friends on the progressive side of the spectrum. Surely, these distinctions shouldn't exist; the only categories should be good and bad in regard to a person's taste. However, there is a school of cynical critics bestowing the unfortunate verdict of "bubblegum" upon anything pleasant or appealing to unsophisticated ears.

Bubblegum

"I can see why some people call us that," says Barry. "But I think we are a lot more intricate than bubblegum. We believe our music is good, and that's the only way we can categorize it."

Main Course defies categorization. It is adventurous and challenging, and will hopefully knock some sense into those previously dismissing the Bee Gees as too saccharine. At the same time, it contains none of the complexity-for-its-own-sake mode of thought present in many current offerings. Without being simplistic, *Main Course* presents music that can be enjoyed and takes little effort to do so.

In the fall, the Bee Gees expect to film a feature called *The Bull on the Barroom Floor*. "It's somewhat of a Western," explains Barry. 'It's about three English boys who emigrate to America in the early days and bring a bull with them and mate it. It's very fast. It's supposed to be a chase film which hasn't been done for a few years. Somewhat along the lines of *It's a Mad Mad Mad Mad World*."

"We're not singing in it, but we'll probably write the theme music," adds Maurice. "We get into Western gear and all that. The town's in trouble and someone tries to steal a wagon train and..."

Had they seen *Monty Python and the Holy Grail* playing not two blocks from their hotel? (seems like the same brand of absurdity) "We haven't had time, being on tour..."

SOUNDS MAGAZINE, August 9, 1975

Tubular Balls

Interviewed in Cambridge, MA

The East Coast boy was on the phone espousing the merits of Bruce Springsteen to his transplanted Californian brother. "He's going to be the next big thing," he gushes. "Forget Springsteen," said the brother with typical West-is-the-best aplomb. "The next big thing is The Tubes."

"We'll make the world forget Bruce Springsteen," shouts Tubes lead singer Fee Waybill (aka "Quay Lewd"). The Tubes just completed their East Coast debut by selling out eight frantic shows at the 350-seat New Theater of Cambridge.

The Tubes opened the show with the musical question "What do you want from life?" The band begins sans Waybill, who makes his entrance in a bright white tuxedo.

"What do you want from life? An Indian guru to show you the inner light? What do you want from life? A meaningless affair with a girl you just met tonight?"

Waybill provides the show's focus; changing costumes to portray his different sides. He rolls onstage in a wheelchair mocking South Pacific's Balai Hai, transmigrating into a cabaret star for a rendition of "It's Not Unusual." The persona of Young Doctor Fee emerged next to perform a delicate operation on a guitar (it failed, she died), and the circus culminated with the character of "Quay Lewd," the super-wasted super-rocker.

The Tubes provide far more than a rock and roll show. They are aided by props, dancers and synchronized TV monitors, with the resulting multi-media potpourri providing a sensory assault.

The Tubes are perhaps most notorious for "Mondo Bondage," in which Fee sings as the ultra-heavyweight rocker clad only in a mask, boots and a thong. He is joined by a similarly dressed Ms. Re Styles for a bondage dance.

The band is a foil for Fee. Prairie Prince is perched on a throne behind plexiglass drums while pounding out ornately frantic rhythms, while Bill Spooner and his Flying V guitar challenge Fee for the stage focus. Spooner loses the battle, and he is running back and forth clearly dissatisfied at being second-best.

The many keyboards of Vince Welnick occupy stage right. Welnick is a wisp in dime-store sunglasses, bouncing madly to Prince's syncopation. Michael Cotton operates a bank of synthesizers opposite Welnick, and Cotton's composed, gum-chewing presence contradicts the outrageous sounds he produces.

Guitarist Roger Steen and bassist Rick Anderson appear restrained in comparison to the rest of the band, these two who are the most concerned with the business of making music. Anderson regards the scene with near-detachment, and Steen is carried into the act only when he is lifted by dancers during the finale, "White Punks on Dope."

"We're white punks on dope. Mom and dad moved to Hollywood. Hang myself when I get enough rope."

This song, another heavy macho rocker, pulls out all the stops on the Tubes' show. Chicly clad female and hermaphroditic dancers do a glitter job on the stage, while Fee as Quay Lewd presides over the prevailing insanity atop silver platform heels.

Clear frustration is conveyed as Fee screams "I go craazy because my folks are SO FUCKING RICH!!!" Art can reflect society, and the middle class -bred Tubes are portraying their own susceptibilities. (Certainly "White Punks" is something we can all identify with).

The Tubes threw a small press party during their Boston sojourn. The band members chatted informally with eager reporters, and the hors d'oeuvres were by all accounts delicious. Fee was there as Quay Lewd, talking to the audience through TV monitors. Those with questions asked them through a microphone passed through the theater while Fee's image armed with a bogus British accent on multiple screens.

The results yielded little about Fee or the Tubes. Fee insisted on playing the Quay character (only one facet of the Waybill catalogue) to the hilt. The questions bordered on the absurd but none were honored with straightforward answers, with Fee stating "we toured the eastern coast of Portugal" and "anything east of Nebraska is still Nebraska." Guitarist Spooner offered the most revealing insight to the Waybill personality when he said "a lot of people have asked me whether Quay is straight or gay and the answer is no, he's bicentennial."

Nevertheless, the Tubes' antics coaxed almost all present into hysterics. Quay soon came onstage with dancer Re ("I'm seventeen years old") Styles, and although the questions were then more serious the answers became sillier. After profoundly muttering "our show appeals to each individually different" the image once again retreated to the dressing room. We all met Quay Lewd, but Fee Waybill is still an enigma.

Bassist Rick Anderson watched benignly, interjecting that Fee "should knock off the Quay bit." I asked Anderson why he thought The Tubes' time had come.

"I think the reason people like us is boredom. Acts like Pink Floyd put me to sleep." Perhaps detecting my cold stare, he continued: "I mean, their records are great but they are dead onstage. So detached." No "The Tubes are a product of a decaying society" crap for Anderson. This is all in the name of rock and roll.

Many rock/theater fusions have been attempted, and the flexibility of both art forms allows for a polarity of results. David Bowie proved that it's no longer enough to sing songs, you have to present them. The Tubes go many steps further than what Bowie dreamed, assaulting all available sensory outlets.

THE BOSTON UNIVERSITY NEWS, December 1975

Starland Vocal Band: Their Voices Make Music

Interviewed at The Tri-State Fair, Amarillo, TX

The Starland Vocal Band, which performed at the Tri-State Fair Arena in Amarillo, establishes an immediate and personal rapport with their audience with their audience through their pleasantly accessible music.

Jon Carroll, Margot Chapman, Bill Danoff and Taffy Danoff have been playing together for about two years, and in that time what began as an experiment has developed into a successful and commercially viable sound. True to their name, the emphasis is on vocals with the instrumentals used only to color the sound.

Starland is easier to listen to than some instrumentally based music, perhaps because the human voice is a natural instrument. Their voices blend naturally, giving the impression that they couldn't sing off-key of they wanted to.

"There is a format to pop music that is like the format of a sonnet," Bill Danoff told the Pampa News. "In French classicism a novel had to take place within a 24-hour period. A writer could do whatever he wanted, but if he wanted the Academy to read his novel, to accept it and publish it, it had to fit the format. We're aiming to make as good music as we can within this particular idiom."

And for a relatively new band, Starland has accomplished a great deal of success. "Afternoon Delight," its first hit single, helped earn the Grammy Award as the best new group of 1976, and this summer they had their own TV show.

They are eager to please their audiences and produce quality music that will be heard by a lot of people.

"A guy who paints your house naturally wants to paint a lot of houses," said Taffy Danoff. "He's very proud of his work wants to be a success in his business. That's what we want to do — sell a lot of records because that's the nature of the art."

The Starland show consists mostly of enthusiastically performed original music such as "Afternoon Delight" and "California Day," a stunning a capella rendition of Paul Simon's "American Tune" (which took Jon Carroll a whole summer to arrange) and a pair of John Denver songs, "Friends With You" and "Take Me Home, Country Roads."

"Country Roads," however, is as much a Starland song as a Denver song, having been written by Bill and Taffy Danoff with Denver. Taffy introduced the song on stage as "the song which made us what we are today, which is very rich."

Their interpretation of the song is more relaxed than Denver's, and due to the intertwining of voices, listening to Starland's version is like hearing the somewhat overplayed song anew.

"I am not sick of any of our songs," said Taffy.

Added Chapman, "It's in the attitude. If you sing a song a dozen-thousand times you have to keep singing it like it was the first time. Otherwise, it's not going to make it. The audience can tell right away if you're bored."

Starland makes its audiences feel good. Its members put a lot of themselves into their show and spend an hour afterwards signing autographs and talking to fans. Carroll said this is a way "to get pieces of many people's lives." In any case, an audience gets a good feeling from Starland as performers and as people, and that's what entertainment is all about.

THE PAMPA DAILY NEWS, September 20, 1977

2

The A List

*E*very time I land a "big fish," I spend hours preparing and I write out all the questions. The difference between George Harrison and Diana Rigg and those that came later is that I no longer feel that I need to ask every question on the list. The best interview always resembles a conversation. And it's better to ask a probing, inappropriate question and have the interviewee decline to answer than to not ask it at all.

The first stories in this chapter are single efforts featuring George Harrison, Roger Daltrey, Roger McGuinn, Ray Davies, Dave Davies and Garth Hudson. The next section takes a wider view representing multiple articles written about a single group. Here, a section about the Beach Boys is followed by a series of stories about Crosby, Stills, Nash and Young. The CSNY section is a series of pieces that sketch out the idiosyncrasies of that particular musical conclave, while the Beach Boys' section traces the discord and drama that occurs when people grow old and greedy and the reason for making music is forgotten.

George Harrison's Cheery Hello

Interviewed at Warner Brothers Records headquarters, Burbank, CA

GEORGE HARRISON has emerged to call attention to his future, but willingly discusses his past.

As a Beatle, Harrison was all hair, knees and teeth, physically and musically overshadowed by Lennon and McCartney. Today he looks heavier and healthier, his medium-length, styled hair is offset by a salt-and-pepper stubble. And his warmth is overwhelming. "I couldn't live in a house full of journalists and have them ask me questions all the time," he said. "But there are occasions like this when I come out and say hello to people."

How did you pick this time to re-emerge?

I wanted to have a little break away from away it. I still continued writing and putting songs on tape I never really stopped doing that, I never put out a record, I had a chance to get away from it for a bit, then I felt much better about the idea of doing it, and then it was a question of finding someone I could work with. It's handy to have someone to bounce ideas off of. I really miss that part of being in a group, where you can come up with all of your own ideas, and you have other people's ideas and they all mix together and they become even a different idea. Here, the whole burden isn't on just myself. I decided it was time to make a new album, but this time I was going to make it with some other producer.

Are they intimidated by you?

No, I just don't really know that many record producers. So I thought who will be good? Someone I really admire and someone who would respect me and my past and not try to turn me into something I'm not. I thought of Jeff Lynne of the Electric Light Orchestra, he'd be fun. If I only knew him....

You'd never met?

I'd never met him. He's a very private person, Jeff, he's one person who I don't think has done interviews or television, or anything. He's just very private. Anyway I got a message to him through Dave Edmunds, that I'd like to meet him. And I met Jeff, and over period of 18 months I got to know him and suggested that I'm going to make a record and just sounded him out. And he said he'd help, (but) he never committed himself. So last November I finally said that's it, I'm going to make a record, at least get some musicians over, and so he said OK, and we worked from January, straight through until August.

But you used pretty much the same musicians.

When I think of who I want to play drums on a track I think of Jim Keltner. I know Jim so well, he's such a great drummer, and at the same time Ringo, because Ringo, I don't have to tell him what I want, he'll just listen to the tune and he'll play like Ringo. So same goes for guitar solos, that should be Eric on that one. So there's a lot of my same old friends. The added influence of Jeff helping to produce worked well indeed, has a good structural sense of songs, he's a composer and a guitarist himself, a lot of similarities.

Were you talking to other producers at the same time?

No, I was just trying to think of who if I had my choice of the people I could think of, and he was the one person I came up with.

You haven't been idle, musically. How did you pick these songs?

I had a lot of demos. I played them to Jeff. He picked them out. I asked him to write me a song too. Since I've been not making albums I've done a lot of other people's songs. Just as demos, some old tunes, I do a quick version. I like the idea of singing somebody else's songs.

Such as?

Dylan's "Every Grain of Sand." A great song, I did a version of that, a couple of other Dylan songs, writing other crazy songs. He wrote me a song, we wrote a couple together, and the song that they're putting out as a single is one that neither of us wrote, from the very early 1960s called "I've Got My Mind Set on You."

Which sounds like nothing you've ever done.

It's true. That came about because Jim Keltner just started playing that drum pattern and the song seemed to fit right on there. Does this bother you? (lights up cigarette)

I'm just surprised you're still smoking.

Well, off and on. You know, something like this, it's, ah, on.

You've recently been a filmmaker, and now you're making your first video. What can we expect?

We haven't made the video, we're not making it until next Wednesday.

What do you have in mind?

We're still just talking about it, it's a bit early for that.

Next week?

That's it. It's silly, isn't it. We'll finalize what's going to happen. It's difficult to make a video that doesn't look like all of the other videos. Occasionally there's a really nice one. Like that Dire Straits or Peter Gabriel. But you can't say "oh I'm going to make one like Peter Gabriel" because he's already done that. This video isn't going to be me making a movie. Maybe later when we start doing different singles off of the album then maybe I'll work more along those lines. I've just finished the record, mixing it, all the art work and mastering it and then it's like 'make a video...'so this video. Gary Weis is making the video. I knew him from the Rutles. Gary has a real good sense of humor, he's done the *Saturday Night Live* stuff as well. It's how to present it so it's funny but at the same time the song isn't particularly a comedy song. Neither was "You Can Call Me Al" but they gave it a comical flavor.

So you want to make people laugh.

Well. I'd like it to not look like the same old videos that just keep coming. At the same time, with the limited time span I'm pretty much in the hands of Gary. It's up to him to do it really good.

What makes you laugh?

A lot of things. I've always liked comedy, back when I was a kid I liked the *Goon Show*, I was a big fan of Peter Sellers, and later on I was a good friend of his. I liked Peter a lot. I loved Monty Python, I couldn't explain how much I liked it. The rut that television gets into, and people lives, Python just blew all that away by making fun of everything. Right down to the style of television we've been watching. The result is that I got to know some of them and we made *The Life of Brian* and *Time Bandits* and a couple of films with Michael Palin, so that kind of stuff makes me laugh.

The Rutles is probably the best Beatles movie.

I think so.

The Compleat Beatles was horrible.

The Compleat Beatles is like taking all the footage they can scrounge and then trying to do a serious thing. The great thing about the Rutles is that even though it was a parody it was the nicest thing about the Beatles. It was done with love, even though it was a send-up. And because of Eric Idle being a friend of mine, it gave him access to things that any other potential Beatle filmmaker wouldn't have. I showed him footage that was obscure, like when we first came into NYC, in the back of a limousine and Paul's listening to a radio and a guy is saying "the Beatles are going to be here at the station to read their poetry." And that isn't a famous bit of footage. So in the Rutles you see them, and he's listening to the radio, and the disk jockey "and the Rutles are coming to talk about their trousers." And also, just the detail, where they got exactly what sort of suits we were wearing on that day, even at Shea Stadium, little marshal's badges, the Rutles even had the psychedelic guitars, it had a good eye for detail. At the same time, it sent up documentaries, the style and those boring questions that they ask.

If I had read every Beatles book and seen every documentary, in a general sense what would I have missed?

Do you want me to tell you something nobody else knows?

No.

A lot of the stuff in the books are wrong. A lot of them are written out of malice, or from people with axes to grind for one reason or another. And they've perverted certain things for their own gain. Not many are actually factual and honest. There is a saying in the old house that I have, it's in Latin, translated it says "those who tell all they have to tell, tells more than they know." So you probably know more about the Beatles, from reading those books, than there actually was.

What would those people who look so closely miss?

Well, there's that expression, you don't see the forest for the trees. Basically the Beatles phenomena was bigger than life. The reality was that we were just four people as much caught up in what was happening at that period of time as anybody else.

Have you listened to the Beatles CDs?

I did buy a CD player when they issued them, yeah. I listened to some of them. I still prefer the old versions, how I remember them on vinyl. There's a lot of stuff that you can hear now that's good. In some cases, there's a lot of stuff that you shouldn't hear so loudly, that's somehow come out in the mix. On *Sgt. Pepper* I keep hearing this horrible-sounding tambourine that leaps out of the right speaker. It was obviously in the original mix, but it was never that loud.

There are still thirty or so songs not on CD. How would you make them available?

Well, it's none of our business any more. When our contract expired we lost any control we had over the Beatles' product.

How would you like to see it done?

I suppose if you took all the songs you could put them order in sequence of years as they were recorded, then as the technology advanced and our technique progressed, then you'd hear them in proper order. Or, you could put all the singles on one, or the B- sides on another.

Does Michael Jackson own your songs as well?

He owns some of mine, up to the *White Album*.

How did "Revolution" end up on a sneaker commercial?

From what I understand, they were just going to use the song, re-record it with Julian Lennon, but Yoko got really pissed off at that idea because I don't think she likes Julian, and she insisted that it be the Beatles version. She has no right to insist that because there's a conflict of interest, it's in the Beatles and

Apple's interest not to have our records touted about on TV commercials, otherwise all the songs we made could be advertising everything from hot dogs to ladies' brassieres. We never took advertising. We could have done our Coca-Cola commercials, just like everybody else. We tried to have a little discretion, keep a little taste, that's what we felt. The four of us tried to keep our songs in running orders on the records, we tried to make good records, we tried to do something as quality, and something to be proud of. When it's out of our hands, it's like we're made into prostitutes.

Capitol's new tapes ruin the running order of your old albums.

This is the problem of not having any control any more. It's unfortunate. We should have been able to retain the control. That's the way it all went.

Derek Taylor said you crave your own space and have a long memory.

Most people need your own space, I still have it, even though occasions like this when I do an album I come out and say hello to people. I couldn't live in a house full of journalists and have them ask me questions all the time. What was the other question?

Memory.

Ah, the memory. Sort of more in the past, a lot of brain cells are missing now. Sometimes you don't want to remember things, sometimes you can't and sometimes they just pop out there.

Is there any unreleased Beatles stuff aside from the "Sessions" album?

Not that I know of. When we made records, everything we made come out. The only things that didn't come out were things that weren't supposed to be recorded. Like if we were rehearsing and they were just rolling the tape. But people want to scrape the bottom of the barrel for anything.

What's next for you?

It'll be pretty much the same. My film company is jogging along, we have a lot of projects. It's the sort of company that doesn't seem to make a lot of blockbuster movies, they seem to be the sort of films that nobody else wants to make. But it still doesn't mean that they shouldn't be made. The only thing that I would like to accomplish is perfect peace in a spiritual sense to be able to consciously leave my body at will.

SONICBOOMERS 2009 from an interview conducted in September 1987

Ah, Daltrey

Roger Daltrey, Seattle, October 2009
Interviewed by phone, Bainbridge Island, WA to somewhere in England.

One of the privileges of my generation is the opportunity to watch the once-mighty play small clubs, but seeing someone of Roger Daltrey's stature didn't seem possible. But it's happening. In preparation for a flurry of activity by the Who in 2010, Daltrey is participating in a two-month jaunt where he promises to mine his own catalog for rare gems, and pull out Who songs that have not seen the light of day for some time. If the purpose is to get ready to grease the tracks for the big Who train, the most dedicated fans will have a chance to hang around the station for awhile.

After a long static period, Daltrey and The Who are hardly over the hill. Three years ago they released *Endless Wire*, the rare occurrence of an old band making new music that actually matches the strength of their earlier efforts. On the side Daltrey has continued acting, such as in an episode of *CSI* in which he

25

played a character that assumes four different disguises. And last year, The Who was honored at a presidential ceremony at the Kennedy Center.

Not so long ago we didn't really expect much more from The Who, aside from another victory lap. So it is nice to know there are still some surprises left.

How are you preparing for the tour?

I'm just sorting through material that I can represent, old solo stuff that I have never done live, and songs that the Who haven't played for years. The idea is to get out there and sing, have some fun, and give people a good time during these miserable economic times.

Do you need to play certain songs that you don't like, or that people will be disappointed to not hear?

There will always be people who will be disappointed, with a catalog like The Who. I want to do songs that The Who haven't done in the last ten years, or if I do them it will be totally different, my version of what they should be. There is a lot that I haven't done live, like from my last solo album (1992's *Rocks in the Head*), which has four good rock songs that I want to play. With all this material it's more like: "What do I leave out?" People will be disappointed that I won't be doing "Won't Get Fooled Again" and I won't. Or "My Generation." If they shout loud enough it will be easy enough to slip them in, but artistically I want to do stuff that is more of a challenge.

What about playing in small clubs?

I'm looking forward to the intimacy and talking to the audience, which is something that I don't really do with the Who. There will be a change in the amount of energy, and ability to reach out and touch the back wall, if you like.

What are you usually thinking onstage?

When I'm onstage with The Who I am always trying to get my brain together for the next song. You live all these words, and play the song as if it were the first time. It takes me to a space where things come naturally and subconsciously, which is much better than having something planned out. I don't think in a real sense. If I start thinking too much about it I lose my way. I forget the words.

Do you use teleprompters?

No.

You've played more guitar with The Who lately. Does that take away from your singing?

No, it's easier for the phrasing and the rhythm, if I am playing guitar. There are a lot of acoustic guitars on Who records, so it's nice to put some of it back. I don't swing the microphone as much, but the old eye and the old shoulder aren't good for that kind of thing anymore. I'm a bit worried about missing it, and whacking someone.

You and Pete were honored last year at the Kennedy Center, where George Bush read a tribute. What were you thinking, then?

I was thinking, "What the fuck am I doing here?" It was not a political event, and it was a not a place to drive in your politics. It was totally surreal. Everyone was very gracious. I just went for the party. It was great to have two days of people entertaining me rather than me having to entertain them. It was a wonderful event, especially with the history of the band over the last ten years, with John going. It's been a hell of a roller coaster.

But when he introduced you Bush didn't seem to know who you were.

It didn't matter. That's all personalities and politics. I don't give a shit about that. It was nice to be honored by America, which I have a great affection for. With all those other people, Morgan Freeman, Barbara Streisand, Twyla Tharp, all who are at the top of their professions, I wondered, how did I end up here?

So we accepted it, graciously. I didn't ever do anything great to deserve this, it's just what I do. I was wonderful to be honored by your country, and I was really proud of Pete. He is one of the great popular music writers of the twentieth century. He's made his mark, that's for sure. And I had the good luck to be the voice for that. And I have never forgotten how lucky I have been. During that time have I added something to the mix? Yes, there's no doubt. The two of us together have always had a lot more strength than either one of us individually.

There has been some friction, though.

There is still a tension between us. We respect each other, but we don't always agree. We have the courage to challenge each other all the time. It's a fiery mix. When Pete and I hit the stage together it's like, "Fuck me, there's something dangerous going on here." We just know if one of us makes a mistake the other will jump right in. There aren't so many arguments anymore, they're just differences of opinion. We don't have the same drive to argue as we did when we were younger, but in some ways we will always be tied to our past.

What about this rumor that Charlie Watts has left the Rolling Stones?

If Charlie leaves the Stones, the Stones are all over. I hope that they do another tour, where they strip down and be like when they started. For me, that would be magic. They're a great band. I hope that Keith can still move his fingers enough to play the way he plays. Mick is singing better than ever. But he should stop running around on those big stages. They don't need the circus anymore. They are great musicians.

What is the future of The Who?

It's very bright, which is the reason why I am doing this tour. We are going to be demoing stuff for a new album in December and I want to be in top voice for that. When we recorded the last one we hadn't been out for three years. But the Who will be gigging next year, we have some big events lined up. We could play *Quadrophenia*, or *Tommy*, or go with the show we have now, which is greatest hits with some more obscure ones put in. My dream would be go on the road and do *Tommy* for a week, *Quadrophenia* for a week and then the hits show the week after. With The Who we are never short of material.

You could go on tour but not tell the fans what they are getting at a particular show.

That's worth a try, isn't it?

What is Zak Starkey's role in The Who? Is he is an official member?

He's not a full member, but he is our drummer of choice. He fits so well into The Who. It's one thing to have someone who musically fits, but Zak's personality fits totally into the band. We have a very cohesive family on the road.

Your CSI appearance was quite a showcase.

I've never seen it, although it was great fun. It was a most extraordinary week. I got to sing Frank Sinatra's "That's Life," which is a great song. I got the script and had some notion what to do with the characters, but had no clear idea until after they put on all the prosthetics. If you don't know what the character looks like it's hard to give them a body language and mannerisms. Then they put in the colored contact lenses, you look at yourself, and you are a complete stranger. I'm not sure that I've ever even seen *CSI* all the way through. It's not that I am not a fan of *CSI*. I'm just not a fan of TV.

SONICBOOMERS, September 11, 2009

Roger McGuinn: Still Flyin' High

Interviewed by phone, Bainbridge Island WA to somewhere in Florida

My mother recently instructed me to dispose of her record collection, but I disobeyed her orders and mailed it to myself instead. When they arrived I was drawn to a pair of albums featuring a pre-Byrds Jim McGuinn. He is pictured on the cover of the Chad Mitchell Trio's *Live at the Bitter End* on banjo, and backed up Judy Collins on versions of two songs that he recorded with the Byrds two years later. At the time, McGuinn was supporting folk's entry into the mainstream, one album at a time. Forty-five years on, the mission continues.

Morphing into Roger, he presided over two stages of The Byrds: the early version that deciphered Dylan for the masses and the latter that lit the spark for country-rock. Since falling back to earth he has mined the traditional vein from which all these were descended, publishing a song each month on for the last 14 years on the Folk Den website, supplementing these homemade recordings with lyrics and chords. Once upon a time the songs were carried between towns by wandering singers. Today, McGuinn blasts out songs to more villagers than a minstrel could reach in a lifetime. As before, everyone still gets to come up with their own version.

McGuinn's own journey now includes Minnesota, California and Washington state, creating a movable Folk Den that draws from disparate sources to provide a cross section of the popular and traditional. Sooner or later, he will make it to your town.

What are you doing on stage these days?

I sometimes do an autobiographical show, and other times I just play a selection of Byrds songs and my solo albums. Sometimes I just mix things up. We design the set on the day of the show, at about two in the afternoon I go out to lunch with my wife and we write out a set list. This is based on what we played when we were in that town before. She has a notebook, where there are set lists from all the shows I've played. If we have never been in that town it comes down to what I feel like singing.

Are there songs you have to play or hate to play?

People would be disappointed if I didn't do some of the Byrds' classics, like "Mr. Tambourine Man," "Turn, Turn, Turn!" and "Eight Miles High." I carry four different instruments, even though it is a solo set it has some variety. These songs are all good songs that I enjoy playing. It's not like they are bubblegum hits that I am going to be forced to play all my life.

Who comes to your shows?

The people who come see me are usually men in their fifties who remember The Byrds. Sometimes they bring their wives, or their kids. Some of the kids are young, and some are in their twenties. If you liked The Byrds you will enjoy the show.

In recent years you have become as much an archivist as a musician.

That's true. The Folk Den is a labor of love that I started, because the traditional side of folk was neglected in favor of the singer-songwriter. That hasn't really changed, although I see more kids interested in roots music. Interest in folk has always been in cycles. It was popular in the 1910s, and the ' 30s and the '40s. It took a hit after that, but came back in the late ' 50s with groups like the Kingston Trio, the Chad Mitchell Trio and the Limeliters. It sort of collapsed under its own weight after the Beatles came in with their electric guitars. That wasn't a bad thing.

Will you ever run out of material for the Folk Den?

No. I've done 170 songs since 1995. There are thousands more; there is no limit to the number of traditional songs that exist. There are enough to keep me going for the rest of my life. All the songs are under the "creative common" designation, so there is no copyright. And I like the Internet, because it makes it easy for me to put songs out where everyone can hear them, and for free. Although some people have the idea that if something is free it can't be very good.

Aside from Internet distribution, how does technology enhance the Folk Den project?

I've always been a technology enthusiast. The new technology makes it easier to record. Where I once needed a whole studio all I need now is a Macbook with ProTools. I can record anywhere, I recorded one song on an ocean liner from Miami to Lisbon.

You wrote a lot of songs about space with the Byrds. Are you disappointed that today's level of space exploration isn't what we once expected?

I'm sorry that the space program got put on the back burner. I know a lot of the astronauts personally because I live in Florida, and have gone over to the Astronaut's Hall of Fame and played for them a few times. They all feel the same way. It's like one moment they were in the Beatles and the next they were in a garage band. It's not the same anymore.

The Byrds did a few songs about space. "Mr. Spaceman" was a comedy song, but we did a few that were serious: "C.T.A. 102" was based on a discovery in space, when we didn't know what a quasar was. We thought that it was beaming out an intelligent signal. After the song came out someone from the Jet Propulsion Laboratories wrote something in one of the astrophysical journals saying we were wrong, that "Dr. McGuinn and (co-writer) Dr. (Bob) Hibbard are mistaken if they think C.T.A. 102 contains any intelligent life." That was pretty funny.

Why are there so many bonus tracks coming out on recent reissues? Are they worthwhile?

There was a physical limit with LPs; they could only fit twelve or thirteen songs. With the cost of publishing they knocked it down to ten, then nine. They didn't want to pay publishing, because at nine cents a song that got into some real money. That was the reason why some of the songs got left off. It wasn't a quality control issue. Although we did try to put our best stuff on the original albums.

Are you the only holdout for a Byrds reunion?

Yes. I'm not interested in being part of an oldies band. I just want to do my own solo thing. My wife and I travel together, it's real romantic and fun. I've been on the road with a bunch of guys, and I prefer traveling with my wife. We've gotten the Byrds together a couple of times in the past 15 years, once to protect the name and another time for a benefit. It hasn't been a bad experience, but it's not something I'd want to take on tour. It's not out of the question, but it's not something that I want to do.

What music do you listen to in your spare time?

Because I make music, I don't listen to music all that much. If I want to hear music I'll just pick up a guitar and play something. I have a lot of sources for music, I have a closet full of CDs, I download from eMusic, and can listen to satellite radio. But if you are involved in making music, listening becomes less of a pleasure. You find yourself dissecting and analyzing the song, and it becomes more like work.

How do you remember the 1960s? It seems like you were more mature than a lot of your contemporaries.

I wasn't really a hippie, although I did do a lot of the same things. My impression is that it was the biggest group of young people on the planet ever. There was a lot of discontent with the hypocrisy of the system, politics and religion, and society in general. So we threw everything out. We threw out the baby with the bathwater, so to speak, and we had to reassemble things. At the time we wanted to rid the world of poverty and hunger. We thought we could do it with music, which turned out to be overly ambitious. It turned out to be a big disappointment, kind of like the space program.

Why didn't the Byrds play Woodstock?

We probably had a gig somewhere else, and didn't know that it was going to be the biggest thing in the world.

SONICBOOMERS September 29, 2009

Ray Davies Gets the Kinks Out Musically

Interviewed by phone, Menlo Park, CA to New York City.

BY VIRTUE of its title, The Kinks' new *Think Visual* album should have a more elaborate cover. Instead it is only an exaggerated supergraphic, with a musclebound woman on the front and a blurry shot of Ray Davies on the reverse.

But this album revitalizes The Kinks musically, and signals Davies' intention to realize the theatrical promise shown in the band's stage shows and concept albums of the seventies.

"I think it will be the most fulfilling time of my career," the 42-year-old Davies says in a telephone interview from New York. "It will evolve me as a visual artist and a storyteller, and bring my career full circle."

This is the first Kinks album for MCA, the band's fourth record label. Their previous associations were not only contracts, but epochs. They were the first rock group signed to Reprise, once a custom label for Frank Sinatra. They began as moderately intelligent British invaders, ending the association with five consecutive masterpieces. RCA signed the band in 1971 on this basis, and was presumably stunned when they turned out six eccentric, neo-operatic concept albums with equally quirky stage presentations. Six subsequent releases on Arista, while occasionally brilliant, ranged from innocuous self-parodies to power-pop restatements.

Each label, in addition, has released one virtually unlistenable live album along with numerous anthologies. Significantly for *Think Visual*, the strongest albums from RCA and Arista — *Muswell Hillbillies* and *Sleepwalker* — were released at the beginning of the respective contracts.

Working with a new company doesn't change his approach as a writer, Davies says. "But it makes everyone else more excited and more anxious to prove themselves and do well," he adds. "There is more adrenalin and more spark on this album."

Of the scores of bands from the 1964 British wave, only The Kinks never tried to sound American. And only The Kinks and the Rolling Stones have continued to record and release original material.

It was once common to follow up a hit single with a similar song, a practice eschewed by the more highbrow bands. The Kinks were never so proud, imitating themselves no less than three times: "You Really Got Me" was followed by "All Day and All of the Night," "A Well Respected Man" evolved into "A Dedicated

Follower of Fashion," and "Lola" begat "Apeman." These were only the hits — the list goes on. At the very least, Davies is guilty of perpetual self-plagiarism.

"I work the same way as a novelist, who will refer to his characters in different works," he says. "Although when I'm writing something, I like to think that it's the first time it's been written. And if I feel it's infringing on something I've done before, I'll shelve it."

Of the four original Kinks, only Davies and his brother Dave, on lead guitar, remain. There has been a succession of bassists, keyboardists and peripheral players. The changes have been relatively insignificant aside from the addition of former Argent bassist Jim Rodford in 1978 and the 1984 defection of drummer Mick Avory.

Between *State of Confusion* in 1983 and *Word of Mouth* in 1984, there was no quiet on The Kinks' front. Dave Davies announced he was leaving, then changed his mind. Months later, Avory, himself part of an early Rolling Stones incarnation, left under a pretense no fan believed — to design golf clubs.

What actually happened, all now admit, is that the continuous bickering between Avory and Dave Davies had come to a head.

"It was Dave who said he really couldn't work with Mick any more," Davies says. "There were a lot of fights, a lot of arguments off stage, about ego, stupid things that had gone back for years. Things that did not make sense. But they built up into major issues.

"They were not getting along. I had to take Mick out. It was tough for me, because he was a real friend."

Asked if "taking Dave out" was ever a possibility, Davies pauses and says: "It was an option I considered at the time."

Avory was replaced by Robert Henrit, also ex-Argent, who had played on Dave Davies' solo albums. Avory makes an appearance on *Think Visual*, drumming on "Rock and Roll Cities" — ironically, a Dave Davies composition.

As survivors, the Rolling Stones and The Kinks beg comparison. The most glaring difference is that the Stones sell a lot more records. Both bands have made debuts on new labels this year, where another contrast becomes apparent: *Think Visual* is vital and optimistic, but the Stones' regressive *Dirty Work* was followed by more than the usual number of breakup rumors.

Both, however, follow the same formula: fine-tuning a concept and signature rather than doing something outrageous or different. Davies perceives the greatest disparity in point of view.

"Where I differ from someone like Mick Jagger, or definitely the Stones, is that one character could sing all their songs," he says. "With this album, I think that I have three, four characters that I use. I write in a different way, maybe like a novelist writes. I'll sing through a character, and it might not necessarily be my philosophy."

There is no fraternity of veteran British rockers, Davies says, because "it would truly turn into boring old farts time."

"I saw Keith Richards recently and he said 'we should get together,' and I said 'all you have to do is phone.' But there is so much distance between people, they get so busy. I mean, the first thing that Keith thinks when he arrives in England isn't going to be 'I must phone Ray Davies.'"

Davies has always kept his personal life private; his three wives have rarely been photographed. After the ambiguous "Lola," in which the protagonist was taken home by a person of undetermined sexual origin, he did nothing to dispel the rumor that he was gay, perhaps to keep people guessing.

This privacy was shattered by a four-year relationship with Pretenders' lead singer Chrissie Hynde, which produced a daughter and loads of publicity, especially when Hynde ended up marrying another man.

"I didn't really feel that I was living with a musician," Davies says of the relationship. "We got together because we liked each other as people. Our jobs were only affected by people outside it . . . I don't really want to comment too much on it, but there was no problem. We didn't fight for the living room so we could both rehearse and write.

"But I don't work that way anyway. I do much of my writing in transit, in cars, on airplanes, in the subway. There were other forces at work. The same forces that any two people have."

There are no immediate tour plans for *Think Visual*. That will come in early 1987. Davies plans something more elaborate and theatrical than the straight-ahead arena rock on which the band has built its recent reputation.

"Commercial success is important in the sense that it's a vehicle to do things that you really want to do," Davies says. "I want to make films, I want to do theatre work, I want to keep writing, obviously. And the occasional commercial success gives you the opportunity to do that."

THE GLOBE AND MAIL, December 6, 1986

Divided Anew, Kinks Online

The Kinks are the only major British Invasion group aside from the Rolling Stones to continue to perform and record, and, like many musicians, have developed a presence on the World Wide Web. True to one of the band's lesser-known anthems — "I'm Not Like Everybody Else" — they have done so in their own fashion.

A large part of the Kinks' allure has always been the sibling rivalry between two of the principals: brothers Ray and Dave Davies. Ray, 54, wrote and sang most of the band's hits, from "You Really Got Me" to "Come Dancing." Dave, 51, is known for his histrionic guitar playing and challenges to Ray's leadership. So it is no surprise that the rivalry continues online, with each brother represented by separate sites — but linked to each other.

Both sites were set up last spring. They focus on the Davies's solo careers, rather than on Kinks music. Mercifully, both are free of the annoying practice, seen in many fan-run Web sites on the Kinks, of substituting the letter "k" when a hard "c" begins a word. Coincidentally, both sites are operated by Kinks fans living in Massachusetts.

Chris Locke, a New Bedford Web site developer, was operating his own Kinks fan site when Christian Davies, Dave Davies's 26-year-old son, approached him with the idea of an official Dave Davies site. Tony Raine, from the Cape Cod town of Chatham, was the one to approach Ray Davies. "None of these guys are overly computer literate," Raine said. "They are just learning."

The Dave Davies Web site (www.davedavies.com) contains the requisite touring information and guitar shots, but Davies logs on regularly to answer the most minutiae-soaked inquiries. Fans are also able to listen to a complete concert. Davies also uses the online forum to expound upon his Eastern-tinged spiritual beliefs and to hawk a related album of ambient music, available only from the Web site. And while turning to a pop star for spiritual guidance may be somewhat misguided, the discourse here is more substantial than the offerings of some other celebrities.

A recent upgrade of Ray Davies's site (www.raydavies.com) is quite an improvement over the initial effort, with flashier graphics and fewer blatant misspellings (although its small white-on-black type does not accommodate the eyesight of the rapidly aging fan base).

Like his brother, Ray Davies is using his site to promote his literary leanings, offering samples that are, for the time being, not available elsewhere. But unlike his brother, Ray Davies seems to treat the Web as a peripheral activity, a 1990's version of a 1960s fan club.

"This whole 'Internet thing' just hasn't piqued Ray's interest like it has Dave's," said Dave Emlen, a systems analyst for the Rochester Institute of Technology who runs a Kinks fan page. "But if I had to choose between Ray spending his free time working on his Web site or working on new recordings and projects, I'd choose the latter."

THE NEW YORK TIMES, December 17, 1998

Dave Davies Embraces His Inner Bug

Interviewed in Seattle,WA

Dave Davies smiles when the inevitable "will-the-Kinks-get-back-together-again" question finally arises. "I think we might do something next year," he said. "Maybe a show in New York. An album would be nice." But in reference to his turbulent relationship with his brother, Kinks co-founder Ray, he adds "we'd have to make sure that we don't kill each other..."

In the meantime there is *Bug*, Davies' first full-fledged album of original material since 1982's *Chosen People* and, like many of the Kinks' best efforts, a concept album. *Bug*, however, is a little more contemporary than some of the Kinks; more archaic themes; discussing the possibility of alien implant, bugs, that are used to monitor people's lives. While Davies has been an observer of the paranormal for some time and has flirted with these ideas in some fragmented web-only releases, the idea for *Bug* came quickly.

"I got what I thought was a horrible mosquito bite that wouldn't go away," he said. "Then I thought 'maybe it's some kind of implant.' Then the songs came quickly. I wrote most of them in three or four weeks, and used my touring band to record them right away."

Bug is quite diverse. Much of it is guitar-driven rock, balanced by the extremes of "Fortis Green" (which would not be out of place on any mid-period Kinks album) and an eight-minute slice of electronica, "Life After Life."

As for the label, he chose Koch, which has ably coordinated the reissue of all the Kinks albums up to 1984's *Word of Mouth*. ("I think they did quite a nice job," he said. "People like to have the original artwork.")

Davies has proven himself with a series of well-received tours, and has beaten his brother by being the first to complete an album. Does this mean, if and when the Kinks reunite, that he will be more of an equal member?

"I always thought I was an equal member," he said. "Although I know what you mean. All the best bands collaborate. I always thought George Harrison was underappreciated."

Unpublished, September 2002

Beyond the Band: Garth Hudson's River of Sound Comes to Port Townsend

Garth Hudson, Port Townsend, WA August 2011
Interviewed by phone, Port Townsend, WA to Woodstock, NY

PORT TOWNSEND — Several weeks ago, Upstage Restaurant and Bistro owner Mark Cole found a used copy of *Cahoots*, The Band's 1971 album, on a courtyard table and set it behind the bar for the owner to claim.

No one took responsibility, but early last week Cole received a call from guitarist Eric Fridrich, executive director of Savor the Sound, asking whether he could carve out a date for The Band's Garth Hudson to perform as part of a benefit meant to subsidize musical education in schools.

It was, according to Cole, "uncanny."

Hudson is scheduled to perform at 8 p.m. on Wednesday at the Upstage, 923 Washington St.

Multi-instrumentalist Hudson, 74, was a co-founder of The Band and was a principal architect of its unique sound, playing the organ, saxophone, accordion and other instruments that were the antithesis of the guitar-based psychedelia that ruled the airwaves when The Band released its first album.

Once they stopped touring eight years later, the five-member group had changed the course of popular music, eventually creating the popular style now known as "Americana."

For this week's appearance, Hudson's vast store of instruments will be accompanied by Fridrich and his wife, Maud Hudson, on on vocals.

"Maud and I will play what is probably not anywhere near the standard Band repertoire, although we do tributes to [deceased Band members] Richard [Manuel] and Rick [Danko]," Hudson said from his home in Woodstock, N.Y., just before getting on the plane to Seattle earlier this week.

"We are taking part in a program which encourages children to care, and hopefully can do it in a manner that can encourage young people to follow music a little more closely."

Savor the Sound raises money to pay for instruments and musical instruction in public schools to replace programs that have been cut back because of decreasing education budgets, Fridrich said.

The money raised by Hudson's performance most likely will support programs in other counties, but the appearance is being used to introduce the program to Jefferson County residents with the hope of establishing it locally, he said.

Aside from its own eight-year career at the top of the charts and a second chapter (without guitarist/composer Robbie Robertson) between 1983 and 1999, The Band is most known for its accompaniment of Bob Dylan, both live and in the studio.

Hudson acknowledges what he calls Dylan's "mythopoetic power."

"He was a mystery, he was a singer, he was here, he was gone, and I don't know anyone else who kept that mystery as consistently as he did," Hudson said.

"As The Band, we were fortunate to work with a top-notch player and one of the greatest popular songwriters of that era."

Many musicians from that era continue to play their songs in a revival format, but Hudson is different and is unique, according to Fridrich, who calls Hudson "an inspiration.

"He's in his 70s, but he's still developing and playing new stuff," Fridrich said.

Hudson said it doesn't come easy.

"Some artists show their talents at age 4 or 5, but some of us have to work at this, and it becomes a lifelong pursuit," he said.

"There is a competitive aspect to what we are doing as musicians. We are always recognizing and appropriating little snippets from here and there.

"We are all composers and we are all songwriters."

To understand a musician, understand what influences him, Hudson said.

"If you want to understand Dylan, you shouldn't just listen to him. You need to find out who he was listening to, what he was reading at the time and what people were singing from the balconies when he was young," he said.

"Right now I am talking with people about jazz metal, and its incredible reiterative patterns," he continued.

Black Sabbath's Tony Iommi "has some masterful guitar fills and great sequences where his grip on the guitar does not cease until the very last note."

Hudson often answers questions about the 1960s and 1970s with comments about the 1940s and the swing era before guitars took over, a time he finds more interesting.

And the "showbiz" story that most interests Hudson happened more than 300 years ago.

"Bach was so fascinated with [composer Dieterich] Buxtehude that he walked 200 miles from Germany to Denmark just to see how he played his music," Hudson said.

"That was amazing, walking all that way, especially when you think about what they wore on their feet in those days."

At the end of the interview with Hudson, the radio coincidentally blared The Band's last big hit single, "Ophelia."

It was, to use Cole's description, "uncanny."

THE PENINSULA DAILY NEWS, August 27, 2011

The World According to Garth

In a previous life you went to several concerts a month, when those who are now rock-and-roll dinosaurs walked the earth. Today you live in a rural area and don't get out as much, but in August the music made a house call.

The month began with a spirited performance by Taj Mahal headlining a local blues festival, and ended with something that promised to be extraordinary: A rare performance by Garth Hudson, the remarkable multi-instrumentalist who was one-fifth of The Band. He was touring with his wife Maud, about whom you knew nothing apart from the fact that she sings and is in a wheelchair.

You are working for the local paper as a news reporter, and one of the perks is to interview Garth. This is eagerly anticipated but becomes one of the most difficult and challenging interviews you have ever done. He talks slowly (which makes transcription a lot easier) and provides detailed answers that border on college musicology lectures. Any attempt to talk about Bob Dylan, or fame, or anything concrete is rebuffed in favor of historical tales about how Bach walked 200 miles to learn from one of his idols.

"This is amazing when you consider what they wore on their feet in those days," he says wryly. He later repeats the line onstage.

"This is great information and a lot of fun," you want to say. "But what I really need is a quote." You ask one question, he answers another. The interaction is more like a history lesson, since the facts are obscure and detailed and you have no real control over the conversation.

You talk to him through a Bluetooth system in your car and tape the conversation with a device on the passenger seat. When it is over you hang up and start the car and the radio blares out "Ophelia," The Band's last big single, and you interpret this as a good sign.

You would not think it to look at him, but Garth was famous long ago as the musical colorist for The Band, a group that rivaled The Beatles or anyone else for their songwriting, performance, and all-around aura.

These days they are reduced on radio to a handful of famous tracks, but their potency cannot be overstated. They first performed "The Weight," now a modern hymn, and a partnership with Bob Dylan offered a peaceful musical refuge amid what could be (not always negatively) described as overwhelming artistic chaos.

The Band made it clear from the beginning that it was not like everybody else. The first notes of the first song of their first album, "Tears of Rage," sounded mournful and dissonant to the average pop fan. Many had to listen to the record several times before we were able to "get it."

Not at all like today, where kids listen to a few notes of one song before skipping to the next. The Band would never have survived such a lack of scrutiny.

There are other similarities between The Band and The Beatles. They both had an eight-year recording career and went out as the crowd called out for more. And they were a unit, where success resulted from an equally configured blend of voices and instruments. Taking one away was akin to removing a car wheel or a table leg.

Which is why many fans welcomed Garth to town, even though he was the functional equivalent of Ringo.

The first inkling that something could go awry comes with a late night call from Eric, the musician who is managing the tour. He is driving into town and wondering where they can go to eat at that hour and you remind him that all restaurants aside from McDonald's close by 10. You hear Maud in the background asking for "a steak to go that we can heat up later," which you are not inclined to supply because you have already loaned them money for a hotel.

You check them in. Later you are chatting with Eric in the parking lot when Garth comes out of the hotel and tells you that Maud is "dreadfully allergic" to mosquitoes and we should go to the front desk to get a vacuum cleaner, so we can suck the insects off of the ceiling. The front desk closed hours before Garth arrived, so that isn't an option. So you lend them your vacuum cleaner and hope you get it back in working order.

The next night Eric's band opens the show and plays until the Hudsons arrive. Eric introduces them and the audience hoots with pleasure and then watches respectfully as Garth wheels Maud into the club and down a ramp to the stage.

After a while the crowd's mood shifts from starstruck fascination to irritation and impatience. Garth putters around the stage setting up as if the audience doesn't exist. No one strikes up a conversation because the man is working, but he's not moving very quickly. Just when you are about to lose patience and go home they start playing, and you have to admit they sound pretty good. Eric's band is crisp, although Maud's vocals are all over the map. She kills on a version of "Don't Do It," and her reading of "The Weight" gives the standard its due.

You enjoy the experience, but several people stop you on the street telling you of their disappointment in the show, and with you for recommending it.

To you, the music sounds great because it almost didn't happen. Eric sent a friend to pick up Garth and Maud but the guy got his signals crossed and used a key to enter the room. This caused the musicians to barricade themselves in their room for a while, finally agreeing to appear for the show after you arrive at the hotel along with Mark, the club owner.

Both of you sit patiently in the hall as the Hudsons prepare for the stage, where the audience is waiting. Mark, who has a lot to lose if it all goes south, isn't especially nervous about the situation. But you are.

The next evening you are once again roped into picking them up at the hotel. This time you wait an hour before they finally emerge, and Maud is luminous. They have just worked out a new arrangement for "This Wheel's On Fire," a Band song they rarely perform. Once at the club it all starts over. Garth takes his time wheeling Maud in and starts tinkering again. You decide to cut your losses, go home, play with your cat, and catch up on your correspondence.

The idea came to you the day before, how you could use this proximity to Garth to write something exclusive and special. You decide to take him to an antique pipe organ that was reconstructed in a local church. If you could get Garth to the church, you would have an exclusive video, a rare taped performance and be able to write a compelling news story about a unique event.

It should be simple enough. You call Stan, the guy who rebuilt the organ, and explain the situation. Mr. Hudson can't be rushed. Stan is accommodating, agreeing on our time range, while only requiring an hour's notice to get things started. Garth is a little harder to convince, but he seems to agree after he talks to Barney, who promises to bring along a tape recorder.

Mindful of Garth's slowness you work backwards: The church building closes at 6 p.m. and Stan says we need an hour, so Garth needs to commit by around 4:30. At 5:30 Eric calls and says Garth is ready. Right now you have more respect for Stan's time than Garth's, so you pull the plug, telling Eric "that ship has sunk."

It docks in another harbor. Eric takes Garth and Maud to an organ site two towns away and well out of your newspaper's circulation area, where they spent several hours making music and discussing history. The event was unrecorded, aside from some pictures and a few moments of video Eric managed to snag for himself.

You are disappointed you were not there, and wonder if a great musician plays an antique organ in an empty house with three people listening and nothing ends up on YouTube, if that makes a sound anymore.

Soon enough the thrill is gone and you are more concerned about getting Garth and Maud out of the hotel in time than attempting to gather more material for any future story. While observing their slow departure, it's clear that Garth doesn't recognize anyone else's authority, so you can either play along or not. But if you play along you'll end up pitching in.

A few days later you run into a local musician who had worked the soundboard for Garth's second night, and witnessed the procrastination firsthand. He does not say what you would expect. He tells you that Garth is a true musical genius and follows his own path, which has nothing to do with what others expect of him.

Later you talk to Mark, whom you would also expect to have a bitter taste, but his strongest impression of Garth has to do with his devotion to Maud. "Whatever he does has to do with taking care of her," he said. Which explains the grand entrance of Garth pushing Maud up to the stage, as he is showing us his priorities. And his insistence to acquire a vacuum cleaner at midnight to suck the mosquitoes off the ceiling evolves into a romantic act.

In a previous life you went to several concerts a month. One high point was in 1971, when Taj Mahal opened for The Band. That night Taj strolled onstage alone in front of 10,000 people and played a casual set of acoustic blues and was followed by a strong set by The Band, which was at the height of its powers.

Forty years on, Garth, at 74, is the casual one. He is only five years older than Taj but the difference is startling. Taj is kinetic throughout: breezing into town in the early afternoon, meeting a group of students, playing a crisp, professional show at night and getting back on the bus.

Garth is deliberate, taking one slow step at a time. Commitments are only suggestions, whether they are to begin playing at the advertised start time, or leave the hotel by checkout. It happens when it happens, or it might not happen at all. We must accept this, since he brings the gift of music that arrives on its own terms.

The Band shone so brightly that a powerful magic stuck to everyone who was around, and Garth is still carrying around his share. There are some who don't see the glow, like the people who wanted to charge extra for the Hudsons being two and a half hours late getting out of their hotel room. Usually Garth says they need to stay later and they don't want to pay any more money. Usually that works, because the one time we see Garth show any real emotion is when the routine fails to convince.

After a few weeks and a certain perspective sets in you get it: Garth ignores the rules because he can. His talent must be a blessing and a burden; he comes to town and people cater to his whims, in return attempting to project their impression of what he should be.

So you feel a bit churlish as you recall Garth's last words to you as he left town. "I hope we meet again," he said in a slow drawl, "when everything will be perfect."

CROSSCUT. September 29, 2011

New Wave of Popularity for The Beach Boys

Interviewed by phone, New York City to Jones Beach, NY

JONES BEACH, NY.—The Beach Boys are taking advantage of this seaside theatre, an idyllic setting for one of their concerts, by beating the audience into blissful surf-music submission. Between songs, a guy in red shorts asks a young dancing girl if Brian Wilson is on stage.

"Uh, no," she says, as if she had just been asked to eat week-old sushi. "He's the one that died, right?"

The band starts up again and the guy shrugs. It's too loud for him to explain that it was Dennis Wilson who drowned. Brian is the older brother, the eccentric genius savant. The fact that he has recently played several high-profile shows made some believe that he'd appear here. But tonight the Brian-less group has pumped out five well-known songs nonstop, as if it was Hooked on Beach Boys.

Some Beach Boys fans care about Brian Wilson and some don't. Most of those who don't are here tonight, yelling for songs recorded before they were born and singing along as if the songs were school cheers or the national anthem. As for the band, this particular bunch of 40-year-old guys is wrapped up in singing about the joys of adolescence.

"They're all great songs," band member Bruce Johnston says the next day. "They sound simple, but they're complex, brilliant and fun. With us, instead of the band members being stars, our songs are the stars, our personalities are our songs."

Fine. But where's Brian?

"It's his choice to not be here. We ask him to play all the time, saying if he's going to come to the really big shows then he should come to the more normal dates. Come into the trenches; don't just go for the easy glory. It's been that way since 1963; this isn't anything new."

When Johnston joined the band in 1965, he thought it would be temporary. He says Wilson's waffling does nothing to the band's equilibrium; the show accommodates his presence but doesn't suffer if he's not there.

There are several precedents on this tour, which stops at Toronto's Kingswood Music Theatre tomorrow night for a "hit and run." ("One of our favorite towns," Johnston says, "and we can't even stay the night.") It is their only scheduled Canadian appearance. And while they have toured incessantly, this is the first time since 1980 they have done so in support of a new album.

The self-titled record is the first the band has made since the death of Dennis Wilson. It is the first one since the very early days to recruit an outside producer, and the first to accept new material from outside sources. It is also their first album since 1973's *Holland* that's worth listening to more than once.

The best of the new album comes not from Brian Wilson but from brother Carl. His three songs, along with one from Johnston, elevate the record from a pleasant musical bauble to real art — lush, mature pop with a purpose.

Like the old joke about an errant husband, the Beach Boys' record companies have never understood them. Capitol, their first label, became antsy when they moved from surf toward art. Warner Brothers signed them for the art, but was piqued when it didn't pay off right away. They hooked up with Columbia in 1978, but almost immediately encountered problems, which eventually discouraged them from recording. Says Johnston: "It didn't make any sense to do something until the label was behind us."

The Beach Boys emerged from the southern California of the early sixties, when Los Angeles was still a boom town. A young, vital President made the United States glad to be alive. The Beach Boys reflected this and brought the California myth to the world. If few surfboards were sold in Saskatoon, there wasn't a kid on the continent who didn't know of the freedom of riding a wave.

Then two things happened. The vigorous, optimistic President was assassinated, letting the steam out of the dream. A few months later the Beatles surfaced, devastating the California myth in favor of somewhat more universal experiences.

The Beach Boys grew. They eschewed and then survived psychedelia, forging ahead while taking chances with their sound, which matched anyone note for creative note. In concert they were proud and stubborn, firmly announcing at the outset of each show that they were not a revival act. They were brash, showing that their new music, with its tonal and lyrical substance, matched the optimism and imagination of the old.

If songs from this time — from *Pet Sounds* to *Holland* — make up the richer part of the group's repertoire, few, if any, will be featured on the current tour. They are putting on the hits, giving the people what they want.

"With us, you have something that can go two ways," Johnston says. "It can go totally as an artsy-craftsy band in terms of the songs you want to play live and the way you want to record. Or we can be overly commercial, like some kind of brilliant amusement park on the road.

"But we want to balance the shows so we have a little of everything, instead of doing 'Barbara Ann' 27 times in a row. We need to give the show dynamics instead of pure power. We're trying to mix new with old, do songs people really want to hear. We hope they'll want to hear songs from the new album too."

Even though it sold less than any of their other records, Johnston's favorite Beach Boys album is 1970's *Sunflower*. He also has special praise for "Til I Die," a Brian Wilson stunner tucked away in 1971's *Surf's Up*. "To me, that's the last great Brian Wilson contribution to music," Johnston says. "The vocal counter-point on the fade-out is as provocative or clever as anything Bach ever did."

In 1976, Wilson returned from his self-imposed exile for an anniversary album, *15 Big Ones*. At that time he had not appeared with the band in two years, and had added only pastel strokes to the most recent albums. His re-emergence was less than anyone expected. It did not invigorate the group with a new series of imaginative sounds. Lyrically, he took the band from "unfolding enveloping missiles of soul" to "honking down the gosh-darn highway." If Wilson was destined to be the twentieth century's Bach, it wasn't going to be for any of this.

Johnston concedes that some of the hype — especially that surrounding *15 Big Ones* — was a mistake. "As Carl now says, that album should have been called *15 Little Ones*. I think it was a gross error on our part to say, 'Brian's back, he's well and wonderful,' when he wasn't. It's one of the most distasteful things that I watched happen to our band. When you are told Brian Wilson is back and in his prime, and you have all those hits you've enjoyed, and you compare them to *15 Big Ones*, you'll know that you got conned."

The band is currently weathering another "Brian is Back" media wave, but, Johnston says, "If Brian were really back 100 per cent, he'd be out here now."

In the video for "Getcha Back," the new album's first single, the hero hits the ocean while inside a plastic bubble constructed by Brian Wilson. This scene could be a metaphor for the band: they are trapped on the ocean with no control, inside Brian's bubble and at his mercy, stuck on the surf with nothing to breathe. When Brian speaks, the group listens, but it's unfortunate that he now has little to say.

THE GLOBE AND MAIL, July 25, 1985

Beach Boys Change, But the Sound Stays the Same

Interviews by phone, Silverton, WA to somewhere in California and in person at Grande Ronde, OR

The Beach Boys, or at least a reasonable facsimile thereof, are on the road again.

The songs are the same, of course, and Mike Love, 57, is front and center. But aside from singer/keyboardist Bruce Johnston, 54, who joined in 1965 as a touring replacement for Brian Wilson, the rest of the band is virtually unrecognizable — even to fans.

Carl Wilson died of cancer in February; Al Jardine is off recording a solo album. Brian Wilson, who hasn't toured regularly with the Beach Boys in decades, is basking in the reviews of his recent solo album, *Imagination*, and living in a quiet suburb of Chicago.

Although those key members are missing, the band is chugging along as it has every summer for 37 years, waving the flag for sun, cars and surf.

"Mike is the only one who really has to be here," guitarist David Marks says. "He has the distinctive voice. You can do without any one of us."

"The Beach Boys are a band with great harmonies that sings the songs everybody knows," Love says. "Most of the audience doesn't even know our names." Don't tell that to Ted Cohen, press agent for the 1976 "Brian's Back" tour. He bristles at the idea of a Beach Boys show with no Wilsons. "What they are doing now is just a hollow continuation of the brand," he says. Cohen, now a Los Angeles media consultant, thinks the current lineup is missing some vital parts. "Brian provided the soul for the Beach Boys, and Carl was the heart."

Marks, 50, now a permanent member, was until recently just a footnote in Beach Boys history. He lived across the street from the Wilsons as a child and played on the band's first five albums; Jardine replaced him in 1964. Love asked Marks to join the road show last year "to lend some authenticity," Marks says. "Without the Wilsons around, it adds something to have one of the founders onstage." How does he feel about being one of the Boys again after all these years? "Sure beats sitting on the couch and flipping through the channels."

"Emotionally there is a void, and it's a drag that Carl's gone," Love says. "But for the rest of us who are still here, life goes on, and we do the best we can. Even if Carl isn't there, it still sounds pretty good." These are, after all, many of the same musicians who've provided instrumental punch for two decades. They strive for exact reproductions of the familiar, albeit at a pace that's more energized than in recent memory. "Carl slowed everything down so it would groove," Marks says. "Now we're going a little faster."

There are no plans to add to the canon, though "I'd like to write with Brian again," Love says. "I would have no interest in doing a Beach Boys album without him." Marks, however, is ready. "I'd love to record," he says. "I've written some great songs. I have friends who've written some great songs. But no one here seems interested."

Still, there's no shortage of product. *Endless Harmony*, a VH-1 documentary airing Sunday, demonstrates that — despite Marks' claim that it doesn't matter who's onstage today — the Beach Boys' music is the result of powerful interlocking personalities. A companion CD, a career-spanning 25-track collection with a healthy dose of compelling rarities and alternate versions, is a balanced cross-section of the group's career.

Symphonic Sounds of the Beach Boys, produced by Johnston with the Royal Philharmonic Orchestra, is a classical treatment that began as part of a symphonic tour but was derailed by Carl Wilson's passing. Johnston is ebullient, chatting the disc up at every opportunity. "I don't care if this sells. It's more of a statement." Capitol also hopes to re-release the band's 1964 Christmas album, combined with tracks from an unreleased 1977 effort, for this holiday season. And that will be followed by new editions of the band's creatively fertile 1970-76 output, with the requisite bonus tracks and expanded liner notes.

"We've been dysfunctional at times," Love says. "We've been self-destructive at times. And time has taken its toll. But the most important thing is that we've created a lot of happy people, millions of memories. These are literal good vibrations. You can pick the group apart, but there is a lot of positivity that has been created."

USA TODAY August 20, 1998

Beach Boys' Family and Friends Give the People What They Want

In 1970, Carnie Wilson and Matt Jardine were toddlers posing on the cover of the Beach Boys' stunning *Sunflower* album along with their respective parents, Brian and Alan. Today, the two have entered the family business, becoming key members of the offshoot "Beach Boys Family and Friends" ensemble.

As anybody who saw them knows, the '90s Beach Boys were in a downward spiral. With no new material or arrangements for years, the shows became anachronistic. The death of founding member Carl Wilson from cancer in February 1998 was the final blow, leaving an empty sound and no Wilson onstage.

That is not a problem here. Carnie is joined by sister Wendy, two-thirds of that band with Phillips. This is an ingenious stroke: With the plethora of soundalike backups the Beach Boys have used for years, why not raid the Wilson gene pool? The band has always promoted musical family values, so this passing of the torch is a natural move.

This group seeks to distance itself from the surf music machine led by Mike Love, setting out to perform lost gems from the group's vast catalogue without concentrating on the predictable hits. But tonight, after reading the surf-oriented promotional material put out by the casino, Alan Jardine (the only original Beach Boy here) changed things around. Out went rarities like "Looking at Tomorrow" and "All Summer Long," in favor of a hastily assembled version of "Kokomo" and other surf-infected hits. This pragmatic step was driven by perceived public tastes, and Jardine is not one to deny the people what they want. So for the moment, he caved.

Even with the change in direction, the show breathes new life into what have become tired old chestnuts — simply with the addition of female harmony. Who really needs to hear "Don't Worry, Baby" again? How about if it's sung by sweet-voiced Wendy Wilson? A third potent-girl sound comes from Owen Elliott, daughter of the late Mama Cass.

Vocal enhancements aside, the women stole the night's focus. Carnie celebrated her thirty-first birthday with an onstage cake, while the eight-and-a-half-months pregnant Elliott tottered crankily around the stage and delivered most of her harmonies sitting down.

The boy zone also exploits the family motif with Alan, Matt and brother Adam Jardine, and support by Beach Boys stalwart multi-instrumentalist (and in-law) Billy Hinsche. The seven voices blend into a harmony that often takes on a life of its own.

Especially powerful was a four-song *Pet Sounds* interlude, leading off with a lush "God Only Knows." The boys and girls traded off the verses, leading into the final section that had, astoundingly enough, more texture than the original. To close the section, they played "You Still Believe in Me," something most have probably never hear the Love-led band play.

"In My Room," driven by Hinsche's gentle acoustic guitar, was similarly transformed by the light harmony of the Wilson/Elliott alliance. Only a "Monday, Monday" cover missed the mark; the harmonies were clear but the overall sound was out of balance.

The "Kokomo" encore, with Carnie taking Carl Wilson's high parts, was injected with new life, but at "In My Room" beat the hits hands down. Throughout, Matt Jardine was the secret weapon. Long ponytail swinging, he provides the vocal parts that, on the original, were performed by three different people. Alan sang lead on "Wouldn't It Be Nice" for years, but now generously bequeaths the part to his son.

"Growing up with the Beach Boys, there was always a sense of family and warmth," Matt said before the show. "But that has gone away in recent years. This band recaptures that feeling."

ROLLING STONE ONLINE, May 1, 1999

Beach Boy vs. Beach Boy

Interviews by phone, from Bainbridge Island, WA to various locations.

While the Beach Boys were once musically illustrious, in the Nineties they've spent more time in the courtroom than the recording studio. Lead singer Mike Love sued his cousin Brian Wilson over composer credits. Carl Wilson led a conservatorship to separate Brian from his controversial therapist, Eugene Landy, while the entire band sued Brian over statements in his biography. Now, the band's management is suing guitarist Al Jardine over his new band's name "The Beach Boys Family and Friends."

The case comes to a head in a few days when Brother Records International (BRI), the owner and administrator of the band's trademark, will enter a Los

Angeles courtroom and attempt to permanently enjoin founding member Jardine, 57, from using any variation of the Beach Boys' name. The action is directed at a New Year's Eve show in Huntington Station, N.Y., and is the third time this year that BRI has filed a similar claim. (The others were dismissed.)

Jardine has filed his own lengthy counterclaim, and has insisted that he is taking considerable pains to differentiate his touring outfit from that headed by Love, 58.

Jardine, was one of five founding Beach Boys, along with Love and the three Wilson brothers — Brian, Dennis and Carl. He did not play on the band's earliest Capitol albums, having left to attend school, but rejoined just before the Beach Boys' peak in the mid-'60s.

He was not as well known as Love or the Wilsons, but was essential nonetheless. He sang lead on "Help Me, Rhonda" and subsequently suggested that Brian Wilson record the folk song "Sloop John B." He also sang many of Brian's lead vocal parts onstage after Brian quit the road in 1965. BRI defines the Beach Boys in legal terms as "smooth four-part harmonies, with all four males at the front of the stage." Up until '98, Jardine was one of those voices.

Love's outfit is now billed as "The Beach Boys" while Jardine travels as "The Beach Boys Family and Friends." BRI objects to Jardine using the Beach Boys name in any format, and has awarded an "exclusive license" to Love for use of the name — even though each band has only one original member.

"Mike is the Beach Boys," said BRI attorney Michael Flynn. "He sang and wrote many of the original songs, and is recognizable to audiences as the band's leader. To have Al out there touring as the Beach Boys dilutes the trademark, but worst of all it confuses the public." Jardine's lawyer, Vincent Chieffo, counters, "Alan is as much of a Beach Boy as Mike, and it is deceptive for Mike to represent himself as 'The Beach Boys.' Mike is touring as he has for years, but is keeping the profits once claimed by Carl and Alan for himself."

Expectations notwithstanding, there is no confusion once you've entered the venue. Love's lieutenants are singer-keyboardist Bruce Johnston and guitarist David Marks, both peripheral players in the band's long history. Jardine brings along his two sons, along with Carnie and Wendy Wilson (Brian Wilson's daughters, formerly with Wilson Phillips). This is a major bone of contention, as BRI objects strenuously to including "girls" in a Beach Boys context. Jardine disagrees, saying that the female voices provide a boost that the music needs.

Love presents a fast-paced 30 songs, drawn predominantly from the surf years, in 90 minutes. Jardine has worked some of the more artistically heralded, yet less commercially successful material from *Pet Sounds* to *Holland* into the set with the surf/car/fun songs.

In doing this, Jardine has run afoul of the corporation.

From the complaint: "Much of Jardine's repertoire with Beach Boys Family and Friends include many songs that the Beach Boys do not regularly play in concert, songs [that] are about many issues that are not traditionally associated with the Beach Boys, i.e. cars, surf, girls and fun." Here, Love may be flouting his own rules, as some of the songs on his set list — "In My Room," "God Only Knows" — don't exactly fit the criteria. Love has also turned much of the set into an all-purpose oldies show, including such classics as "Duke of Earl" and "Why Do Fools Fall In Love?"

Jardine's inability to convince either Brian Wilson or Carl Wilson's estate — the other shareholders — to vote with him cripples his position (to convince either would bring about a deadlock). According to Flynn, the Wilsons' position has little to do with family or friendship. "Mike has maybe five years of touring left, and he generates a lot of income," he said.

Carl Wilson died in February 1998. As the band's longtime mediator, he had held a balance between its arguing factions, and, according to several sources, his death allowed these situations to become fractious.

If this band has become a corporation, it is also an institution. "I think the Beach Boys should go on even if only Mike Love is in it," said former Byrds leader Roger McGuinn, in an e-mail to *Rolling Stone*. "It would be sad for the world not to have a Beach Boys band. I wouldn't be in a band like that myself, but if Mike wants to do it, it's okay with me."

At this point in the band's history, it's sad that the two men who collaborated on the lyric "omnipresent love surrounds you/Wisdom warming as the sun/You and I are truly one" (from 1972's "All This Is That") can now only snarl at each other from across a courtroom.

ROLLING STONE ONLINE, December 8, 1999

Keeping the Beach Boys Alive

There are some really good reasons to loathe Mike Love's Beach Boys. There is the authenticity problem: There is no one named Wilson onstage, and Love is the only founding member present. We can get personal: Love sued his cousin

Brian Wilson for songwriting credit, refused to tour with Carl Wilson when he was sick and legally prevented founding member Alan Jardine from using any part of the Beach Boys name. Then there's the show: The band's current set list concentrates on its surf years, with only a cursory nod to its richest music. Finally, there is something really ludicrous about a nearly sixty-year-old guy prancing around, singing songs about high school and pretending to be a "boy."

The complaints may be irrelevant. Brian Wilson partisans have long since stopped attending these shows. As for authenticity, there are no veteran bands now touring who still have all of their original guys. All this certainly didn't matter to the sellout crowd who gathered at Seattle's Pier 62. As the sun set over Puget Sound, this music machine cranked out a sped-up set of surf oldies and assorted gems, following its now-established pattern of 30 songs in 90 minutes.

Throughout, Love seemed to want to give us even more reasons not to like him. He went off on several sophomoric pro-Bush/anti-Clinton rants. This was so strident that it probably made even the Bush people in the audience feel creepy (and last we looked, Bush was running against Gore). He then dedicated "Why Do Fools Fall In Love" to Diana Ross, "who isn't feeling too good right now." Then, his smarmy lieutenant, Bruce Johnston, razzed the "rental Supremes." Careful, Bruce. Beleaguered as the recent Supremes tour may have been, it still had a greater percentage of original members than these Beach Boys.

Still, this version of the Beach Boys plays crisp, clean and competent music. That is to say, close your eyes and this could be the old days. Guitarists Adrian Baker and Philip Bardowell bracketed Love and Johnston onstage, adding passion and enthusiasm to the mix. Bassist Chris Farmer — who looked like a healthy Brian Wilson — and drummer Mike Kowalski gave the band depth. In fact, Love and Johnston (who spent much of the set singing off-mike) only went through the motions, becoming vestigial organs in the band they are supposed to lead.

While it's obvious that Love won't grow up, he also can't last forever. Documents filed last year in the court case versus Jardine stated that Love has about five years of touring left. But that doesn't mean the Beach Boys should pack it in. Love has already tossed authenticity out the window, and proven that a group of ringers can perform these songs very well indeed. One by one, the Wilson brothers and Jardine went away, with no appreciable change in the sound. So it goes to follow that Love could leave and much of the audience wouldn't really notice.

One day Bruce Johnston could become leader. This is doubly horrifying, as they would probably have to let him play his "I Write the Songs" all the way through. But maybe it really doesn't matter. As repugnant as it may be to purists, an officially sanctioned cover band bringing Brian Wilson's music to a new generation of fans may not be entirely a bad thing. (The precedent for this behavior is called the Glenn Miller Orchestra.)

What would Love do if he were no longer up front? We will surely miss witticisms such as his perspective on Brian Wilson: "My cousin is such a genius. He's stayed home since 1965 and we send him money." He may be angling for a job in the Bush cabinet. Failing that, he threatened to move to Seattle for a month, get a condo (perhaps forgetting Jimi Hendrix's admonition that the planet should "never hear surf music again") and spend the time visiting the Experience Music Project. "That place is amazing," he said. "It would take weeks for you to see everything that's in there."

"I wish," Johnston piped up, "that we were in there."

ROLLING STONE ONLINE, August 4, 2000

Beach Boys Not in Harmony

Lifetime Grammy award comes at chilly time for Beach Boys

There seems to be scant possibility that special "Lifetime Achievement" recognition at tonight's Grammy Awards will soothe the acrimony that has divided the Beach Boys in recent years.

"Thank God we don't have to perform," said founding member Alan Jardine before yesterday's non-televised ceremony, a day before the Grammys. "Hopefully, we can just pick up our awards and not run into each other. I'm just delighted that the original band is getting this recognition, as opposed to that fake thing that is playing today."

Jardine's son Matt, who attended yesterday's ceremony, said that his father barely spoke to his former colleagues. "Unfortunately, they seemed to have as little as possible to do with each other," he said. "There was a lot of tension, but it was all glossed over because of the thrill of the Grammys."

The Lifetime Achievement award honors Carl and Dennis Wilson, both deceased, along with Jardine, Brian Wilson, Mike Love and Bruce Johnston. Yesterday's award was received by Love, Jardine and Johnston, along with Carl

Wilson's sons and Dennis Wilson's daughter and grandson. Also in the audience was Jardine's mother, Virginia, who put up $300 for the first Beach Boys' session.

Brian Wilson skipped yesterday's ceremony due to scheduling conflicts, according to a spokesperson, but is expected to attend tonight's event. "It is a great honor," he said.

The ill feelings that split the band into three factions (Love, Jardine and Brian Wilson) originated after the 1998 death of Carl Wilson, who acted as peacemaker. "The group split up a little bit after Carl died," Brian said. "We didn't officially make any statements about it, but I think people have figured it out for themselves. It's too bad."

Since that time Brian Wilson has stayed neutral. Not so for the other survivors. Alan Jardine's animosity is directed at Love and Johnston, who continue to tour as the Beach Boys but successfully enjoined Jardine to prevent him from performing under any form of the name. One year after that decision, Jardine was encouraged by a California ruling that allowed Steppenwolf bassist Nick St. Nicholas to use his old band's name. Jardine feels this sets a precedent for the re-opening of his own case.

If things fell apart after Carl Wilson's death, Jardine noted that Dennis Wilson was also an effective (although unconventional) mediator.

"Dennis was a real karma corrector," Jardine recalled. "If Mike ever got out of hand Dennis would take him off of the plane and punch him in the nose. Then he'd behave for a few weeks, until Dennis would have to do it again."

ROLLING STONE ONLINE, February 21, 2001

Beach Boy Charges Former Bandmates With Excluding Him From Concerts

More than a year after a California court ruled that he couldn't tour under the moniker "The Beach Boys' Family and Friends," Beach Boys founding member Alan Jardine has sued his former bandmates for $4 million, claiming that he has been excluded from recent concerts.

The defendants in the suit are Mike Love, Brian Wilson, the Carl Wilson Trust and Brother Records Inc., the owner and administrator of the Beach Boys trademark. An initial ruling is expected July 23.

"This is frivolous harassment, where Alan is trying to get money that he does not deserve," said Brother Records attorney Michael Flynn.

"The entire premise of the Beach Boys has been to promote love, harmony and music," Jardine said as he prepared for a show at an Indian casino in Bow, Washington. "But right now the 'Beach Boys' are taking the financial rather than the creative route, and Mike is making an end run to grab all of the income. This is a moral issue."

Jardine had no desire to bill himself as "The Beach Boys," instead opting for "The Beach Boys' Family and Friends." But in granting a license to Love, Brother Records prevented any use of the name by Jardine, a decision that was upheld by a California court in December 1999. Jardine claims that he was offered use of the name in 1998, but the offer was withdrawn.

Currently, the band formerly known as the Beach Boys can be seen in three performing ensembles, each with one original band member: The licensed version with Love and touring replacement Bruce Johnston; Brian Wilson's touring band; and Jardine's Family and Friends, which includes Brian Wilson's daughters Carnie and Wendy.

That Jardine has filed suit against his former bandmates has not affected what he calls the "wonderful spiritual connection" that occurs onstage. Says Billy Hinsche, the music director of Jardine's band, "The topic never comes up. It's only business and has nothing to do with anything personal."

Upon returning to California from this week's show, Jardine plans to do the final mixing for *Live in Las Vegas*, a recording of a 1999 concert to be sold on his Web site (www.aljardine.com). While the album has many of the expected hits played by the other iterations it also includes more obscure selections like "Breakaway" and "Wild Honey."

Despite all the ill feeling, Jardine said he would play with Love and/or Wilson if they could bury their differences. "These guys are my lifelong partners," he said.

ROLLING STONE ONLINE, July 5, 2001

Founding Member Can't Use Band's Name

Founding Beach Boy Alan Jardine received a severe legal setback Monday when a U.S. District Court ruling prohibited him from touring with his band under the name the "Beach Boys Family and Friends," as he did throughout 1999. Instead, he may continue as the "Family and Friends Beach Band." "The Beach Boys" moniker is used by the touring band featuring another founding member, Mike Love.

"We are happy with the result," said attorney Mike Flynn, who represents Brother Records International (BRI), the Beach Boys' corporate entity. "This terminates his entire case."

Jardine's, attorney Jeffrey Benice, said the ruling will be appealed. Furthermore, this ruling will not affect the $4 million lawsuit Jardine filed June 30 against Love and Brian Wilson, alleging that he was excluded from recent Beach Boys concerts.

Benice, hired by Jardine in June, takes over from Vincent Chieffo, who handled Jardine's legal affairs for several years. Benice said this move will allow Chieffo to testify during the upcoming appeal.

Flynn said that Jardine receives revenue from the Love-led Beach Boys tour, per the initial corporate agreement. He added that BRI had offered to settle financially with Jardine several times, but will not grant him use of the Beach Boys name.

Jardine could not be reached for comment.

ROLLING STONE ONLINE, August 3, 2001

Billy Hinsche: From Dino, Desi & Billy to the Beach Boys

Interviewed by phone, Bainbridge Island, WA to Las Vegas, NV

The Beach Boys were at a turning point in 1974. They had spent the previous six years in the commercial wilderness cranking out arty, clever albums, but a renewed interest emerged in the surf/car sounds that first built their reputation. So this particular tour, presented in an often-ragged video directed by band member Billy Hinsche as part of a film school project, is basically the last gasp of the more cerebral version of the Beach Boys.

Hinsche has spent his postgraduate days providing backup for the Beach Boys — an occasional member of the regular band followed by a spot as musical director for Al Jardine's Beach Boys offshoot. He's now pulled together *1974-On the Road With the Beach Boys* from the raw tape, much of which features the Beach Boys and their backing band fooling around offstage. He's blended this with current interviews with some of the participants, shot in black-and-white in order to match the original footage.

Hinsche, 58, has been onstage since he was 13, when he was the one member of Dino, Desi & Billy without a famous relative. That changed when his sister married Carl Wilson, and he has been a member of the Beach Boys' extended family since. In the meantime, he's had a front row to all the band's highs and lows, legal squabbles and musical triumphs.

He spoke to us from his home in Nevada, where he teaches music in between calls to play with one old friend or another.

How did this project happen?

In 1974, I was working toward a degree at UCLA and it was a class project. I got a lot of film, put it away and forgot about it. Recently, I was looking through my garage and found the video reels and turned them into this movie. I tightened up a lot of the scenes that dragged on a bit, and edited it into the final product. In a lot of it I was just getting the feel of the camera, so it's pretty loose.

For my next project I'd like to do something about Carl. I have a lot of home movies, Super 8 stuff that doesn't have any sound, but it's in color. I'd like to pull that all together. I'd really like to share this; I think it would be a great project.

How did people feel about being filmed back then?

They loved it. The camera was like a magnet. People would run up and want to be filmed. It was a novelty. People in the Midwest would see these guys from Hollywood, come up and say, "Hey, we want to be in your movie." It was all very innocent, not like some of the malicious stuff that goes on today.

What was it like being in the Beach Boys in 1974?

It was a great time. *Rolling Stone* had just named us band of the year. There was a lot of room to stretch out and take prolonged solos. It was a really interesting configuration, a very tight unit. It was different every night, depending on where we were playing. We had our "meat and potatoes" set, where we would do the surfing songs, or the longer set that had more of the later stuff.

How was it different from how the band is today?

I did see the band recently, and they sounded pretty good. I enjoyed the show. It has more to do with the songs themselves than who is in the band. The audience loved it; they don't care about the band's history or the politics. The music is still strong. I'm still friendly with most of the guys. And I've known

(Mike Love's son and current band member) Christian Love all his life. He's a good kid, and has as much right to be onstage as anyone. He's family.

SB: If Al Jardine were to sing with the new band would it necessarily improve the sound?

BH: I think so. It would mean a lot for the fans because Al was one of the main voices, and his voice is still in excellent shape. I can actually see both sides here. I understand why Al feels what he does, and I understand Mike too. But the good news is that everyone is talking to each other; they are more friendly and there has been a rapprochement. It may be time to make peace, considering that the 50th anniversary of when the band started is coming up. I'm not trying to tease you here, I don't have any inside information. I'm just saying that something could happen.

What do you think when you listen to the Dino, Desi & Billy records?

I don't listen to them very often. When I do, they sound good, they were a lot of fun. We had a good time recording them. We had a great band, the whole Wrecking Crew. Although we were shocked at first when we arrived at the studio we were surprised that we weren't going to be playing our own instruments. We didn't understand how this could happen. We had these teenage dreams that we could play our own instruments competently. We were wrong.

But it's pretty raw, and sounds like you could be playing.

They played like a trio, with three pieces. There were not a lot of keyboard fills in there, which would have suggested that it wasn't us. There was a lot of percussion, and drum fills everywhere. You would listen to the record and think "Hey, that Desi really can play the drums." It wasn't Desi. But the thing was, he really could play the drums. Dino, Desi & Billy aren't in the Rock Hall of Fame, and we never sold a million records. But we were on the Ed Sullivan Show, which was a big deal. There were some people who said we only were a success because of who our families were, that we had an instant success. But our first record, which we played on *Hollywood Palace*, went nowhere. "I'm A Fool" sold a lot because it was a good record. You can't make people buy something they don't like.

We are like a lot of groups from that time that cannot reunite, since one of our members has died. But he didn't die of a drug overdose or in some other embarrassing way; he died defending his country. That was pretty strong, a good way to go.

Your first album had three Dylan songs. How did that happen?

The way we picked out the songs is that producer Lee Hazlewood would come in and give us all copies of Billboard and Cash Box charts. He'd tell us to pick out the songs we liked and we would learn to play them. It wasn't so much picking Dylan, it was picking the Byrds. We loved the Byrds. It was all connected. We'd go to Dino's house, and Terry Melcher was over there because he was seeing one of the Martin girls, and he'd bring Roger McGuinn, who was called Jim back then. Roger and I have stayed in touch. He just sent me an e-mail, to join his Linkedin network.

Did you ever meet Dylan?

A couple of times, in passing. He was very quiet. One time I was walking into a club with Rodney Bingenheimer and Dylan was walking out. There's a picture of that.

A picture of you and Dylan?

No, I took the picture of Dylan and Rodney.

Do you see a lot of the people you knew in the 1960s?

I see a lot of people when they come to Las Vegas. There are a lot of survivors. Mark Volman and Howard Kaylan from the Turtles, Paul Revere and the Raiders, Peter Noone. We are all survivors, like if we were all in the same class together. We all had some great moments.

You are one of the few people in your "class" to have gone to college, much less get a degree. What has that meant to you?

It has really helped me in life. I know how to get a project done, which is something you learn from writing a term paper. I learned a lot about history, language, art and a lot of other subjects. Even though I never had an office job it made me a better person.

I had gotten an offer to join the Beach Boys as a full-time member in the late 1960s, which I accepted. But the manager of the band and my parents got together and decided that it would be better if I went to college. It was a shaky time for the Beach Boys, and the future of that job was uncertain. As it turned out I played with the band while I was in college, in the summertime.

But I was living at home, under my parents' roof. My parents had not attended college. My sister had married young, to Carl, and had not gotten her college degree. So it fell to me to bring one home for the family.

How did people treat you, when you were in school?

No one knew who I was. I hadn't been on TV for a few years and wasn't really recognizable. There were 20,000 kids there, and it was a big campus.

What does it mean to have played in the Beach Boys?

That you are pretty darn good at what you do, and that you must be doing something right to get an opportunity to play in one of the greatest bands ever. It's a credit to you that you were invited to participate, and that you made the cut. It also means that you can get the call to come back any time. I joke about this, but unless you've been fired and rehired, and fired and rehired, you really haven't been in the Beach Boys.

SONICBOOMERS, April 2010

GRAHAM NASH:
A Technology to Teach the Children Well

Graham Nash, Tacoma, WA April 2004
Interviewed by phone, Silverton, OR to somewhere in California

In the information age, powerful technology without compelling content is an empty experience indeed. This realization by the singer Graham Nash led to his partnership with Silicon Graphics Inc., the maker of powerful graphical work stations based in Mountain View, California. With the backing of the company, Mr. Nash has created Lifesighs, which he describes as "a one-man historical, musical, informative, empowering stage show," which he intends to take on the road this summer to college campuses and small theaters.

Lifesighs, developed in conjunction with Rand Weatherwax, a producer and software programmer, uses multimedia technology to present Mr. Nash's life and times in story, video and song — from his birth in wartime England, through his childhood in Manchester, his musical career with the Hollies and then Crosby, Stills & Nash, and then as a solo artist and social activist. He now lives in Encino, California.

During a Lifesighs performance, Mr. Nash intends to take the stage live, to assume the role of host and teacher for this digitally driven, personal examination of modern history. Flourishes will include 25-foot-high computer generated images of historical figures like Churchill, Stalin and Hitler, who, with the aid of actors speaking off stage, will appear to answer questions from the audience.

Where did the idea for Lifesighs originate?

It came from a series of college lectures I did several years ago. The kids had a lot of questions, about Watergate, Woodstock, and everything in between. I wanted to find a way that I could make them visualize what I was talking about. I set about to create a database of all the information, one that I could manipulate in real time. So I can talk about a subject for 10 minutes one night, and give it one minute the next.

What is a typical Lifesighs encounter?

I talk about Manchester, and how World War II affected me on a personal level. So I bring up world leaders of the time — Stalin, Hitler, Roosevelt, and Churchill — and interact with them.

What technical obstacles have you faced?

We had to figure out what the database and interface should look like. We had to make it clear that I was reacting to this information in real time, rather than responding to information on a tape or a videodisk. And we wanted to do something unique. People have used digital video, huge screens and three-dimensional objects, but never simultaneously and in a live stage show.

How do college students react to you and your music?

They are most curious about the 1960s. It was the last time the youth of this country felt that they had any control over their own destiny. Kids want to know about that time and how they can retain that power. I will provide them with information about how to take action, giving them the ammunition to become involved with projects in this country without giving them some tools to deal with them

What are the benefits of today's technology?

It's making the world more accessible. The world is shrinking, and technology brings you closer to other people. This decreases the propensity to kick the hell out of them and kill them. The internet gives you a better sense of community as well as your fellow human beings.

THE NEW YORK TIMES, March 13, 1995

CSN To Cover Pre-CSN Tunes

Thirty years after they left their respective bands, David Crosby, Stephen Stills and Graham Nash, better known as Crosby, Stills & Nash, are harking back to their early careers by re-recording some of their pre-CSN tunes for an upcoming album.

Crosby, Stills & Nash came together respectively from the '60s psychedelic folk-rock bands the Byrds, Buffalo Springfield and the Hollies. Now, the trio is acknowledging that pedigree with plans to re-record one or more songs from each of their old bands as part of a new album they are now recording in Los Angeles.

"Last year, when we asked our fans what they wanted to hear, several of them asked for 'Turn! Turn! Turn!'" Nash said, referring to their last tour during which members of the audience put in requests for songs. "It sounded great, so we decided to try some Buffalo Springfield and Hollies songs."

Among the songs that kept coming up was "Turn! Turn! Turn!" which Crosby recorded with the Byrds. The idea to incorporate Hollies and Buffalo Springfield tunes as part of their upcoming project followed, after they realized how well the Pete Seeger-penned song turned out. "Since a lot of our fans are very young, these songs will be new to them," Nash said.

Whether the project will include one song from each band or an entire album of CSN covers of its members' vintage hits will depend on how well the songs work in the studio, he added. Meanwhile, each member has about 30 new songs from which to choose for the next project.

The trio has not chosen which vintage songs they will use for the new album, due out this summer at the earliest. But Nash did list his preferences from each act. Among his choices were "Turn! Turn! Turn!" and "Eight Miles High" from the Byrds, "Uno Mundo" and "Rock and Roll Woman" from Buffalo Springfield, and "I Can't Let Go" and "King Midas in Reverse" from his own early band, the Hollies.

He also indicated that CSN may record some songs written and performed by other members of their previous bands, such as his former Hollies mate Allan Clarke.

The as-yet-untitled album would follow a just-completed effort from Crosby's side project Crosby, Pevar and Raymond, an album that Crosby recorded with his newly discovered biological son. It would also be the first CSN album since 1994's *After the Storm* and the first since the group dissolved its long-term partnership with Atlantic Records, which had released every album since 1969's landmark *Crosby, Stills & Nash*.

SONICNET, April 1998

Rockin' in the Free World

Neil Young, David Crosby, Tacoma WA April 2004

During the intermission at Wednesday's Crosby, Stills, Nash & Young performance, Susan Nash turned Portland's Rose Quarter into a birthday tribute to her husband. She passed out hats to eager fans and supervised the arrangement of fifty-eight candles along the proscenium. This number is astounding. Not only does Graham Nash hardly act his age, he has spent more than half of that time associated with a band that is only now achieving its full potential.

Five dates into their reunion tour, these rocking seniors have found a groove more energetic and enlightening than what they displayed more than half a lifetime ago. They scrambled expectations: The traditional openers and closers, "Suite: Judy Blue Eyes" and "Find the Cost of Freedom," respectively about lost love and early death, were scrapped in favor of the optimistic and redemptive "Carry On" and "Long May You Run." Instead of long acoustic and electric sets, they started out hard, downshifted into a softer set after an intermission, and then kicked into a deconstructive seven-song sequence that began with "Woodstock" and crashed into "Rockin' in the Free World."

There, Neil Young took control. While he floated on the balls of his feet in the acoustic set, he flew upward when he plugged in, tossed his guitar in the air, and caught it on the way down. This may be a familiar occurrence to his fans, but having Stephen Stills challenging his every note, bouncing and laughing together as their guitars screamed in cacophonous duel, is a rare and exhilarating sight.

Backed only by legendary Stax Records bassist Duck Dunn and drummer Jim Keltner — who packed his propulsive punch while inexplicably positioned between an antique lamp and a wooden Indian — CSN&Y acted as generous equals. Birthday boy Nash, who led stellar renditions of his own "Teach Your Children," "Marrakesh Express" and "Our House," has always ceded the spotlight to his more aggressive bandmates. On this tour, however, all four have adopted that same attitude. They acknowledged each other throughout, adding the patented four-part harmony to such unlikely targets as "For What It's Worth" and a pipe organ-driven "After the Goldrush."

On this night, however, Young was slightly more than an equal and Stills slightly less. Young's guitar insinuated itself into every aural opening, while Stills — aside from the aforementioned guitar duels — seemed more intent on managing the sound than sharing the spotlight.

While there were plenty of popular crowd pleasers, nine songs — about one-third of the concert — came from the recent *Looking Forward* CD. While new, the songs aren't completely unfamiliar. Nash's "Heartland" borrows a line from the Beatles' "I'm Only Sleeping" in making a case for slowing down, while the cheers of recognition for Young's "Slowpoke" came from fans who thought they were getting "Heart of Gold." But, by the first harmonica break, the song was earning its own applause.

Some improved over the recorded versions. Stills' "Seen Enough," an annoying polemic on record, gained new depth live as the backing vocals were brought front and center. Similarly, Young's jazz-tinged guitar lifted "Dream for Him" into another realm. The song, David Crosby's paean to his young son, offered an unaffected look at senior parenting. At the song's end, Crosby kicked his legs out from his stool and smiled shyly, offering up a pretty good idea of how he looked at age five.

Crosby's over-documented drug problems have made him a curiosity, but judging by this performance it's well past time to remove him from the sympathy list. He held his own with his compatriots — not an easy feat considering Nash's vocal ebullience and the Stills/Young guitar interplay. He would often slam rather than play his guitar, but he also turned in a slowed-down, subtle rendition of the raga-tinged "Guinnevere" and added appropriate touches of fury to "Long Time Gone" and "Almost Cut My Hair."

The "Long May You Run" encore closed the show with a big smile. In another life, Stills and Young incurred some well-deserved Crosby/Nash wrath when their vocals were cut from the recorded version. Here, they set that record straight. And even if they cannot rewrite their fractious history, CSN&Y are now reaching all of the grace notes.

ROLLING STONE ONLINE, February 4, 2000

"It's Better Now, I'm Not Wasted"

Interviewed in Portland, OR

David Crosby and Graham Nash have lived at the cultural flashpoint for more than 30 years. As they edge toward 60, the musicians haven't lost their passion for social causes, even if much of the world seems to be less involved than in the 1960s.

For his part, Crosby can't seem to stay out of the headlines. His well-publicized bout with drugs was barely out of mind when he revealed himself as the biological father of singer Melissa Etheridge's children. His latest book, *Stand and Be Counted*, examines the role of music in modern social protest.

Their new album with Stephen Stills and Neil Young is titled, appropriately enough, *Looking Forward*. They sat down to discuss the past, the future, getting wasted and the new family structure.

It seems like the time 30 years ago was better than today, more interesting.

Crosby: For me it's better now. I'm not wasted. I'm having a lot more fun as a grownup with a family. Back then I was obsessed with getting as much sex as possible, getting as loaded as I possibly could. That was a pleasure, but nothing compared to the pleasures that I have right now. Like you just saw my little boy, right? Those other pleasures don't measure up to what it's like to be a father to a child like that.

If you were 20 today, knowing what you do now, how would it be different?

Crosby: I'd get a lot more work done in a lot less time. I wasted all that time getting loaded. I could have been making music. I almost died, so every day becomes precious. Right now, I'm conscious of the fact that we have a limited amount of time here. I don't waste a second. I don't waste time being mad at people. I don't waste time competing with people who have nothing to do with me. I don't waste time putting up a shell, I spend time on the things that are really important to me, my music, my family, other things that I live to do.

What would motivate you to write another "Ohio?"

Crosby: Hopefully we won't have that kind of stimulus staring us in the face anytime soon. We react to the world as it happens. We want to applaud the people who perform exemplary acts of humanity, if we see injustice we want to point it out and say that it seems wrong.

Nash: You were talking about "Ohio?" With all due respect, what happened in Columbine was way more tragic than what happened anywhere else. The media changes the way people live and leaves very little room to really react.

Your website is providing some pretty good tour information. Do you talk to a lot of fans online?

Nash: Yes. You're not black on the Internet. You're not Jewish, or gay. You are only your words. If your brain is in gear and you type good words, people will respond.

Crosby: People who are flustered when they meet us face-to-face aren't when they send us e-mail. They'll tell us what they are thinking. The Internet is unbelievably powerful, and what we are seeing now are just the baby steps. It is going to be huge. Everything is going to change.

Have we made too much of this sperm donor thing?

Crosby: It's a little bit overblown because Melissa and I are both in the public eye. If it had been two families that nobody knew, nobody would have said squat about it. But it's a perfectly normal thing for a straight family and a gay family to do, if they like each other.

Nash: You should look at the sociological impact here, of what David has done. He's been on the front edge of so many things for so many years, and has stumbled onto something that could have a very profound effect on the way that families are raised. I was deeply moved by the *Rolling Stone* cover, and the headline that called it "the start of a new American family." I said, "Goddamn it, Crosby's done it again."

MYPRIMETIME.COM, February 6, 2000

Will Buffalo Springfield Roam Again?

Stephen Stills, Tacoma WA April 2002
Interviews by phone from Silverton, OR to various locations and in person in LA (Dewey Martin).

Neil Young's new album, *Silver and Gold*, features a plaintive ballad titled "Buffalo Springfield Again," where he expresses nostalgia for the band that first put him on the map. Singing "I'd like to see those guys again and give it a shot / Maybe now we can show the world what we've got," he hints toward a reunion, which would neatly dovetail the recently completed Crosby, Stills, Nash and Young road show and give legs to the long-awaited Buffalo Springfield box set. Indeed, now that CSN&Y have re-lit their flame, it would seem to be the perfect time for Young and Springfield cohort Stephen Stills to dig a little deeper into the past.

Fans shouldn't hold their breath. Members of the often brilliant band that was derailed by intramural jealousies and individual ambition still carry considerable baggage. And while the contentious competition between Young and Stills is now resolved, getting the other three members on the same stage — or even the same room — is a dicey proposition.

For a band with such a spectral influence, the Buffalo Springfield were exceedingly short-lived. The five members first met in an L.A. traffic jam in April 1966 and played their last show just two years later. Along the way there were three albums: A self-titled debut, the diverse *Buffalo Springfield Again* and *Last Time Around*, more a collection of individually produced tracks than a group effort. "The first album was the best we made and captured how we sounded as a band," guitarist/singer Richie Furay recalls. "The others were piecemeal."

Furay, who later led Poco, holds the key to any reunion. Unique as former rockers go, he is now the pastor of a Colorado church. He acknowledges his past but isn't waiting around for the call to reunite. In fact, when the CSN&Y tour visited nearby Denver, Furay didn't think the occasion was important enough to reschedule the regular Bible study class. But Furay is at least open to the idea of playing with his old pals — even though his offer to put together an opening band for the CSN&Y tour was rebuffed. Would he participate in a Springfield reunion? He supplies an enthusiastic "Yes!" but adds, "I would have to know the details and have some input."

Drummer Dewey Martin is another story. Ebullient at sixty, he is still riding the reputation of his finest hour, two short years that ended more than thirty years ago. He doesn't play much anymore, but has invented and patented a variable height drum rim that he says "will change how drummers play." But while Martin certainly has time on his hands, he still holds a grudge against Stills for "defrauding" him out of royalties and preventing his use of the Buffalo Springfield name (which is actually a position shared by Furay and Young).

Bassist Bruce Palmer, who was in and out of the band due to drug convictions, is now living on 100 acres near Bancroft, Ont., where he isn't doing much of anything. Palmer is coy about how long it would take him to get into musical shape, saying, "Great players never divulge that information," but Martin estimates that "it would take about three weeks for him to get his chops together."

Even so, Furay, Stills and Young with another rhythm section would satisfy at least the promoters. Furay won't rule out such an arrangement, but points out, "It wouldn't be a Buffalo Springfield reunion then, would it?"

If there is little chance of an actual reunion, the box set — now slated for a November release — will go a long way toward establishing Springfield on a level comparable to their contemporaries, such as the already anthologized and canonized Byrds, Doors and Jefferson Airplane. Said Young in an unused promotional interview supplied by Reprise Records to *Rolling Stone*: "We didn't know what we were doing. We didn't have the kind of direction we needed and didn't have the production assistance we needed. We were too young and didn't reach our potential."

The box set has been on and off of Elektra's release schedule for the past two years (Elektra gobbled up Atco, for which Springfield recorded). Last slated for late 1999, it was further delayed when Young invite Stills is Woodside, Calif., ranch for a listen. The two got sidetracked into a session with David Crosby and Graham Nash, which led to an album and a successful tour. "If it wasn't for Stephen and Neil working together on the box set and realizing they could get along in the same room for five minutes, this whole CSN&Y thing wouldn't have happened," says Palmer.

Few official details on the box are available aside from the projected release date, which could again change. "It has been ready for more than a year," says John Einarson, a Winnipeg high school history teacher who co-wrote a book about the band with Furay. "Neil has given the project a lot of care and attention. He remembers this period with much fondness."

The four-CD set will not contain every track from the band's albums. Instead, it will be composed of some previously released songs, alternate versions of the familiar and about one third unreleased or newly discovered material.

"It's a chronological history of the group from the demos all the way through the albums," Young said in the Reprise interview. "You can see the development of the group from the beginning to its hottest points, to when it starting splintering apart to when it became a vanilla shake or something."

"Neighbour Don't Worry" and a Stills-sung version of Young's "Down to the Wire" are the best-known rarities, along with a long jam titled "Raga." Others include "Whatever Happened To Saturday," a Young track intended for the third Springfield album; "We'll See," which Einarson calls "a great Stills song that represents one of the last examples of the unison singing they did so well"; up to four songs later recorded by Poco, including a take of "I Guess You Made It" and a Stills rendition of the buoyant "What a Day." Furay calls this particular track "a nice surprise."

As good as these newly released recordings may be, the band's best work — live performance — is lost in the ephemera. Beach Boys sound man Steve Desper said he recorded every one of the Springfield's shows when the two bands were on tour in 1967 and 1968, but erased the tapes after a standard performance critique. These shows sounded great because both bands used Desper's "doubling" technique to enrich the vocal sound.

One set of Springfield tapes that exists in some form captures their performance at 1967's Monterey Pop Festival, where David Crosby filled in for the then-departed (and soon to return) Young. While the tapes might have some historical significance, Einarson says their presence on the box set is "not likely" because of Young's absence.

It is ironic that Young has taken on the archivist task, as he essentially scuttled the band. He quit several times — once on the eve of a *Tonight Show* appearance — and deflated the band's momentum. But the others don't object to his prodigal interest. "Neil's in charge here because of his initiative, and his proclivity for collecting and preserving things," says Palmer. Furay agrees: "Neil doesn't do things halfway. He's done a great job with this."

At the same time, all participants approach any reunion talk with extreme caution. In 1988, the five met and played informally, planning to meet a few months later. Feelings about the session were mixed. Palmer recalls the session as "terrific," and Furay says it was nice to get reacquainted. "It could have had some magic," says Martin, "but Bruce's chops weren't up, and I was sick with the flu. We should have warmed up on something familiar, but were playing all this new stuff."

They all agree, however, as to what happened next. Young didn't show for the next rehearsal. "He just forgot," Palmer said. "So we all said, 'What's the use?'"

ROLLING STONE ONLINE, April 29, 2000

Crosby, Stills, Nash and Young: Auburn, Washington, July 27, 2006

"Do you think there are any Republicans here?"

We are on the queue for Crosby, Stills, Nash &Young's *Freedom of Speech* show, and the woman behind us has chosen to make conversation. My companion, herself belonging to the party of both Lincoln and Bush, squeezes my hand and rolls her eyes as if to say "do not engage...." It's a gesture our neighbor does not detect.

"Statistically speaking, with all of the Republicans who are in the general population, there must be a few," she prattles on. "And there are so many of the band's songs on the soft-rock stations. So I bet they are all over the place." So as far as the audience goes, "freedom of speech" translates in the freedom to criticize Bush and the war.

The prevailing politics here follow a simple syllogism: "War and lies are bad. Bush supports the war and has not told the truth. So let's impeach the president for lying." The real world is somewhat more complicated. But that doesn't really matter when you get a chance to hear songs like "Carry Me" and "Immigration Man" done by the full foursome, along with an album's worth of vibrant and passionate new Neil Young songs.

And if Young's new stuff is a tad one-sided, it's still a lot more profound than Crosby's eternally dumb "Almost Cut My Hair."

Earlier this year Young made a big noise with the protest album *Living With War*, for its confrontational politics and for the fact that it was written and recorded in two weeks. He got a second bump by loaning it to his sometimes compatriots as the featured segment of this tour, with the ultimate purpose of using music to stir things up like in the old days. This goes along with the tendency to play a healthy portion of new songs on every tour, something that not very many of the older groups still do. Young's contributions are a lot more exciting than the last CSNY studio album, *Looking Forward*, which was flogged to death on the 2000 tour. (Those songs, along with 1988's equally limp *American Dream*, are unplayed here.)

Not to mess with Neil's vision, but he could have taken a different path. Recording the songs with CSN in the first place would have given us a better record that more people would hear. The concert versions of these songs are no less powerful or argumentative, but more polished and palatable. Young is revered for his raggedness and spontaneity, but sweet things are always easier to swallow. Especially for the Republicans who listen to soft-rock radio, or those not already converted to this point of view.

Pick your cliché: Young is the straw that stirs the drink. He is the only one of the four who keeps growing. He pushes the others to another level. Truth is, the other three do as much for Young as he does for them. They all sublimate their notorious egos, making Young just one-fourth of the equation, part of the team.

And CSN accommodates the singleminded message by updating songs from their catalogue that fit the theme and added little anti-Bushisms to those that didn't.

The sweetening of Young's new songs and the enhancement of through-the-years solo material are the second and third best reasons to come out tonight. Number one is to see Young and Stills play with – and against – each other. The notes run together, individually and collectively, and are never out of sync. Watching these balanced duels you would never guess that one is revered as one of our greatest living songwriters and guitarists, while the other draws an overwhelming lack of respect from the general public: "Stills. Isn't he the one who almost died?"

If it chaps Stills' ass that he plays a perceived second string to Young, he acts as the head honcho here. You remember the notation on the Buffalo Springfield LP, "Steve is the leader, but we all are." It's as true as it ever was. Stills is more relaxed, seeming less grumpy than in the past. His playing is extraordinary, although lacking the recognizable tones of his old buddy Hendrix or Young. I haven't seen Stills this cheerful since CSNY's 1970 tour. And while many claim to have come only to see Neil, it is clear that Crosby, Nash and Young would be a comparatively dull ride.

There are some missteps, most noticeably a minor Young guitar flub followed by a major Nash meltdown on 'Our House'. They started again, not before Crosby announced "when someone fucks up in this band it is usually me. For the perfect Englishman to make a mistake....." Young then interrupts, handing Crosby money as if paying off a bet. We laugh, not quite sure why. "Guinnevere," which followed, sounded good enough but was ruined (at least for those of us close enough to see) by Nash's painfully pretentious pantomime. This recalls the worst part of the 1960s, where people overemoted, pretending that straw was gold.

But there are enough highlights, so you are grateful for the chance to breathe or go pee. Stills' "Treetop Flier" is boosted by Young, while the obscure jam "What Are Their Names?" becomes a deranged barbershop quartet. The always too brief "Find the Cost of Freedom" gets the three-verse treatment and segues into the most passionate of Young's new songs, "Let's Impeach the President." With a giant microphone and a smoke machine, they are using humor to get the message across. So even the Republicans and their soft-rock leanings can go home smiling.

All evening Young was reined in by the bounds of melody, but during the "Rockin' in the Free World" coda they let him out of the cage. He rebels with an extended stretch of feedback where he seeks to break all his strings. We are in the parking lot by then. Priorities are different since their first tours. Instead of lapping up every note and screaming for more we now care about beating the traffic and getting to work the next day. (Among these changes is the tendency to wait a few months for the DVD, where we can skip through "Guinnevere" or whatever else doesn't blow our thinning hair back at that particular moment.)

If CSNY had stayed together since Woodstock they'd be sick of each other by now, and we'd be sick of them. As it stands, their performances are rare enough to stay valuable. And notwithstanding the politics, personalities and pharmaceuticals throughout the intervening years, they have never sounded this good.

Set list: *Flags of Freedom/ Carry On/ Wooden Ships/ Long Time Gone/ Military Madness/ After the Garden/ Living With War/ Restless Consumer/ Shock and Awe/ Wounded World/ Almost Cut My Hair/ Immigration Man/ Families/ Deja Vu/ Helplessly Hoping/ Our House/ Only Love Can Break Your Heart/ Guinnevere/ Milky Way Tonight/ Treetop Flier/ Roger and Out/ Southbound Train/ Old Man Trouble/ Carry Me/ Teach Your Children/ Find the Cost of Freedom/ Let's Impeach the President/ For What it's Worth/ Chicago/ Ohio/ What are Their Names?/ Rockin' in the Free World/ Woodstock*

ROCK'S BACKPAGES, August 15, 2006

Taking Aim:

Unforgettable Rock 'n' Roll Photographs Selected by Graham Nash

With "Taking Aim," an exhibit of rock music photography that opened recently at the Experience Music Project in Seattle, guest curator Graham Nash has assembled a selection of pictures that portray the passion and intensity shared by musicians of a certain age.

"Rock and roll is no different from photography, or composing classical music," Nash said. "You tap into this incredible energy, and use it to create something magical."

Nash, best known as the skinny part of Crosby, Stills & Nash, has been involved in making pictures since he was ten years old--well before his storied music career began. Since then he has taken thousands of photographs, including people whom which he shared a stage or a personal experience.

After nearly a decade as a museum, this is first time any kind of rock star has been directly involved in creating an EMP exhibit, according to Nash's curatorial director Jasen Emmons, who shepherded the project.

"Graham is as much of an artist as he is a musician," Emmons said. "He has access to a tremendous amount of fantastic images, and was able to pull together a remarkable collection of photographs by himself and others."

The exhibit will be at EMP through May, and will subsequently visit three or four other cities, according to Emmons. In the meantime, there is a posh coffee-table volume that has all the included photographs peppered with commentary and context supplied by Nash.

There are a few obvious shots. Annie Leibovitz's "John and Yoko," days before he died. Johnny Cash flipping the bird. Janis Joplin, reflective on a couch with a bottle of Southern Comfort. "She wasn't the prettiest girl," said Jim Marshall, who took the picture. "But she wasn't afraid of the camera. I took another shot 90 minutes after this one, and her mood was 180 degrees in the other direction."

Most of the pictures are black and white, which the photographers believe is more evocative. Said Nash: "I don't think in color, I think in black and white. The images are a lot sharper, and more interesting."

Nash led a discussion after the opening, telling stories and singing two songs played on Buddy Holly's stickered acoustic guitar. He was articulate and relaxed, speaking directly to the audience in a familiar way.

It is only later you realize they basically performed the book. Emmons asked the questions that elicited the right stories, and Nash told them as if it were the first time.

Well, more or less. He occasionally wandered off-script, alluding to the era's recreational drug use and describing the first time he met The Mamas and the Papas; "I knew who they were," he said, "I'd seen that album cover and I wanted to fuck Michelle (Phillips) just like everybody else."

Afterward, attendees previewed the exhibition, mingling with all the photographers, carting around books and cadging signatures like it was their high school yearbook. At one point, all the photographers gathered in front of the exhibit for a photo shoot, as bystanders took pictures of the people who were taking pictures of the photographers who took the pictures; recalling the Kinks, who once sang "People take pictures of each other. Just in case someone thought they had missed it. Just to prove that they really existed….."

The following day, archivist Joel Bernstein led a discussion about photographing Neil Young, followed by a panel discussion featuring all of the photographers.

Throughout, they repeated many of the same stories, adding a layer of detail each time.

These shots succeed because they were taken in an atmosphere of trust and open access. Nash always got his subjects to cooperate because he was one of them. As a musician backstage he was able to point a camera across the room and shoot his pals. Bernstein, who began as a fan and then an associate of Young and Mitchell, was vetted as someone who could be trusted.

The panel had a certain geezer-on-a-park-bench quality, with all of these old guys lamenting how much better it all was back then. Before the cold, digital age began and friendly competition was the rule and acting greedy was the exception. When pictures weren't technically perfect, but evoked emotions that complemented the music.

"When I was shooting all these pictures, photographers were given a certain amount of trust," Bernstein said. "Today, you print one picture the artist perceives as unflattering, they will cut off your access. Photographers used to determine which shots to use, now you need to get approval of management for each shot."

Marshall doesn't follow the new rules, especially the one that only permits photography during the first three songs.

"I will only work with a band that gives me absolute trust and access," he said. "If my body of work means nothing, then fuck them. Trust is something that you don't ask for, it just happens. Today, everything is so contrived and controlled."

SONICBOOMERS, February 2010

3

1983-1989

*T*he *freelancing process is pretty simple. You first figure out what, or who, you want to write about. The next step is to determine a market for the story and pitch it to the publication. Once successful, you approach the artist's management with the proposal, which will be accepted, or not. This is again simple: If you are working for Rolling Stone or the New York Times you'll get in, while efforts on behalf of the Port Orchard Independent might not be successful.*

This has been turned sideways by the recent blogging phenomenon. There are so many writers that you're lucky to get any kind of answer out of a publication, and an artist will never respond to a request from a blog. That might not matter in some cases, since a blogger can write what they want without the cumbersome responsibility of having to actually interview the subject or confirm any facts.

This process worked better when you didn't have to sell the piece to a publication, someone was willing to take your ideas and respond positively without making you wait weeks for an answer. During this era my preferred music client was the Toronto Globe and Mail, a high-class Canadian paper with capable copy editors and good taste for stories. Which meant that it coincided with what I was offering.

Nils Lofgren's School Spirit

Interviewed in Potomac, MD

Photo from Walter Johnson High School 1972 yearbook

Nils Lofgren's life can best be described by a poignant line from "Like Rain," a song he wrote in his teens that he will probably sing all his life: "When I fall sleepin' I dream of good things but I always wake up the same."

Nils has release thirteen albums, counting two greatest hits packages, both with the band Grin and as a solo. He's blessed. While most musicians never get the chance to be heard Nils, at 32, has been touring and recording for all of his adult life. Simultaneously he is cursed. He has been bubbling under since 1970 and has been thought of as the "next big thing" for as long as many rock fans have been alive.

Thirteen years ago Grin was a band with unlimited promise, Washington's Great Rock Hope. But they never caught on outside the Boston/Washington axis. Some blame this on the narrow and obtuse tastes of the record-buying public. But the principals now admit that Grin's albums never fulfilled the promise of their live shows. When we got the records home and tore off the shrink wrap, the magic was gone.

He's back now, with renewed desires. He'd like to play live clear through the spring and then cut another record. No more two-year spaces between albums. But there is no reason to believe this will be Nils' year. It's happened before: He has put out first rate records, put on kick-ass shows, and still languished at the bottom of public awareness.

Wonderland, released approximately thirteen years after Grin's first record, is both a step forward and back. It's stripped down and revved up; a visceral melodic album that rocks hard without a trace of heavy metal and then turns around and underlines the best of his harmonic gifts. Nils calls it "by far the best record I've ever made," and while some of this can be attributed to enthusiasm for the moment it's not that far off the mark.

It was on his last album, 1981's *Night Fades Away*, the style he first originated — melodic rock songs punctuated by aggressively wailing guitars and a rollicking pop piano — was finally perfected. Sales were, as usual, unimpressive, With *Wonderland* he's switched gears. It's apparent by the cover: the colors are clear and bright in contrast to the black-and-white grunge of *Night Fades Away.*

On *Wonderland* he's clean-shaven and almost smiling. He has pared down the music; there are no flourishes. The guitar is cranked up, pushing everything but the three lead pieces into deep background. Simply put, Lofgren fans haven't felt a punch in the stomach like this since early Grin.

I entered Bethesda's Walter Johnson High School in 1969, where Nils had dropped out less than thirteen months before. His most incidental actions — how he stood propped against the lunchroom door bumming cigarettes and change, for example — were already legend. Those who knew him were a few rungs up the social ladder from those of us who didn't. And while the crowd in the back parking lot would hoot mercilessly if you accused them of harboring anything akin to school spirit, their reverence toward the departed guitar hero was just that.

I saw Grin on countless occasions and was never bored. Even though my eventual personal contact with Nils was peripheral at best, I was among those who rooted for him in the same way others supported the high school team. I gossiped about him as if he were the president of the class, and surely made him wish that I would leave him alone.

I even bought a guitar from him, but it was a sorry trophy. One of the cutaways was chopped off, the result of what I imagined to be an early Pete Townshend emulation. Two years later I sold it to another unsuspecting Nils fan at a profit.

Nils arrives, carting a thirteen-pound two-thirds size "travel" guitar. It's portable and harmonically accurate. On a long flight he'd rather practice scales than read a book. During the interview, he brings it along so he'll have something to do with his hands while answering questions. But his hands are mostly still, poised on one chord at a time—unless there's a lull in the conversation or when the talk takes an uncomfortable turn.

Such as why, after thirteen years of recording fair-to-great albums on three labels, touring worldwide (with Grin, as a solo and part of Neil Young's band) and accruing a smattering of session work, does he still fail to make cash registers sing?

"I make records for the people," he said. "I'd love to reach more of them. I'd much rather my records sell. It does get frustrating sometimes. But the only thing that I can control is the music. I just have to work at getting better, write better songs, and keep working at it. If it's destined to be then it will happen."

He won't say anything bad about anybody. When asked about a particular album or stage in his life he addresses the specific instance rather than what it meant generally. He talks about people who made that time special, as if to say "I'd like to thank the producer and all the members of the Academy...

Outwardly he claims to accept his lot, waiting patiently for his turn under the big lamp. Inside, though, he must be churning. While he hasn't always batted .1000, lesser acts have taken the money and ran during the time he was clamoring for the same attention. He used to compare himself to other musicians, he said, bit then realized that as far as success went "luck has something to do with it, Politics have something to do with it. A lot of elements are involved.'

When Nils buttonholed Neil at the Cellar Door in 1969 he played what became the first Grin album. Young was spellbound. They've been friends ever since, and Nils has played on three of Young's albums. *Wonderland*, in fact, would have been released a year ago but Young asked Nils to join his European tour.

Young, when he first met Nils, was on the brink of his own substantial success, The invitation to join Crosby, Stills & Nash precluded his producing the first Grin album. Today, Nils is still perched on that same brink; waiting for a time when he can be perceived as more than a rock footnote or a Joker to Young's King.

It took a lot of balls for the 17-year-old Nils to confront Young in his dressing room. It is that very gutsiness, in his persona and his music that makes him special.

Those of us who rooted for Nils in the early days have grown up. We have learned that he was not the Great Rock Hope. But he has grown up too. His last three studio albums show that the maturity is here to stay. He is no longer trying so hard to impress. He has decided, essentially, to shut up and play his guitar. Unfortunately, as he has refined his art, many fans stopped listening.

He still craves a shot at fame, claiming it's not for the wealth or other trappings. He says he already has the essentials: enough money, plenty of friends and a place to sleep. But his grand ideas about lighting and staging will translate only to an arena format. Visions of trampolines, tunnels and trap doors can't exist without the money to realize these schemes.

"One of the reasons I'm still recording," he said, "is that people in the record companies realize that I'm very serious about this. I'm in for the count. This is something I'm going to do all my life, for better or worse."

Along with the decline in audience interest, many of the writers who initially pleaded Nils' case have given up. He was once a critic's darling, perhaps because it took a critic to appreciate his potential. But when he didn't follow the good notices with record sales, the fickle critics jumped ship, as if to acknowledge that the ignoring audiences were right all along.

I thought that a piece about Nils would be an easy sale. I found otherwise, after approaching several publications. Most turned the idea down flat. One editor told me that Nils' failure to sell records was a direct result of his own "bad career decisions." Another was simply unimpressed with *Wonderland* and decided, as is the editor's privilege, that it didn't warrant any attention. A third editor said bluntly, "You don't tell me why I should even be interested in this guy."

Rather than lose any more sleep, I decided that the failure to sell big wasn't all my fault. The monolithic rock press has lost interest in Nils. Ironically, this comes at a time where he is closest to achieving what critics and fans knew he could.

The three factors that determine success, as Nils himself mentioned, are talent, politics and luck. He has the talent, although it hasn't always been presented properly. He is not so good at playing politics. He knows his own strengths and isn't inclined toward sycophantic maneuvering—especially when he'd rather be playing racquetball.

That leaves luck. Stated simply, Nils is one unlucky soul. He has, with only a few exceptions, been at the wrong places at the worst times. He has been ahead of or behind his times, missed musical trends by five years or more, was born too early or too late.

Still, he's given Washington something to crow about. He set an early example for local musicians, and the continuing stubbornly original nature of local rock owes a lot to Nils. Thirteen years ago, he showed that a Bethesda boy could turn out music as fresh and original as anything coming out of New York or San Francisco. He's instilled a regional pride, and helped make the early 1970s worth remembering.

For that, we are very lucky.

UNICORN TIMES January 1984

Tori Amos' Happy Hour

Interviewed in Washington, DC

Cocktail pianists occupy the lowest rung in the musician's hierarchy. While there are some whose performances approach true art, and others whose reputations place them ahead of the pack, they often battle condescension from their fellow musicians. Stereotypically, the cocktail pianist is stranded in a seedy lounge, playing limp renditions of "Melancholy Baby" as requested by drunk patrons.

But as there are fewer and fewer jobs for musicians, many young pianists have decided they would rather play in a cocktail lounge than not play at all. Some, like Georgetown Marbury House's Ellen Amos, are first-rate composers and performers, clearly headed for bigger and better things. Others, like Rib-It's

Michael Moore-Kelly, are engaging, ingratiating performers who neither challenge nor offend the ear. And even if most cocktail performers don't have as much to offer as these two, the city's numerous piano bars feature a variety of keyboard artists, each earning an honorable living pounding the 88s.

"There are times, while playing with other people, when you are really cooking," says Moore-Kelly, who has performed in many Top 40 bands. "You know you have it musically. Here, you only have 10 fingers. But you can still get that feeling, when you know that everything's right." Cocktail pianists are solo artists in the truest sense of the word, responsible for not only the music but their own unelaborated sound and light arrangements. If radio or tapes are played between sets, they cue it up themselves. And when they play the result is all their own; the strengths and weaknesses of the final sound emanate from only one source.

With the help of synthesizers and rhythm machines, one person can almost sound like a whole band. But these props can't salvage a no-talent. A bad cocktail pianist, synthesized, sounds worse than a monkey on an ocarina. Used skillfully, however, the new toys augment solo sound, flushing out paces and turning one musician into several.

Moore-Kelly has taken the artificial percussion concept one step further, prerecording about 20 rhythms with live drums and punching the cassettes into a piano side deck at whim. It sounds more realistic than a drum machine, but still has an automated feel. Rhythm machines, and this revision, succeed because the musical moves are so predictable. All the songs are familiar and the beat is steady. But some musicians disdain the technology. Amos refuses to use the new machine. If she can't play with a band she'll brave it alone.

"I don't like the sound of rhythm machines," Moore-Kelly says. "I use it only as a backup, as opposed to a structure to build the song upon. I mix it accordingly."

During happy hour, many patrons are still absorbed in the day's leftover business. A pianist is often ignored, becoming little more than live Muzak. Cocktail piano, then, is not the right format for those who perceive themselves as "artists" who need total silence during the performance.

Amos and Moore-Kelly demand feedback from the audience, even if they have to yank it out of them. "This is like election night," Moore-Kelly said during one slow evening. "A little applause for each of the states."

Moore-Kelly, who is situated close to the door, actively acknowledges the sometimes shocked patrons, forcing them to respond to him and his music as they arrive and depart. "I want to get people involved with me," he says. "I want to play songs that they'll recognize. That's all that entertainment is. People should feel comfortable when I'm playing. If I get a feeling they don't want to get involved with me I'll just play background."

Cocktail pianists are often long on musical skill, yet short on the natural talent that catapults performers to stardom. But while original musicians maintain a sacred integrity by playing only their own tunes, they are usually sentenced to day jobs until they land their big break. Cocktail piano provides more lucrative, steadier work that allows freedom during the day and a chance to perform regularly—albeit in front of less than attentive audiences.

Amos is using her six-night-a-week gig to hone her performing skills, and while she is a good cocktail pianist she is hoping that the experience will help to make her a great performer. She doesn't expect to be playing dimly lit lounges for the rest of her life, but while she does it will get her best shot.

"You have to be satisfied where you are," she says. "While I'm playing the Marbury House it is the most important thing. The Capitol Center might be my eventual goal, but that's down the road. Tonight, this has to be my best performance."

If it is a pleasant surprise to chance upon Amos in the Marbury House, it's a shock to discover her future plans. Raw ambition in a cocktail pianist is rare. Amos wants to perform to huge audiences, doing running jumps over the piano and the speakers—a cross between Elton John and the Flying Wallendas. Her idols include Tina Turner and Billie Holliday.

"Playing lounges teaches you so much," she says. "When you are playing in a bar no one really wants to listen. When people pay to see you then they will pay attention. But when no one is listening it takes 10 times the effort. Audiences are much more critical of bar singers."

While every performer has a threshold of pain, requests are a part of a pianist's life. Amos will field a request, mutter that she doesn't really like that particular song, then turn in a near-flawless rendition. If she doesn't know the song she'll do her best to figure it out on the spot. It's musical roulette, and it's remarkable how often it succeeds.

"If someone walks out of here and says that I didn't play what they wanted to hear, then I'm not doing my job," she says. "You shouldn't be able to tell that I'm playing what I don't like, even though on something I like, or on my originals. My enthusiasm will shine through. Otherwise, I'll fake it, give people what they want to hear. My tastes really don't matter. I might hate a song, but three people are in the corner crying because it means a lot to them."

"I know a lot of songs," Moore-Kelly says. "If someone asks for a particular song there is a 70 percent chance that I can play it. Either that, or I can play something related, by the same artist or from the same album."

Cocktail pianists take their music seriously and hope it will take them to bigger and better places. Amos manages to sneak a couple of her originals in every night. Sometimes nobody notices, as the originals are written and performed in typical cocktail lounge style.

Amos, however, is trying to break all of the rules. She seems to parody cocktail pianists, trying so hard to please, asking for requests and then peppering the expected "feelings, whoa, whoa, whoa feelings" fare with her own acerbic observations.

Her originals are gutsy and gritty, projecting a sensuality that belies her frail form. She may start with a song about how hard it is for a woman to go home alone, then swing into an accented "Thank Heaven for Little Girls."

"I would like to be able to write songs and sell then," Moore-Kelly says. "I want to be known locally as a good musician. As a musician you can either move forward or back. You can never be static."

"I'm a minister's daughter," Amos says, priming her tip jar with five dollars of her own money. "I teach music in Sunday school. I never saw this side of life. But I have learned to talk to people."

THE WASHINGTON TIMES, September 2, 1983

T-Bone Burnett's Chapter and Verse

Interviewed in Washington, DC

T-Bone Burnett strides onstage alone, immediately sitting at the piano. He strikes a few soulful chords, wincing at every sound. He stands up, falls to his knees and twists his face into a sharp grimace. Suddenly he breaks character and walks away, as the piano keeps playing itself. Later, he tells the crowd, "Remember Lenny Bruce, how they called him a sick comedian? Well, I'm a sick troubadour."

Forgive them Father, for they know not what they do. --Luke 23:34

He is "born again," and it has been said that he helped convert Bob Dylan, But holding him responsible for Dylan's religious albums is like blaming Yoko for breaking up the Beatles. It was bound to happen anyway, and Burnett was around to see that it was done right.

Despite the hype, a sheep in the valley of wolves, Burnett says that he's actually "not a real religious person." He calls the matter a non-issue, adding that journalists are lazy. They opt to "do a story on this guy, here's the handle." Then pick up their fifty bucks for cranking out another lame piece.

"I just have a very specific point of view that doesn't mesh with rock and roll. I couldn't tell you what it is, that's why I write songs, but I can tell you what it isn't. It's not sex, drugs and rock and roll. It's not 'rock and roll is the answer.' I don't think rock and roll gives life meaning in and of itself.

"People need perspective. We live in such a relativistic age where you have to check everything you say with everybody else. People don't take responsibility for their own point of view. I've had a lot of kids come up to me and say 'T-Bone, your last record was terrifying, but keep doing it because somebody has to say something.' They're just happy to hear someone not apologizing for their point of view."

In reality, his religion has as much to do with his music as his astrological sign or his shoe size, his songs are musical daguerreotypes, void of proselytizing or religious reference. Still, even if he doesn't push his beliefs they set him apart, turning him into a rock oddity.

But journalists are stubborn. The Sunday prior to his latest appearance here the Washington Post previewed him as a "pop moralist."

"People say more about themselves when they say I make judgments," he said. "I look at myself very much as a journalist, imagine Walter Winchell doing the last verse of "Fatally Beautiful" as a news flash: 'In a restaurant in Brussels she pulls back her hair and lights a cigarette.' It's got that element. But I can tell you, from my point of view I'm not making judgments of people.

"Everybody's a moralist, everyone has some set of morals they live by. Moral codes from person to person are slightly different, but they are amazingly the same, throughout history, across the face of the earth. On the other hand I think people have a lot of preconceptions. If you go to anything with a preconception you can find what you want.

"God, what a terrible thing, to be a pop moralist," he laughs. "I'd rather be a pop Marxist."

A man can never step in the same river twice, as the man changes and the river changes. **-American Indian proverb.**

If Burnett were in fact a journalist, his favorite words would be "get me rewrite." His revisionism extends from the pop standards he performs (a line from Cole Porter's "Anything Goes" becomes "he who has a platinum album seems to always have some talcum under his nose") to his own songs. In "The Sixties," Jackie Kennedy, John Kennedy and Jackie Bisset evolve into Squeaky Fromme, Eric Fromme and Erica Jong.

He always asked audiences for requests, offering interpretations that fall flat on their face. But his batting average is good enough to forgive the clunkers.

Last fall he stunned audiences with a band that featured Tom Petty drummer Stan Lynch, bassist David Miner and the Williams Brothers, modern Everly Brothers clones who are, according to Burnett, "either Andy Williams' nephews or Hank Williams' nephews." A few months later he toured the East Coast alone, suitcase and guitar in hand, playing stripped down versions of the same songs to fanatic loyalists in small clubs.

He draws fresh sounds from the same old progressions. He can't say exactly how this is done, saying "it's a matter of commitment to the note."

Burnett isn't the only one to show a commitment to these particular notes. His latest album features guest appearances from Pete Townshend, Richard Thompson, Mick Ronson and Ry Cooder, mostly sounding like generic session men. ("I don't know if that is bad or good," he mugs. "What do you think?") He downplays the importance of having famous guest stars, saying "we are just in the same business."

"Do you remember what rock and roll was like before Dylan?" he asks. "He walked out with an acoustic guitar and it was like he was from Mars. David Bowie even said he was from Mars. I've noticed something about every performer I ever admired. They have done the impossible by becoming really single-minded. Dylan, Bowie, Townshend. They all did the impossible."

In the future, Burnett plans to produce other bands, using the same instinctual informality that he brings to his own songwriting. And there may be a new album in 1984.

"My new songs are really funny," he said. "I tried to rid them of any trace of cynicism. I'm trying to be more open and generous, and take myself less seriously."

Two of these songs, incidentally, are called "My Life and the Women Who Lived It" and "Having A Wonderful Time, Wish You Were Her."

Gave proof through the night that our flag was still there. —**Francis Scott Key**

Burnett performed in a Hamburg club soon after the Pershing missiles were deployed in Germany. He didn't think it was right for an American performer to be there at that time and not address the issue.

So he dedicated his sparse version of Dolly Parton's "I Will Always Love You" to "the people who have their fingers on the button." Some of the words: I hope life treats you kind/I wish you joy and happiness/but most of all I wish you love." The feeling in the room, Burnett recalls, was intense.

"It was a radical statement to be making at that point," he said. "It wasn't taking a stand. It was just telling the guy who had his finger on the button that I hoped he got everything he ever dreamed of."

If Burnett's religious leanings are obscure, his patriotism is clear. He refers to the Constitution as "the greatest social document ever framed," though one that has recently been compromised beyond belief. He thinks that Ronald Reagan pales in comparison to past presidents, but can't say who might be any better.

He was still seething about Reagan's post-Super Bowl TV appearance, in which the president mixed political and sports metaphors.

"He was trying to make all these jokes about something that's just not funny," Burnett said. "He will use any opportunity to spread his garbled perspective on life. It was humiliating to watch, that we've sunk to making bad jokes about nuclear disaster on the Super Bowl broadcast.

"If I thought the people I wrote about on *Proof Through the Night* were really bad I would have made them politicians," he mused. "I think I'll say that onstage tonight."

The line is revised. He is soft-spoken and laconic offstage, but the guitar becomes the ultimate confidence-builder. His personality changes, and he becomes simultaneously ingratiating and aggressive. He retells the story onstage, tying it to a song called "Ridiculous Man" then saying "you'd think that he'd have enough grace to not use every single opportunity to promote his wretched life."

Check Your Levels. —**Roger the Engineer**

"This better be a good article," he smirks. "This is real payola."

I've asked him to tape a message for my answering machine and we, along with a borrowed dobro, are holed up in the john.

"Charlie's in the bathroom of the 9:30 Club right now," he deadpans over a fingerpicked folk riff. "He can't get to the phone because it's over at his house. If you'd care to leave a message…he can't stay in that bathroom forever."

"This is really great!" he said during the playback, grinning widely. "No one's ever asked me to do that before." But when I transfer the tape to the answering machine the effects are hardly spectacular. The guitar drowned out the vocals, and turned everything into gibberish. I knew we should have done two takes.

The next day he was on the road to New York, probably unrecognized, where he is due to play at Gerde's Folk City. It will be a thrill, as Gerde's is the birthplace of contemporary folk. And he is in the midst of his own reverse evolution, from rock and roller to folk singer.

In my imagination he is again revising the Sixties: "There is a new breed of man…he works behind a desk, next to a computer….when so-called celebrities come to town, he asks them to record personal messages on his answering machine….."

I'd be embarrassed, except it's a privilege to be part of T-Bone Burnett's America.

UNICORN TIMES, March 1984

Exclusive: The Go-Go's Papers

Explicit scenes of a writer's downfall

Interviewed in Columbia, MD

EDITOR'S NOTE: Three days after deadline, two Unicorn Times editors sought out contributor Charlie Bermant, whose promised Go-Go-s piece was past due. We found the door to his fashionable apartment ajar. He was in a semi-conscious state, sitting in a dry bathtub, fully clothed and clutching a grimy little folder.

Yes, he had done the interview. No, he had not finished the piece. Everything he had written so far was in the folder and he mumbled something about needing three weeks to pull it together. We told him that was impossible, wrenched away the folder from his arms and called an ambulance.

Two days later the doctor called with sad news. They said he wouldn't come out of his hospital room. He was alone with his Walkman and a tape of the Go-Go's Talk Show, which he listened to continuously, day and night. As the alternate cover story for this month, "Great Rock Bands From Wheaton," had already fallen through we decided to print the folder's legible contents.

Some of it is a little rough, and we ask the readers to bear with us. Maybe when Charlie reads this he'll snap out of it and begin what is bound to be a long, uphill struggle to return to the semblance of a productive member of society he once was.

THERE ARE DIFFERENCES between the sexes that neither we nor the band should forget. While a male rocker might try to incite a crowd to dance by shaking his gut and shouting "let's get down," singer Belinda Carlisle slips out of her high heels, holds them up and shouts, "These shoes have got to go."

Talk Show isn't "women's music, however"; it's major-league rock 'n' roll, free of blatant gender delineations or (except for "Mercenary," reverse sexual posing). But if this record offers the most convincing argument for equality since the Nineteenth Amendment, it takes a while to forget the silliness in which the band indulged to get attention before they built up their confidence.

There's no telling how it will sound in 15 years, but right now it feels like the Beatles' *Revolver*, the Who's *Who's Next* or the Bee Gees' *Main Course*: a richly textured release that not only holds up well after repeated listenings, but offers something new each time out.

As punks, the Go-Go's probably would have found their current level of success hard to visualize. They also could never have foreseen another development: the acquisitions of a sense of poise and style that a male band would be unable to fake, much less convey. And this grace can be appreciated by men and women alike.

Transcript Part One:

Belinda Carlisle: "People think that Go-Go's songs are just love songs, which is really a lot of bull. Go-Go's songs are about things that happen in life. It's not just love songs. It's not just parties. It's people's experiences. That's what makes me mad. A lot of people don't bother to read our lyrics, because they assume that we're just...."

Charlotte Caffey: But we're not.

Not what?

Carlisle: Airheads. Too many people write off our lyrics like they're not important.

What are some other misconceptions about the band?

Caffey: You read them all and you hear them all. They're all misconceptions. We're just a bunch of normal girls in a rock 'n' roll band.

Carlisle: We're just normal people, people who have fun, who have problems.

Caffey: It's normal to me. I can't think of anything else to do.

Carlisle: It is sort of an unrealistic profession. It's not "real," but it's fun.

Caffey: I thrive on it.

Carlisle: I definitely feel lucky.

Every minute of it?

Caffey: Yeah.

Carlisle: But sometimes.....

At this point in the manuscript we uncover the first clue to Charlie's unraveling. In a shaky, largely unintelligible scrawl we were able to piece together about what appeared to be about half of an unmailed letter to Charlotte Caffey. There is a reference to an unpleasant experience and an apology, something about how interviews don't do them justice and phrases like "you answered questions that I hadn't even asked" and "I never said you were 'airheads.'" The letter ends with a plea for Caffey "to not be so defensive."

Belinda Talks

"I was completely willing to pose in my underwear for Rolling Stone, it was funny. We weren't trying top pull it off as sexpots or anything. It was Hanes underwear, you know, Fruit of the Loom—I mean, how sexy can that be? Sometimes we get in trouble with our sense of humor; we have a warped sense of humor that people don't really understand.

With that picture, we were poking fun at ourselves and at the whole ideas of how a girl group should be packaged

Like sex kittens, it was like ha-ha-ha, taking the piss out of everybody. It didn't work out, a lot of people took it wrong and really did think we were selling out, you know, trying to use 'that,...'"

It's a classic identity crisis. The Go-Go's refer to ear other as "girls," but bristle when too much is made about their gender. They make straightforward rock 'n' roll albums, yet have appeared in videos as dipsy-doodle dames. They want to be the world's biggest party band, while being taken seriously as musicians.

The Go-Go's have accomplished what only the most creative rock bands have been able to pull off — arriving with something new, then creating a special niche for their music. But after almost four years in the limelight, they're still on the defensive.

IF THE GO-GO'S RECALL the Beatles and the Who in power and spirit, they are also similar to those seminal bands in their sense of musical democracy. First impressions, from the substantive (guitarist Jane Wiedlin is the most important songwriter) to the incidental (Caffey is the most traditionally attractive), fall apart under closer scrutiny. The band is an interlocking puzzle: to remove or separate one piece is to leave a gaping hole.

In concert the band serves up a supercharged hour or so, suggesting that the new album only scratched the surface of the hard-rock potential of the Go-Go's. Gina Schock attacks each song with metronomic precision; if it were not for the flourishes, one would swear she was finely tuned percussion machine. She's louder than most drummers and her interplay with Kathy Valentine's bass suggest a rhythm section bursting at the seams, thrusting the band into overdrive,

Guitarist Wiedlin's eager effervescence and delicate manner contrast with counterpart Caffey's toughness. Wiedlin's high vocal harmonies complement Carlisle, and her well-scrubbed demeanor makes it hard to believe she was once a punk known as "Jane Drano." Caffey is the visual weak link, for she is obviously preoccupied with the business of making music. But she is the one around whom the other four seem to revolve musically.

The three guitarists' use of transmitters instead of guitar cords leaves them unencumbered and unrestrained. While some bands use this modern invention merely as a conveniences, the Go-Go's take it as a license to start some action, chasing each other around the stage and crawling to the very brink of the audience.

Nevertheless, most Go-Go's songs are about love in one form or another, with a majority of the others about rock 'n' roll. On this particular afternoon, no one has suggested that there is anything wrong with this mix. And no one has called them "airheads." Carlisle has cast the first stone at herself.

THE GO-GO's ("I guess it's just illiterate, " Carlisle says when asked why the band's name is a possessive and not a plural. "We really should take that apostrophe out") will show just how "normal" they are Thursday, when they perform at the World's Fair Amphitheater.

When the band—Carlisle, Caffey, bassist Kathy Valentine, guitarist Jane Wiedlin and drummer Gina Schock— started during the 1970s punk movement, they were admittedly awful. But at that time, sloppiness was chic and women playing hard rock were still a novelty, so they pushed onward. Their perseverance was eventually rewarded. In 1981, *Beauty and the Beat* became the first No. 1 album by an all–female rock band.

By then, they had cast off the punk pose, but continued to mine the sexual novelty. They essentially became a surf group: short and concise leads, happy and bouncy melodies, as uncomplicated attitude toward music and life. Having fun was the most important thing, but the surfboards and cars message of their surf-music ancestors was replaced by a dose of cautious 1980's pessimism.

Vacation, a melancholy collection masquerading as an archetypal summer album, came out in 1982. It pales in comparison to the band's other two records, for even though it is often thoughtful and witty, it suffers from a lack of direction. It also features a pair of genuine clinkers, "Cool Jerk" and Bikini Beach." Which detract from the cynical brilliance of the other songs. The public was underwhelmed, and *Vacation* was soon banished to the budget catalog.

All involved were ready to chart a third album's course more than a year ago. But there were management problems, and Caffey developed a hand ailment which made it difficult, if not impossible, to play the guitar. After *Talk Show* (so named to acknowledge the increasing influence of videos on music) was finally recorded, the 26-year-old Schock had a heart operation, which delayed the band's current tour and its ability to cash in immediately on the album's March release.

Talk Show is a rare triumph from an unexpected quarter — blistering, forward looking rock album with equal parts of raucousness and melody.

Although Carlisle is the only band member with no songwriter credit on the new album, she has shown the most growth recently. Her singing in a lower register has eliminated her previous chipmunk-like styling, and she now projects an appealing blend of aggression and restraint. Her "I must be loooosing it" growl lifts "Head Over Heels" into a special realm, cluing the listener in to *Talk Show*'s exceptional quality on the very first track.

"THE ONLY THING that never changes is what the Go-Gos really are," Carlisle said. "A melodic, pop sort of escapist music in a way. Of course, we get happier, you get thinner. You wear red, you wear blue. But we've been together for seven years, we hope that we've changed and grown."At the end of this tour a lot more people will know about the Go-Go's. Those who give *Talk Show* more than a cursory listen will come back for more, and the energy of the band's shows cannot help but impress. Carlisle feels they still have to "sell ourselves, let people know we can play our instruments, so they will take us seriously."

"Seeing people enjoy your music is the bottom line," Caffey says. "Selling records is part of the whole process: that happens when you play well and people like you."

Talk Show's sales, however, have fallen off; They could be revitalized by the new single, the bombastic "Turn to You," or the band's tireless touring, but even if sales do not rebound the band feels this is still its best album.

"We know we gave our 100 percent with this album," Carlisle says. "We are artistically satisfied with it. If people want to enjoy it, that's wonderful. If they don't want to like it, that's fine too. The bottom line is that we're very happy with our work."

"After all we've been through as a band we've come out with a great album," Caffey said. "That means a lot to us."

IN THE IMMEDIATE future the Go-Go's plan to tour worldwide until February, when they'll take a few months off to "cool it and write new songs." They will then begin the rehearsal and recording process anew. Carlisle and Caffey said they'd like to again use producer Martin Rushent, who is credited with giving *Talk Show* its punch.

"He worked out great," Carlisle said. "It was nice to go over to England, get away from all the distractions and bad influences. The frame of mind was work and only work, no boyfriends, no friends...."

"Just us surviving," Caffey chimes in.

"And it worked out really well," Carlisle continues. "That's what was on our minds, all day. Twenty-four hours a day, all we thought about was our album."

"Except," Caffey interrupts, "when we went shopping."

UNICORN TIMES, August, 1984

Linda and Richard Find There's Life After Divorce

Interviewed in person, New York City (Richard) and by phone (Linda)

LINDA Thompson's memories of touring the United States with her soon-to-be ex-husband Richard are filtered through an alcoholic haze and a skewed sense of delight. The marriage had already soured. She'd stalk off stage when her vocals weren't needed, and would often trip him up purposely on stage. "I was a monster," she recalls. "It was like a Chekhov play."

Richard Thompson (performing with a new band next Wednesday at The Diamond in Toronto and Friday at Montreal's Club Soda) plays agile and articulate guitar, albeit in what many rock fans view as a foreign tongue. Those quick to find English accents fascinating have been less eager to embrace his particular musical dialect. But changes are ringing, and listeners who once rejected the music's perceived dissonance now embrace it for that same quality.

The Thompsons' 1982 breakup was a textbook case of bad professional timing. Years of playing for a handful of fans were paying off. Their album, *Shoot Out the Lights*, was hot, and the tour (complete with on-stage family feud) brought out more admirers than anyone dreamed existed.

Three years after the breakup, personal feelings have subsided to what Linda calls "passive indifference," and the two have issued simultaneous solo albums that are poles apart but still invite comparison and contrast. Her glossy *One Clear Moment* is melodic and melancholy — eerie, fashionable modern pop with an international feel. His jagged *Across A Crowded Room* continues his blending of traditional and contemporary elements.

Both are on major labels, and the Thompsons have already achieved an element of commercial success that eluded them in their partnership. "On an independent label, there's a definite ceiling," Richard says. "My last two albums sold X amount and no more. To have done a third one the same way would have seemed a little stale. A move was necessary, somehow, somewhere."

Linda agrees: "Being on homegrown labels wasn't a great experience. *Shoot Out the Lights* was a great album, it got good write-ups, but people couldn't get it. I wanted to be with a major label after the split. It was personal."

They may not be Liz and Dick, but breaking up in the spotlight did turn the Thompsons' private trials into fair public game. The Dynasty-mad listener wonders who "Twists the Knife Again" into whom, or who must suffer her exhortation to "rot in hell." She admittedly based some of her songs on the split, while he demurs: "I don't know why songwriters are taken so personally. You wouldn't do that to a novelist or a film director or even a poet — assume that everything they wrote was autobiographical."

He grudgingly concedes his relationship with Linda is "what people want to write about. Nobody asks me what strings I use." However, he brightens noticeably at the suggestion that his good nature and sense of humor contradict the dark content of his best songs.

His stutter suddenly disappears ("I think he stutters when he's nervous," Linda says. "He used to stutter a lot around me"), as he says: "I don't know if this is allowed in popular music, to write something that's non-teenage in subject. There's room in the three-minute popular song to cram in a few tidbits of real life. I don't think it's being depressing or a downer, or belaboring the point."

In concert he draws from his 17-year repertoire, accenting the fast and loud. The notes are everywhere; his subtle side stayed home this time. The show includes the late Sandy Denny's "John the Gun," but vocalist Christine Collister does not perform the songs that bear Linda's trademark. Instead, Thompson reclaims them for his own gruff voice. With a new album, a crack band and a new wife, he might as well tattoo "I don't miss her" across his arm.

He has made a career of dodging the spotlight, but now seems proud that he has, at last, been accepted on his own terms — this, along with a feeling that it should have happened long ago. Simon Nicol, with whom he founded Fairport Convention in 1967, recently observed, "If anyone from our circle makes it, it will be Richard." Fairport, like The Byrds and early Jefferson Airplane, filtered folk impulses through rock 'n' roll. The English folk tradition is richer than that in North America, but stateside ears didn't appreciate the experiment. Thompson now says of Fairport's early U.S. tours, "It was difficult. We thought we were playing alien music and people didn't know what we were doing, as if it was a strange form.

"Celtic folk music and the twentieth century are, I think, anathema to each other. With the amount of media and communication we now have in the world, I don't know that you can have real folk music. It ends up being Barry Manilow or Wayne Newton or something."

He quit Fairport in the early 1970s but never really left, continuing to draw from the same pool of musicians. It's a loose aggregation that has, at times, included Montreal's Kate and Anna McGarrigle.

Linda, meanwhile, still holds the Fairport family in high regard, but is voluntarily playing the role of ex-in-law. For her album, she went out of her way to record with a new crowd.

"I couldn't use the same musicians. It's bad enough to have these incredible parallels between Richard and myself. It would be too painful to be singing a song about him, and have Simon on guitar. It would have been a nest of incest. I worked with those people for too long. They're great, but now I want to surround myself with gorgeous bass players and have a wild time on tour."

As for their new records, neither will admit to being impressed by the other's. Of hers, he says only, "I've heard it briefly." She counters with: "It's my least favorite of his albums. The guitar work is fabulous but, as far as the songs, I couldn't find one that I loved."

As for the future, Linda feels that her own identity has been established although, with three children, "there is a parallel running through our lives. We'll go on forever."

The current tour is his third solo outing in as many years, but hers will have to wait. Acting commitments will keep her away from music through the spring, when she'd like to record another album and then hit the road in the fall. She concedes the delay may well cost her some momentum, but doesn't think she'll be forgotten by the audience she and Richard seem destined to share.

"I still love his songs. I thought of asking him to write one for my next album, but he might just hit me over the head with his Rickenbacker."

THE GLOBE AND MAIL, APRIL 6, 1985

The KBC Band: Steered By Old Airplane Crew

Interviewed by phone, San Francisco, CA to San Rafael, CA and in person in San Rafael.

THE KBC BAND breezed through the first part of rehearsal, but was stymied by "In the Midnight Hour," a late addition to the New Year's Eve repertoire. Everybody knew the garage-band classic, but re-creating its original precision took a while.

It eventually clicked. After a half hour, the converted church owned by singer Marty Balin had become the ultimate garage. "I've played that with a lot of people," sax player Keith Crossan said of "Midnight Hour.". "This one has meat."

Members of the KBC Band fall into two camps. There are the names — Balin, Paul Kantner and Jack Casady. Their collective pedigree includes founding membership in Jefferson Airplane, stints with Jefferson Starship and Hot

Tuna, and various solo projects. Crossan is one of four seasoned semi-unknowns whose presence ensures this will never be a revival act or a dinosaur show.

KBC has dutifully played San Francisco-area bars for two years, since Kantner's acrimonious split with Starship. The band is consolidating its national push (a record has been released, and a tour is planned this spring) exactly two decades after Airplane's breakthrough album, *Surrealistic Pillow*.

The musical comparison, Kantner says, should be made with *Jefferson Airplane Takes Off*, the album that preceded *Surrealistic Pillow*.

"On the second record of whatever band I've been in, it's congealed," Kantner says. "*Pillow* was the second record. (Jefferson Starship's) *Red Octopus* was the second record. I would expect our next one to be more daring. This was a little conservative."

Surrealistic Pillow, the clarion call for turbulent times, had a lot in common with a blockbuster album of a decade later, Fleetwood Mac's *Rumours*. Both were accessible melds of modern U.S. folk music and rock, using several disparate songwriting voices.

"We were like broadside balladeers," Kantner says of *Surrealistic Pillow*. "It really reflected our time quite intensely, more so than a regular band. It was a lot more topical. That was the transition from folk music to rock 'n' roll."

Elements of folk music, he adds, are still present in his work, for example, KBC's first single, the cynically patriotic "America."

"It's a story song," Kantner says, "the most basic of folk traditions, rather than an ooh-baby-I-love-you-won't-you-do-this-that-or-the-other-thing. This song helps to tell a story and create a picture, which stems from the folk tradition."

Once, during the Nixon years, Kantner drove Grace Slick and Abbie Hoffman to a White House reception to which Slick had been inadvertently invited; they intended to spike the punch with LSD. They were denied entrance to the ladies-only event, and Kantner insists the attempt was not a vicious act.

"I think we self-destructed it intentionally by bringing Abbie Hoffman along with her, to a woman's tea at Tricia Nixon's back door," he says. "So it was more for the comedic, Merry Prankster effect. It was just more conceptual humor."

His feelings for his country have evolved. "As you grow and go," Kantner says, "you learn that America is not a bad place to be, although it has a lot of imperfections. But even in the '60s when everyone was saying whatever they were saying, it wasn't in damning or wanting destruction. It was more reconstructive, taking care of business. There were some things that needed to be fixed."

The tradition of "fixing" things with music continues, with Live Aid, Amnesty International and other activities by musicians "concerned with doing more than just f---ing off," Kantner says. This borrows from another folk music tradition, he adds, the blending of social responsibility and party spirit.

What is most remarkable about watching the KBC Band play is how much better the new songs sound live. The record is pleasant, yet uninvolving. Generic music. It never actually sounds bad, except when compared to *Surrealistic Pillow* or 1967's *After Bathing at Baxters*, perhaps Jefferson Airplane's most exciting album.

Kantner admits that the live/studio dichotomy has always thwarted him, but feels this album turned out well. He says records are a two-dimensional representation of music, and that live shows always sound better.

"We don't know how to make records," he says. "We can get by, and make OK records. One of the drawbacks has been trying to re-create — to use the corny word — the 'magic' that goes into it, all the thunder and the chaos and the swirling harmonics that go on in an uncontrollable live venue, compared to a recording studio, which can be very clinical."

At this rehearsal, all the soft edges (presumably added to make the music more palatable to the masses) are brushed aside, giving everything more depth and bite. It's also apparent that the band's range extends well beyond the album's contents. The only song that doesn't sound better here than on the record is "Mariel," perhaps because it seems a touch over-rehearsed. And Kantner would probably rather be singing "If we don't care now Chile could happen here" to something other than a carpeted wall.

Throughout, the irascible Balin sits next to that wall, drinking mineral water, and not even leaving the perch when the more ambulatory band members take a 20-minute break. During this time, two of the new guys tell him they've lost enthusiasm for one of the new tunes, one that Balin sings but did not write.

They approach him gingerly, but he is gracious. "No problem. We'll do something else." He is either secure or bored. Earlier, the band's publicist had said Balin did not give interviews, something he is quick to deny.

"Hell, I'll talk to anyone," he says after the rehearsal. "When I'm working, I'll do interviews. But the rest of the band doesn't want me to talk because I'll tell the truth. Then they'll be mad at me."

Some of Balin's truths: He doesn't like the album. He doesn't like the album cover. He thinks the band should have a name, instead of initials. He didn't like the production, and sneaked in a favored take of one song when the producer was attending to a family crisis. He doesn't like the finished sound and would have liked the opportunity to do some remixing.

His word for the album is "appalled," throwing tacit blame Kantner's way by accenting the second syllable and adding "excuse the pun."

"I don't know what his pleasure or lack of pleasure is," Kantner responds later. "I don't think he's liked any album that we've ever done."

Balin says he has "no desire to be part of a corporate rock band," pointing out that his agreement with KBC leaves room for his solo activity. (Other than Kantner and Casady, the KBC Band is Balin's regular backup group.) Balin's presence injects an element of danger, for he could always leave, as he did with Airplane and Starship, when the group seems to be at an apex.

Kantner still harbors resentment toward Starship, which can no longer use the "Jefferson" prefix due to Kantner's ownership of the name. He calls the falling-out "pretty terminal," adding there will be no further musical cross-pollination without "a major groveling apology" from the Starship crew.

"The original split was your basic musical differences," he says. "But it got into them being rude and wanting to have the name, and trying to keep any of my money tied up in the band from getting to me so I would sell the name out cheap. That was the wrong thing to do to me. I would rather fight to the death than give in to something like that."

THE GLOBE AND MAIL, January 9, 1987

Ronnie Lane Determined That Disease Won't Beat Him

Interviewed in person, San Francisco, CA

SAN FRANCISCO — The last time Ronnie Lane performed here it was for 16,000 people in a sold-out arena. On this night, he has managed to draw only about 100 stalwarts to a small club.

Numbers are irrelevant here; this is a much happier occasion. Four years ago, several of Lane's musician friends — including Eric Clapton, Jeff Beck and Jimmy Page — headed the Action Research against Multiple Sclerosis (ARMS) tour. Lane, who suffers from MS, closed each show by singing "Goodnight Irene" from a wheelchair.

Lane, 41, hasn't licked the debilitating disease, but he's put together a band and taken it on the road. He's on the verge of signing a recording contract. And in fighting MS, he's managed to avoid the pessimism that envelops many sufferers.

"It's fantastic to be on stage again," said Lane, now a resident of Austin, Tex. During the interview in his matchbox-sized hotel room, he lay on the bed, shoes on, answering questions in a soft, weak voice. "I never thought I'd be able to do it. Perhaps I shouldn't be doing it. But I want to. So that's that."

Lane played bass and wrote songs for the Small Faces, a British band that became famous west of the Atlantic only when Steve Marriott left to form Humble Pie and was replaced by Rod Stewart and Ron Wood. The rechristened Faces evolved into an ersatz Rolling Stones, and Lane left in 1973 for the prototypical solo career.

His records caused nary a commercial ripple, perhaps because the blustery folk-oriented sound was closer to Fairport Convention than the Faces. He made albums with Ron Wood and with Pete Townshend. But in 1978, he developed symptoms that were later diagnosed as MS.

In simplest terms, Lane's brain works as well as it always did but his body doesn't always respond. He can't play guitar. He can hardly walk. But he has proven that he can still sing.

When Lane was wheeled onstage at a Faces reunion last year, he thought he would never perform again. While he was in England, however, a doctor suggested that the mercury fillings in his teeth might be the source of some discomfort. The fillings were replaced, and he felt the difference immediately.

"I'm still a cripple," he said. "But I don't have that fatigue any more."

He speaks slowly. Carefully. Whimsically. He peppers his speech with British slang and inserts the F-word everywhere.

"I've been on the track of MS for years. I knew the first thing was not to let it make me negative, because I'd seen it do that to people. And it helps the f---ing disease. I've tried to get to the bottom of this disease and it's so stupid. This country has managed to get to the f---ing moon and hasn't managed to get to the bottom of the disease. I was always waiting for this country to crack it but it never has. I found out more about it than what the poxy doctors know. In Britain it's even worse."

Earlier this year Lane was approached by an Austin alternative newspaper with a request to perform a few numbers at its annual awards banquet. He accepted before he was sure he could make it work. He recruited a slick local band, the Tremors, along with another Texan, occasional Rolling Stones sax player Bobby Keys. It sounded good, and Lane followed that success with two short U.S. tours.

On stage Lane is the benign bandleader, perched on a center-stage stool while singing and making small faces at the more active band members. Without knowing anything about his past, you might merely think he is someone who chooses to sing sitting down. The only clue that something is amiss is the unfocused glaze that clouds his eyes.

He opened the show with two songs from his last record, 1979's *See Me*. "You're So Rude" and a remarkable "Ooh La La" were borrowed from the Faces, and Lane filled out the set with solo rarities, unrecorded songs and odd covers like "Shakin' All Over" and "Tired of Waiting for You."

Lane's singing voice is clear and strong. It's apparent he is not as fragile as he looked earlier in the day, and that his restraint then was a way to save his energy for the stage.

Using rock music as a fundraising tool did not begin with ARMS, but the group certainly set the stage for the now-commonplace large-scale benefit concerts. ARMS, however, missed its happy ending. The tour raised about $1 million for the cause, but there were problems involving the money and the people who handled it. Little money ended up going to MS, and the matter is now in litigation.

"I don't want to do anything like that (benefit) again," Lane said. "I want to help people who've been suddenly told they've got MS." I don't want people to be in the same situation as I was in when they told me. They told me, 'Don't do anything.' That's all they said. I was not encouraged to exercise; I was not encouraged to do anything."

The purpose of ARMS had been to establish a hyperbaric oxygen treatment center for MS in Houston. The efficacy of HBO treatments for MS patients is still being debated. Part of the controversy is due to the inconsistent nature of the disease. The symptoms can suddenly subside, and the patient never knows if the remission has anything to do with the treatment.

HBO recently received attention when it was revealed that Michael Jackson uses an HBO chamber in an effort to prevent aging. Lane, who still swears by the process, doesn't begrudge Jackson its cosmetic use but can't afford to pay for his own treatments. (Costs run to $90 a half-hour; about 15 sessions of 90 minutes each are needed before the treatment does any good.)

While talking about HBO, Lane's eyes wander, like an addict discussing a particularly powerful opiate.

"Good stuff, pure oxygen under pressure. It helps indeed. I go in and take a dive once in a blue moon when I've got the money. Before I had the HBO I couldn't talk. I was slurring my speech like a drunkard. I wasn't drinking, but I couldn't get my mouth around the words."

Manager Chesley Milliken said several major labels have shown interest in signing Lane, and an album could be out by the end of the year. Lane's vision of his future is less precise. He'd like to play the guitar again, but needs to regain his ability to walk first.

"My attitude toward music hasn't really changed," he said. "My health is not that good, although it's not as bad as it was. And it's hard to kill a vermin. I'm here to prove that point."

THE GLOBE AND MAIL, July 27, 1987

Benefit for Amnesty Keeps Doors Open

SAN FRANCISCO— A CONSPIRACY OF HOPE, a package tour benefiting the human rights organization Amnesty International, kicked off at the Cow Palace Wednesday night with more than five hours of luminescent, socially aware rock and roll.

The performers, in order of appearance, were The Neville Brothers, Joan Baez, Lou Reed, Jackson Browne, Peter Gabriel, Bryan Adams, Sting and U2. Other artists and special guests are expected to join as the tour progresses through Los Angeles, Denver, Atlanta and Chicago, along with a finale originating from East Rutherford, N.J., on June 15. (Pay-TV channel, MuchMusic, is planning to telecast part of the New Jersey concert.)

No new anthems have been written to celebrate the cause; none is needed. These are performers who have already spoken through their music, seven smart bands who, in Joan Baez's words, "are taking an intelligent stand and offer some commitment to human decency and caring."

Rock has long boasted a social conscience, with most performers playing a benefit at some point — even if it was for a local clinic or a friend's lost equipment. Recently, however, rockers have rediscovered this power in a big way. Causes for the spate of rock-based benefits have been diverse, tied together with the "- Aid" suffix. First Band Aid, then Live, Farm, Sport and Drive. The idea has even made its way to the USSR, where Russian rock bands recently played to benefit nuclear accident victims. The social conscience aspect of rock, then, has added a suffix of its own: since many of these efforts seek to help the less fortunate through redistribution of wealth, it can be said that rock has now developed a socialist conscience. Some fans find this new awareness an intrusion, but not for ideological reasons.

"There are those who have wished that the doors that have opened with Band Aid and Live Aid would close," U2's Bono told a San Francisco press conference Tuesday. "Some people have suggested that we get this charity business over with, get back to rock and roll's redundant behavior, like we had in the 1970s. But there are those of us anxious to keep those doors open, by refusing to go back to sleep."

The events seek to balance Amnesty's low visibility in the United States with a higher European and Third World profile. Adams, the sole Canadian participant, thinks the situation is even more acute in his homeland.

"Canadians live a very sheltered existence," he said. "We don't know a lot about these things. Young people aren't educated, they aren't made to know about things like torture, and governments in Third World countries taking advantage of artists and poets. We have to make them aware."

Amnesty exerts pressure on governments on behalf of those tortured or imprisoned because of their beliefs. The tour is dedicated to six specific prisoners of conscience. Pre-addressed postcards, to be signed and returned to the dictator in question, are distributed at each show.

The concert lineup is a fitting cross-section of the best in modern rock. Both Sting and Bono sang with Band Aid; at the time they were considerably less famous. Reed, Browne and Gabriel are veterans who have recently shown vitality with strong new records.

There are tips of the hat: Gabriel's years of art/rock experimentation made groups like the Police and U2 possible. Once with Genesis, Gabriel in turn owes a lot to Reed and his first group, the Velvet Underground. And every socially aware rocker, whether they know it or not, owes something to Joan Baez.

After Gabriel took the stage everything changed. He played longer than anyone except U2, ending with "Biko," an ode to a prisoner of conscience Amnesty was unable to help. As the song finished, the band departed the stage, leaving the audience chanting along with an overpowering synthesized drum.

To suggest that anyone is here to further careers would be the worst form of cynicism. But by the time this tour is over, Gabriel should be a major star — these performances will expose him to the masses he has yet failed to reach, and his musical loquaciousness and fiery performance will gain him scores of new fans. While many people will leave these shows with the urge to send $25 to Amnesty, suspicions are that far more will first choose to spend their money on Gabriel's phenomenal new album.

One of Gabriel's co-stars, Sting, arrived late at the press conference Tuesday; there was no doubt he would rather have been in bed. Nevertheless, every other question seemed directed toward him, and his brisk statements tore right through the twaddle. Some quotations from Chairman Sting:

— "There is a direct link between musicians and communicators and Amnesty. That is, without freedom of expression we can't do our jobs. Quite selfishly, it's a way of protecting our position as artists. It's for us as well as the people who are being tortured."

— "I really don't like organizations very much — political, religious or otherwise. But I regard Amnesty International as probably the most civilized organization in the history of the world, because of its support for human rights."

— "It's essential that these events all be unique. There's no sense in repeating things year after year. If we had done Live Aid again this year we would have gotten diminishing returns. If musicians and artists are going to be involved in human rights and causes, then each time we do it we have to be creative, innovative, because people get bored. It's our responsibility to make them interested, constantly excited by what's happening."

Meaning, perhaps, that rock benefits will never approach the flavor of the Jerry Lewis Telethon. It is then suggested that this need for perpetual entertainment doesn't say a whole lot for the audience's intelligence or commitment.

"No," Sting responded sourly. "It doesn't."

At the concert, Sting, backed by a slick, six-piece band, played four songs with nary a word in between. Rumors of a Police reunion were quickly forgotten, blown away by this band's vivid jazz/rock.

Compared to most of the veterans, Bryan Adams was the new kid on the block, yet he performed in the third-to-last spot. He seemed a little overwhelmed by the setting, while playing a fast-paced set of his best-known songs. The day before he had said he would have special guests, but none materialized.

"The music is basically what's bringing everybody here," he said. "We have to play the songs that people are familiar with. The songs themselves don't have to be political; it is the music that's bringing people together to make them aware of the situation."

If most of the bands stuck with what was expected, show closer U2's passionate cacophony tore all of the conventions down. While the band highlighted its own material, there were some extraordinary covers: "Sun City," Eddie Cochran's "C'mon Everybody," a slowed-down reading of The Beatles' "Help" and a medley of "Maggie's Farm," "Old McDonald" and "Cold Turkey."

The now-traditional finale, where all take a bow, was a gently appropriate reminder of what the evening was all about — Bob Dylan's "I Shall Be Released."

Promoter extraordinaire Bill Graham, whose efforts ensure that the events don't turn into a Conspiracy of Hype, said that after Live Aid there was a feeling of "Gee, what a great concert, what's Ethiopia?" Steps were being taken, he added, to make sure that doesn't happen here. Many, however, have already missed the point. To judge from the piles of postcards discarded after the show, there were quite a few people who savored the music but ignored the message.

This is something the participants expect. They are playing for the cause, in the hope that the audience will hear about Amnesty at the concerts and, through the accompanying media blitz, investigate the cause on their own. Knowledge acquired through effort, then, is all the more profound.

"We are admired and followed by our public," said Adams. "We should bear some responsibility for other human beings. Being a musician, I'm in a position where I can tell the people who buy my records the things I believe. Even if they don't agree, at least I'm making them aware."

THE GLOBE AND MAIL June 6. 1986

Like a Rolling Clone:
Peter Landecker's Dylan Show

SAN FRANCISCO — IN 1981, college student Peter Landecker spotted Bob Dylan at a Los Angeles gas station. Dylan is accustomed to approaches by strangers, but Landecker's impromptu overture was unique: he had portrayed Dylan in a play he had written, and wanted to turn the school project into a professional production.

Dylan's referral then led Landecker to what turned out to be a series of dead ends. A year or so later Landecker was driving the Pacific Coast Highway when he saw Dylan riding a bicycle. He reintroduced himself, and the two talked at length about what such a show should and should not be.

"He told me then I could have the rights," said Landecker, now 26. "But it took me another two years to get those rights legally. I had created a property out of someone else's work. . . . and it was complicated by the fact that he doesn't own the rights to many of his songs, and other rights for other material had to be obtained."

Dylan: Words and Music, which opened last night at the Zephyr IV Theatre for a six-week run, combines elements of modern media archetypes to yield a new one, a live documentary. Every word in the show was at one time written, sung or spoken by Dylan. Landecker assembled the various scraps from years of songs, interviews, concert programs, liner notes and private correspondence. Throughout the process he submitted the script to Dylan, who is also receiving a royalty.

With the presence of actor Bob Miles, a Dylan lookalike, the show is similar to other solo portrayals of characters from literature or history, although Miles is not always on stage. Projected images turn the show into an audio- visual experience, and there are enough songs to qualify it as a concert.

According to producer John Neal, the biggest obstacle has been acquiring rights for each of the projected images. When a first choice (such as a sequence from D. A. Pennebaker's *Don't Look Back*) was too expensive, other visuals had to be found.

The show features a necessarily incomplete but predictable cross-section of 22 songs, from "Song to Woody," to the finale, "Forever Young." Some are in rapid-fire medley, and many have verses cut.

"There are certain songs you have to include," Landecker said. "'Like a Rolling Stone,' 'Mr. Tambourine Man,' 'Blowin' in the Wind,' the classics. Then there are the ones that are representative of certain times. Like 'It Ain't Me, Babe' is representative of the love songs, the semi-love songs or the anti-love songs he was writing at the time."

But Landecker never sought to provide the last word on Dylan's life and music. "I didn't want to make some definitive statement or biography or come up with a whole new version of what happened," he said. "All we're doing is taking a selection of his words and piecing them together in a theatrical setting to create a tribute which can re-create his spirit."

The most significant difference between *Words and Music* and *Beatlemania*, frequently cited by this crew as a benchmark of what *Words and Music* is not, is the co-operation of the subject.

"Words and Music" is a sanitized affair, as close to an authorized biography as we are likely to get for some time. Dylan, according to Landecker, forbade the use of early unpublished songs and anything that invaded his privacy.

"He's very protective about his personal life," Landecker said. "Some people might be upset that there isn't more about his family. But if you listen to the songs, we tell the whole story."

Like a folk song, the end product is rife with exaggeration. "Some of the things in the script, like his being in jail, aren't necessarily the truth," Landecker acknowledged. "But they are his words. It's part of his story. That's how he became a legend at age 21."

It has never been necessary to actually resemble Dylan to look like him: A tousled head, a raw voice and a guitar provide a running start. Miles. 35, has the right look but tries to play the role from the inside.

"I don't think I look like him," Miles said, not breaking character. "More people tell me I look like Roman Polanski."

Miles has met Dylan, having housesat for him in 1969 during a concert tour, so his portrayal comes from more than secondhand sources. (Dylan also had actor approval; it was muster that Miles, who has no regular understudy, easily passed.)

"I'm not doing a caricature," Miles said. "It's an interpretation of his words and music, how he approaches public life and audiences. The play does not delve into his personal life; there is nothing that I'm doing that I wouldn't do in front of him."

Four of the best seats are to be held in his name each night until 15 minutes before showtime.

"If he sees his material performed and feels it has been treated with respect I think he'll be happy," Landecker said.

Lending the show further credibility is the presence of musical director Bob Johnston, who produced what many consider to be Dylan's best albums, from 1965's "Highway 61 Revisited" to "New Morning" six years later.

Some of Johnston's arrangements are faithful to Dylan's own, while others use the crack house band and two gospel vocalists to search for new interpretations. "Masters of War" becomes a heavy metal drone, while "Subterranean Homesick Blues" sounds like an outtake from an early Elvis Presley session.

"This is a celebration of Dylan," says Johnston. "If he were dead we'd be praising him but he's not dead so we are praising him while he is alive It's become fashionable to give credit to those who have worked so hard before they're dead. I like that fashion."

"There is something in this show for everybody," Landecker says. Fanatics will find many things that please them while someone who knows nothing about Dylan can come to this show and not be lost."

After viewing *Words and Music*, theatergoers may have a feeling for the man and his art, along with a sense of his obscurity-for-its-own-sake poses. Consider this re-created mid-1960s exchange between Dylan and a reporter, who had asked what piqued his interest in rock 'n' roll:

"I lost my one true love. I started drinking. First thing I know I'm in a card game, then I'm in a crap game. I wake up in a pool hall and this big Mexican lady drags me off the table and takes me to Philadelphia. She leaves me alone in her house and it burns down.

"I wind up in Phoenix. I get a job as a Chinaman and start working in a dime store, and move in with a 13-year-old girl. Then the big Mexican lady from Philadelphia comes and burns the house down. I go down to Dallas and get a job as a 'before' in a Charles Atlas 'before and after' ad, and move in with a delivery boy who cooks fantastic chili and hot dogs. Then the 13-year-old girl from Phoenix comes and burns the house down. The delivery boy, he ain't so mild, he gives her the knife.

"Next thing I know I'm in Omaha. It's so cold there. By this time, I'm robbing my own bicycles and frying my own fish. I stumbled on to some luck. I get a job as a carburetor out at the hot rod races every Thursday night and move in with a high-school English teacher, who does some plumbing on the side, who ain't much to look at, but who's building some kind of refrigerator that turns newspaper into lettuce. Things go good until that delivery boy shows up and tries to knife me. Needless to say, he burnt the house down. The first guy that picked me up asked me if I wanted to be a rock 'n' roll star."

And that, the bewildered interviewer asks, is how he became a rock 'n' roll singer?

"No," Miles-as-Dylan deadpans. "That's how I got tuberculosis."

THE WASHINGTON POST, May 3, 1987

Career Heats Up For Joe Ely

Interviewed by phone, San Francisco, CA to somewhere in Texas

COTATI, CA—With its own hot brand of Texas rock and roll, the Joe Ely Band has transformed the tiny stage of this rural club into a musical sauna.

It's been a diverse week for Ely. Two days prior, he headlined the San Francisco Blues Festival, playing to a large crowd in an open meadow. The day before, he closed Apple Computer's company picnic, where staff and their families, lulled into complacency by an afternoon of family entertainment, were in a dancing frenzy by the third note.

Tonight he is playing the type of venue he prefers, a large wooden floor jammed with a few hundred rowdy people. It is an environment in which the 40-year-old Austin, Texas-based singer-songwriter may soon be less visible. After seven albums since the late 1970s, his new album and streamlined shows are gaining wider attention.

Ely appeared in Vancouver in early September, following this with a tour of the western United States. More Canadian dates — including Toronto — are now in the planning stages.

The impetus comes from more than a record and a tour.

On Nov. 13, Ely and three other Texas songwriters — Terry Allen, Butch Hancock and Jimmie Dale Gilmore — will perform their yet-to-be-written new U.S. national anthem at the Smithsonian Institution in Washington, D.C.

Of the new anthem, commissioned by the Washington Project for the Arts (WPA), Ely will say only that it should be danceable, and sound good at ballgames.

There is common perception that the current anthem is outdated and hard to sing. But Jock Reynolds, executive director for the WPA, says the effort is not meant to denigrate "The Star Spangled Banner," nor to force the new song down anyone's throat.

"Who knows what will happen to it after it's written?" Reynolds asked. "We are not trying to say it should be adopted. It will only be out there for people to do what they want."

This could be a metaphor for Ely's own sound, as his seven previous albums have served up a picturesque brand of Americana; a blend of folk, blues, country and rock 'n' roll. "It's tough for me to categorize my own music," he says. "I let other people make those distinctions."

His records pale in comparison to his performances, but the new album, *Lord of the Highway*, ups the ante. Released by an independent California label, it blends influences from Jimi Hendrix to the Sons of the Pioneers, resulting in a rock 'n' roll album that actually sweats.

"We didn't expect it to turn out this well," Ely said. "We just did it and threw it out there. This is the first album that I've ever done that was not produced but only recorded. There was no pressure, no clock running."

For spontaneity's sake, Ely did not excise all glitches like missed notes, sudden tempo changes and false starts. In addition he almost added a deliberate defect, a pre-recorded "skip" at the end of the compact disc.

The album was completed without record company money; costs were supported by live shows while the band's time was divided between the studio and the road.

"It captures the energy of the band like none of my other albums did, even my live one," Ely said. "We had the best of both worlds. We were playing some of the songs before we recorded them, and knew they were working in live shows. It was a continuous process."

The last Ely album was 1984's *Hi-Res*, which tossed his Texas punk into a high-tech blender. It was by no means a bad record, but made few waves in a year dominated by Michael Jackson and Prince.

He then recorded *Dig All Night*, which his former record company, MCA, first subjected to extensive production work and then declined to release at all. It was recorded when Ely's current band had not yet solidified; sidemen included former Little Feat keyboard player Billy Payne and members of the Cruzados and Los Lobos.

Dig All Night's perpetual limbo is still a cause of frustration. Its ownership was supposed to revert to Ely after a year, but that hasn't happened. Contractual fine print, he says, prevents him from re-recording any of the songs himself.

Still, Ely and band perform six of the hardest-hitting songs from *Dig All Night* onstage. If the album is ever released, he says, "I'll remix it and take off the schmaltzy garbage."

Ely's regional appeal has not always translated well to outsiders. Most of the world, for instance, perceives "New Mexico line" as three terse words about an unfamiliar place. To initiates, it is more eloquent, evoking 360 degrees of clear sky and plains with the faint western mountain haze.

"Somehow it gets across," he said of his songs' Texas flavor. "Whether it's completely accurate I can't judge. The real Texas has a lot more 7-Elevens than I put in my songs."

He recently found, on a tour of Norway, that the Texas experience is not confined to the boundaries of the Lone Star state.

"Even in remote villages near the Arctic circle there were raging fans," he said. "A lot of their images of the Southwest came from movies and records. It was unsettling to think that the culture revolves around a music that comes from a different place." Texas flavor notwithstanding, this isn't redneck rock.

"I'm not trying to convey the physical appearance of mainstream USA, but the spirit of what moves people. I'm not just a gung-ho Texan. I'm a writer. I take whatever where I am and turn it into a song without explaining it too much. I want to leave mystery in there.

"If characters and landscape jump into my songs it's only from my natural habitat, all over New Mexico and Texas. I like to ramble around. But I don't want it to be a song like, 'If you don't wear boots you ain't s ***.' I don't like that kind of segregation in music."

The new album's success, despite the odds, gives Ely a sense of accomplishment. "It makes me feel great," he said. "I know that it can be done. Maybe it will be an inspiration to someone else who feels that the forces of the record company are against them."

THE GLOBE AND MAIL, September 29, 1987

Todd Rundgren: I've Got My Own Operating System to Do

Interviewed in person, Sausalito, CA

I'm not sure of the exact circumstances surrounding this transcript. I interviewed Rundgren several times between 1985 and 1988, during which time he became a "close acquaintance." This was probably done at his house in Sausalito, at 69 Sunshine Lane. This address was always a source of amusement to me, and now that he has moved away I can share the oh-so-little joke.

It is easy to slide Todd Rundgren into an artist-as-technoweenie buttonhole, but to do so is to forget that were he not an artist his technoweenie instincts would not even be worth discussing.

Rundgren is in some circles as well known for his computer acumen as his music. He was one of the first to elevate overdubbing beyond the curiosity level, well before MIDI. He never had the urge to express himself on canvas, but has become an expert on programs that turn a PC into a paintbrush. He is proficient in both process and product; his high tech impulses complement his innate pop smarts.

He first emerged in the late 1960s with Nazz, a band which, he now says, "wanted to be The Who." Subsequent records, both as a solo and with Utopia, ranged from the great to the curious; running the course from cloying pop tunes to sophisticated aural noodles. Throughout, there have been few hits; the last was 1983's "Bang the Drum All Day," and he constantly derides — and ostensibly refuses to play — his most famous song, "Hello, It's Me."

Still, he inspires adoration rivaling the most ardent Boss booster or Deadhead, with the Todd-Is-God-Squad wallowing in his every move. His fans cite the injustice of his low profile, stating that he is entitled to a far larger slice of the commercial pie. But it is he who has blocked his own shot at the top. He obviously has the commercial instincts, but chooses to thwart them with elements of eccentricity and humor that are somewhat less than universal.

There may be other factors here, but as Rundgren has delved more deeply into the computer universe there have been fewer records. For over a decade he cranked out more than an album a year. Today, his most recent new record is *Acappella*, released September 1985.

Currently, he is writing the music for a Broadway production of the late Joe Orton's *Up Against It* (once intended as the third Beatles movie). And he is always adding to his production credits, which range from Badfinger to XTC (his latest is Bourgeois Tagg). All along, he reflects the transition into the personal computer age, proving the new machines need not lack soul.

It is said that a struggling performer can nearly starve; once he makes the grade everyone is buying him dinner. A famous guitarist can always get free guitars. Similarly, Rundgren's stature earns him free access to a lot of new systems and software. A manufacturer lending him equipment will get more than warm fuzzies from the fact that Todd is using his stuff, at least for the moment. He is brutal in his pushing of equipment to its limits, and pulls no punches when discussing its shortcomings.

"What he uses has to be the best, or he's not satisfied," said PC Magazine technical art director Gerard Kunkel, who has worked with Rundgren. "He takes the machines to their highest level, immediately finding ways to improve them, and writing programs that will improve them for his own use."

What was your first involvement with computers?

High school. I used to go after school to the Bell Telephone billing office. They were indulgent because everyone was a Bell Telephone customer, also because it was unusual for somebody who was just getting into high school to show some interest in this.

When I was growing up there were two things that I wanted to be, either a computer programmer or to be in a band. The real reason I became a musician is because it was something that required a natural talent that I had, and I didn't have to go to school. All I had to do was "woodshed," take my guitar and practice it until I got good.

In the same way, the people who are writing the good software today are good not because they went to school, they taught themselves. These are the people who are providing the creative force behind the whole industry.

There are so many predilections you're born with, some things come naturally. I constantly need to have some kind of input, I enjoy thinking about convoluted things. I'm not intimidated by technology, but it's not that I have some kind of patent desire for things technological.

Do you always need to have the newest stuff?

I used to. Nowadays I tend more to wait. Before personal computers, video was my thing. I spent every cent I had on it. If there was some new thing I had to have it.

That was where the first million went?

No. The first million went to a recording studio, and the next two million went to a video studio.

If you were ten years younger, doing Something/Anything *with* MIDI, *say, what would be different?*

If I was younger I would have gone directly into computers. Personal computers weren't capable, or at least the affordable ones, of doing the things I wanted to do when I first got into video. Now I would have no compunction about spending several hundred thousand dollars on a computer. But it isn't even necessary nowadays.

What doesn't software do, that it should?

Interfaces in general need work. They still require a certain amount of computer consciousness on the part of the user. It doesn't take a lot to become a software publisher. A lot of it is just rehashed versions of things that already exist, rearranged and changed around. It is easier to come up with an operating piece of software than a valid theory of interface or application design that the software adheres to.

Everyone has what they believe to be a philosophy of user interface, but usually it's coming from the wrong direction. It's usually "we're capable of doing this, so we'll build a front end that allows us to control the things we're capable of." That doesn't always conform to the attitude that the user has about the software.

A user has an understanding of the area that he's operating in. If someone want to use a word processor they already have a familiar metaphor for that, pencil and paper or a typewriter or stacks of pages. Ultimately when you're word processing it's supposed to end up in that format anyway. Most people do their word processing to be published somewhere else than on the screen of a computer.

So there is already a metaphor for that. A computer screen is flat and two-dimensional, and a sheet of paper is also flat and two-dimensional. When you start to get into other things where the metaphor is a little less flat that's when people have trouble thinking up interfaces that make sense.

Why do computer graphics in the first place?

For me, obviously, it's artistic expression, but it can be used for engineering simulation. In order to free up the computer as an artistic tool certain engineering concepts have to be built in. The artist doesn't want to have to worry about taking a ball-shaped object and throwing it at wall-shaped object, he doesn't want to have to play God and detect the point where the ball hits the wall and tell it explicitly to change direction. This has to be a result of natural physics. Very few interfaces have that built in.

This stuff is so expensive, so using computer graphics becomes an elitist practice.

It's definitely an elitist tool. But anything less is a waste of your time. With some systems I'm trying to be creative, but at the same time I'm spending equal or more energy trying to overcome limitations in the system. I suppose there is that aspect of any medium, but if I was just using a canvas and paints I would not be limited by the number of colors. I would only be limited in resolution in how small the brush was and how much control I had over my hands.

Being a musician nowadays doesn't necessarily require a whole lot of musical talent. Same thing with visual artists; technique takes a back seat to so-called inspiration. Whatever it is you are trying to convey is the most important thing. When you're recording music the most important thing is the song, the technique by which you perform are secondary.

What's the biggest difference between music people and computer people?

Computer people have a different sense of personal style. They dress the same than when they were in junior high school. In the rock world, style is one of the things that's necessary, you have to have some kind of look because that's what you're selling. In computers, nobody cares what you look like, but there are programmers who look like rock stars. And there are people like Husker Dü, who look like computer nerds but play heavy metal.

Onstage, you use an IBM compatible to control the music, but a Macintosh for the graphics. What's the difference between the two environments?

The IBM was made for the business world and since I'm not a businessman I don't have much interest in their line of computers or the method of marketing, I'm really essentially involved in personal computing, I don't care what the business world does.

Everything in the IBM scheme of things is based less on a philosophy of computing than a philosophy of marketing. The only reason that the new IBMs have graphics and MIDI is marketing, everybody else has them and IBM is going to look pretty antediluvian if they don't.

Nobody knows what goes on inside IBM, so no one can say for sure. It's an impression you get from all available things. There's always a lot of software for IBM but it's the type that really defines the personality of the machine. There's such a great preponderance of business software, and the available programming tools are for people who want to write more business software.

IBM has never been interested in the causal user of computers, those who use them at home, or hackers. It's interested in people in a good solid rich dependable market, the business community. IBM wasn't thinking of me when they made the machine. Steve Wozniak was thinking of someone like me, the guys at Atari and Commodore are thinking of people more like me than IBM is.

I also know for a fact that IBM is never going to give me a machine. I've gotten machines from Apple, Atari, and a lot of others. I know I'm never going to get any kind of personal treatment from IBM.

But you use an IBM compatible onstage.

Because it runs (music sequencing program written by Utopia bandmate Roger Powell) Texture. And it doesn't belong to me. My sound man, Chris Andersen, bought it when he needed to do his accounting, or something.

What is the difference between taping music and copying software?

In order for anything to be subsidized there is marketing involved. I don't care if people tape my records and pass them around because I made them to be heard. If I don't make money off that's unfortunate, but it's not the reason I make music.

The reason I get involved in designing interfaces is that I want people to be ultimately to be doing those things. I want to make pictures myself, but I also want to see the pictures that other people make. Some other people have a more wacky visual sense, and I enjoy looking at those things.

Are you always playing catch-up with new equipment?

Artists will seek tools that enable them to express their ideas with a greater degree of accuracy. After that, a technology will develop. Once he becomes familiar to that he realizes other things that he wants. Then the technology has catch up with that, and after this make demands on the artist again. The artist wants something, then the technology attempts to catch up, then the artist has to become abreast of the technology again. It's a herky-jerky thing.

How will compact discs change how records are made?

The central issue continues to be whether the music is any good to start with. The advantage to me is not the purported increase in fidelity, because what people hear is always a subjective thing. The real advantage is that they have a longer playing time and that they don't degrade. I see just as much as validity in remastering all the old Motown things, no matter how noisy they are the noise is not the issue, it's the quality of the music.

I don't see that the existence of CDs will change the way that people make music, except that you don't have the previous time limitation. Before, there was a gray area between single and double albums, eventually you can just make an album as long as you want.

You've made some long albums, and some short ones.

I've made too many short ones. *Todd* was two albums, it was too long for a single but not long enough for a double, so there were a couple 15-minute sides. With me, it depends on how much music gets recorded for a particular concept, I have to make music until it's adequately defined. With conventional plastic, there always has to be a certain time limit.

Is there a method to your solo albums?

I set aside times to record and prime my consciousness for that time. It involves a lot of front-end work, like refining the concept and the lyrical subject matter before I start record. The concepts are more a question of potential rather than a concrete thing. Before I do any record I don't have a bunch of songs. What I have are potential concepts; when I sit down to realize them that's when they take form.

Do you have a concept for your next album?

I have a vague idea, it could change. It won't be another a cappella album. I'm still writing songs.

And Utopia?

It's still on sabbatical, sort of suspended animation, It's not death but the next best thing. There doesn't seem to be any need for any of us to do it right now. Instead of making records because we enjoy it we have always had it in the back of our minds that this was our financial well-being was on the line. We will not make another record until we can do it without this pressure.

What about fame? Your fans all think you should be better-known.

A lot of that has to do with the extent where you're willing to promote yourself. I don't care to promote myself, I'd like to be financially comfortable. The biggest drag in the world is having to think about money. I have no patent desire to be famous.

It wasn't always that way. With Something/Anything *you seemed to be begging for attention.*

It was a game. When I got the fame from *Something/Anything* I realized all the bad things that came with it, and it pigeonholed me. When I did an album that I really wanted to do, (like) *Wizard*, I got a bunch of shit for it.

Famous people get flack from all directions. People will not let you alone when you're in a restaurant and want to eat. When you don't want to think about it you don't have a choice. Somebody as famous as Bruce Springsteen or Prince, a certain part of their life is gone forever. They can't just get up and pretend to be normal. People are always going to be reminding them of what it is they do and what they are and what they mean.

It makes it hard to get a certain equilibrium. I don't want to be constantly reminded of what other people think I am, I have too much trouble trying to figure it out myself.

FULL TRANSCRIPT UNPUBLISHED, SEPT. 1988

For Folkies: The Times They Are A- Changin'

Interviews by phone from Portland, OR

Folk music was big business in the 1960s. Descended from centuries of British and American idioms, it became a sounding board for social commentary. The folkies even had their own TV show, *Hootenanny*, which provided a direct line into middle America.

The sounds of social change have died down, and folk's popularity has been eclipsed several times over. The category has assimilated into other forms or has been banished to a dark corner of the record store.

To many, however, the music still speaks. Artists forgotten by the mass market still tour regularly and play to small but eager gatherings. One occurs Friday at 8 p.m. when Peter, Paul and Mary perform at the Arlene Schnitzer Concert Hall.

Peter Yarrow, Paul Stookey and Mary Travers waved the folk flag throughout the 1960s, folded it in 1970 and unfurled it again in 1978. Since then, they have steadily regained an audience through diligent, regular touring and are now on a roll: A holiday album recently was released and the group hosted a PBS special.

"There is no doubt that folk music isn't dead," Stookey said. "It's just looking out from a different window. And the market is changing so fast that it's possible that what we do today might soon be thought of as unusual."

Stookey (born Noel Paul Stookey) said the group will draw from its regular repertoire for its Portland show. "There will be the usual solo section: Peter will lead a singalong, Mary will talk about her granddaughter. And I'll probably sing a song about a child with Down syndrome and do some sound effects. This is the blessing and the curse of folk music, you do things that are so diverse that they become strange bedfellows."

Peter, Paul and Mary are the lucky ones, still performing to audiences that want to hear them. Others have been left behind by the public or by their own inability to produce individual music. For every prominent artist with roots in the folk movement — Bob Dylan, Paul Simon or Joni Mitchell — there are many others who eke out a living on the smaller club circuit, reminding smaller crowds that they too once were relevant.

Many of these artists have suffered a common indignity. When it became apparent that their selling power had waned, they were dropped by their record labels. Consequently they have sought alternative outlets, smaller labels and mail order sales, to reach audiences that have diminished in size but not enthusiasm.

Proof of interest comes from the success of similarly influenced artists such as Suzanne Vega and Tracy Chapman. U2, perhaps the most popular band in the world, emulates both the social commitment and musical inclinations of modern folk.

"In popular music we hear some of the elements that have always been there in folk music," Stookey said. "Politically we've moved into an era where we are being forced to examine the disparity between the aspirations of the country and the reality we see on the streets. Much of the citizenry is out of step from the direction that the administration takes, and the music is a rallying point."

Fewer people, however, are rallying. John Stewart, once a member of the Kingston Trio and later a solo artist, feels that folk music's inability to gather a popular majority saddles it with an innate cultural disadvantage. "Everyone shops at malls all over America," he said. "You have the same stores everywhere and they only stock what they can regularly sell.

"As far as records go, you have a few artists who are bought by a lot of people. Occasionally someone like Tracy Chapman will sneak through and sell a lot of records but she's perceived as a novelty."

Stewart verbalizes what must echo in every once-popular songwriter's mind.

"This is a business that you are lucky to stay in for 10 years," he said. "Even Bob Dylan is having trouble and he was a god in the 1960s. Peter, Paul and Mary sell a lot of records but it's as if their success doesn't count. They go against the natural order by trying to stay in the business longer than the average."

In many ways folk music is no different at the dawn of the George Bush era than it was during the Kennedy years. The music still originates from outrage against all types of social injustice. Nevertheless the differences abound, many having to do with the size of the audience. Folk peaked well before the days of arena concerts, but artists who once drew crowds of 5,000 might not fill a 500-seat hall today.

There is the danger that singing the same songs for decades will turn an artist into a nostalgia act, but doing so also can result in a wondrous symmetry. Peter, Paul and Mary still perform "The Marvelous Toy," a life-goes-on ballad about a mechanical knick-knack that a man remembers from his childhood. He gives it to his own child who is just as fascinated by its magic. The song, like the toy, is passed from one generation to the next.

"Blowin' in the Wind" is still their performance centerpiece, written by Bob Dylan and enhanced by their signature reading. The group's performance is of the song is basically unchanged, but Stookey said the song is changed by audience perception and mood.

"The moment is always rare," he said. "You cannot ever recreate the song's effect on that mix of people with the news of that evening. It matters how you think the current administration fits into the peace process or freedom of choice process or self-determination. But the subject matter is contemporary and the songs are timeless."

Stewart's belief in the music is as strong as it ever was, but he perceives talk of a folk revival as so much hype. Despite good reviews for his last album and his multigenerational audience, he has no plans to make another record. And he has no desire to join the current, nostalgia-driven Kingston Trio, singing listless versions of "Tom Dooley" wearing the same striped shirts.

"What we're looking for is not happening," he said. "The music is as healthy as ever. Acoustic guitars are in. But the '60s aren't going to happen again.

"It's like when people ask you to bring your guitar to a party, but when you get there you get the vibe that no one really wants you to play."

THE OREGONIAN, January 22, 1989

1996-2003

*T*he years surrounding the turn of the century were prime time for my freelance work, much of which appeared in Rolling Stone Online. There were a lot of stories and I was in the geographical proximity to tell them; Seattle was no longer the center of new music, but the presence of the new Experience Music Project and the tendency for major artists to begin their tours on the upper left coast put me in the right place and at the right time.

This led me down another fortuitous path, covering the dispute over Jimi Hendrix' estate between his stepsister and brother. This resembled the Beach Boys' controversy which I covered at the same time; how people fight about money and control in ways that have little to do with art.

Kevin Moore Makes A Name For Himself As Blues Singer Keb' Mo

Keb' Mo,' Cayamo Cruise February 2012
Interviewed in person, Portland, OR.

JUST LIKE YOU, the second album from singer-songwriter Keb' Mo', raises a question: why is a 44-year-old, who's been playing music all his life, just now releasing his second album? Musicians half his age boast many more recordings. Then again, it didn't take them thirty-five years to realize that playing music was what they were meant to do.

Keb' Mo', aka Kevin Moore, was born in Texas and raised in Compton, California, a blue-collar town just south of Los Angeles. Compton's streets would eventually give rise to the brutal West Coast rap music of Ice Cube and Dr. Dre, but life there was pretty idyllic for Mo', and it shows in his music, a sweet blend of traditional blues guitar and soulful vocals. "It was a cool community," says Mo', who lives in New Orleans now with his wife and young son.

"I was just one of those kids in school — a good kid, quiet, not loud and crazy. I liked to eat a lot."

After he graduated from high school, Mo' attended a trade college with the intent of studying architecture, but he lost interest in the subject and dropped out. A few years later, he enrolled in a computer repair school, but the idea of fixing computers for a living didn't thrill him much either. All the while, he kept playing music, working as a part-time arranger at A&M, and sitting in with a local club's house band now and then. It was some ten years ago, when Mo' agreed to play the part of a Delta bluesman in an L.A. production of *Rabbit Foot*, that he had his musical epiphany.

"It took me a long time to realize that I loved music, and could make a good living at it," says Mo'. "When I was about thirty-five, I realized that it was a gift from God and that I may as well enjoy it and let it take me as far as it will."

The good thing about getting such a late start in the business, explains Mo', is that "I've already had twenty years of normal adulthood. I have some perspective on how to appreciate it. Whatever happens now, I'm equipped."

In the grand tradition of "noms de blues" such as Muddy Waters, Son House, and Taj Mahal, Mo' picked up his moniker in clubs along the way. He always liked the nickname, but he never imagined using it professionally. Then, says Mo', "I made a demo tape for the label [Epic] called Kevin Moore, AKA Keb' Mo'. Even though I was just kidding around, the label picked up on Keb' Mo' and didn't want to hear about Kevin Moore."

He has come to find the double identity useful. "It separates the stage from real life. Keb' Mo' is an alter ego, although I don't think of him as a fictitious character. But Kevin Moore is more grounded in reality. He knows how to treat people. He remembers having only two fans. So if Keb' Mo' gets out of line, Kevin Moore will be there to straighten him out."

The new album from Moore (and Mo') embraces three musical idioms. There's searing blues-rock that would be right at home in any roadhouse; radio-friendly ballads such as the title track, which features Bonnie Raitt and Jackson Browne; and a handful of imaginative solo blues selections that showcase his simple, expressive guitar playing and commanding voice. The latter is what you'll hear if you catch Keb' Mo' on tour this summer and fall. (He'll be working the blues-festival circuit, headlining club dates, and opening a few shows for the Allman Brothers.)

"We actually thought about doing (*Just Like You*) as a solo record, but we started to add various instruments for their texture, and I like that emotional variation," says Mo', who welcomed the chance to work with musicians such as

Raitt and Browne. Mo' also recognizes that experimentation is something sorely lacking in much of today's blues. "There is a stagnation in the blues," he admits. "It's hard to listen to twelve-bar blues all day. At some of these festivals, after about the third act, you start yawning. So I try to add a few different chords and things where they are least expected."

These nontraditional twists have been well-received by the genre's elder statesmen. "They aren't that small-minded," says Mo'. And while Keb' Mo' is gaining a reputation for redefining the blues, he isn't afraid to be categorized by it, either. "If you want to put me in the blues box, I'll get in," he says. "Getting in the box gives you focus." And, he adds, "people know where to find you."

MR. SHOWBIZ, August 1996

Rickie Lee Jones Follows Own Beat

Interviewed by email from Silverton, OR

IT HAS BEEN 18 years since Rickie Lee Jones breezed in with the eccentric bop of "Chuck E's in Love." A one-hit wonder on radio, she has followed that spotlight moment with richly textured, lyrical albums that draw from myriad musical and verbal influences. She has eluded categorization throughout and probably couldn't be more unique if she tried.

So does she try?

"That's like asking a beautiful girl if she's purposefully beautiful," she says in an e-mail. "I think I have always been, personally, a bit offbeat. But I do not strive to be weird in music."

Ghostyhead, out June 17, borrows modern aural elements without compromising an existing and distinctive style. Jones incorporates trip-hop, electronica and a host of effects but still sounds most like herself. Her honeyed voice, which has gained considerable strength and depth over the years, alternates between the strident and the ethereal.

Ghostyhead is her first all-new album since 1993's *Traffic From Paradise* (1995's *Naked Songs*, her understated entry in the unplugged sweepstakes, featured stripped-down versions of her best songs).

Elements of her lyrical and musical vocabulary pepper the work of many modern singers. Jewel's "Who Will Save Your Soul" came from the rib of "Chuck

E.'s in Love." And anyone hearing Sheryl Crow's "All I Want to Do" at a noisy party might think it was an early Rickie Lee outtake.

She finds this kind of borrowing "gratifying, but sometimes it can be bewildering." The obligatory website (http://www.ghostyhead.com), to premiere with the album, will contain more than standard promotional fodder. Jones' poems, stories and miscellaneous faxes to friends will be posted, and the site will be the only place listeners can access lyrics, which aren't printed in the CD booklet.

Jones, 42, has always disliked printed lyrics and would prefer to omit them entirely, forcing people to listen. This will certainly frustrate some fans, as her diction isn't always clear.

Jones' own writing, however, is intended just to prime the pump. The idea is to create a literary magazine, an on-line sponsor of poetry, prose and, perhaps, multimedia manifestations of modern creativity.

She's wary of the online process, saying "advertising has quickly polluted the water. I go into chat rooms and people are illiterate or insulting or both. People have this marvelous opportunity to open amazing dialogues, and all they have to say is "what do you look like?'"

That's a question she prefers to dodge. The skeletal drawing on the *Ghostyhead* cover continues the Jones tendency to obscure her image. Though her first album boasted a clear head shot, attention was drawn to her beret and cigarette, eclipsing any sense of her true appearance. Seeing her in concert or on the street doesn't really clear things up: she looks like all and none of her pictures, as if you need to see her in motion to get the whole story.

"I prefer people do not know what I look like unless they are really involved in my music," she says. "Now, if someone knows me, they are close to me, at least they have experienced their lives with the songs I have written, and so I am not threatened by their attention or advances."

Still, she maintains a certain protective wall.

"When you least expect it, someone will say something really cruel... and you'll have been open and unprepared. And the cruel words will devastate you. Then you have to go on, pick your kid up from school, talk to the people who work with you, buy milk, you know, and you're wiped out.

"So I keep both the flattering stuff and the criticism out of my realm of thought. But if you need to tell me where you were when you heard some song, I will stop and listen."

USA TODAY, June 5, 1997

Keeping Up With Rickie Lee Jones

Interviewed by email, from Bainbridge Island, WA

Since her 1979 emergence, Rickie Lee Jones has always whipped myriad influences into her own musical blender. Now she's turning the tables. Her next album (tentatively titled *It's Like This*, due in September on Artemis Records) is all covers, paying tribute to Marvin Gaye ("Trouble Man"), Steely Dan ("Show Biz Kids"), Traffic ("The Low Spark of High Heeled Boys"), the Beatles ("For No One") and Broadway ("One Hand, One Heart" from *West Side Story* and "On the Street Where You Live" from *My Fair Lady*), among others. This is a far cry from her last effort, 1997 wildly experimental *Ghostyhead*, which was bounced between two record labels and is now out of print. Jones, who now lives in Tacoma, Wash., is greasing the skids with an appearance at the opening of the Experience Music Project in Seattle, the $240 million rock & roll museum named in honor of Jimi Hendrix's famed band.

What did Jimi Hendrix mean to you?

I have the sense of Jimi as not being like the rest of us, as being super-energized, moving differently, fitting in space just a little suspect. I saw him once, and he fit in the air. Like when you're on acid. Except I wasn't on acid. And he moved different. We were truly blessed to have Jimi Hendrix here, I think. I remember his singing was funny. He was not so smooth, so perfect, but something came through him that was profound. *Electric Ladyland* is the greatest record ever made.

Ghostyhead was your most experimental album; this new one is your most traditional. How did you get from one place to the other?

I think it's a question of picking me up and putting me back together after every album experience, and I always come out a little different. One thing seems to send me in the direction of another.

How did you pick these songs?

There was no apparent sense to this list as far as I can tell. I think the main thing was: Do I sing these well? Do I love to sing these songs? I suppose that is true of every one. I feel very joyful singing.

How did you put your own stamp on these songs?

Well, it's my record, so it's no great feat to put my stamp on each one. It was hard to wrestle "Low Spark" out of Steve Winwood's house, the musical house, in which it has hidden for so many years. I got to that bridge and had to work hard not to sing it like him. Even if I had sung it like him, you know, it's a different recording, a different time, it means a different thing.

When you began, it was thought that a bad original song was worth more than a good cover. When did this change?

I have always seen myself as a singer first; singing comes much easier than writing, and songs other people have written are very much a part of who I am. So I have no problem with the concept in my workplace — I never did — though I did realize that it was confusing. People like to see you as simply a singer-songwriter or a singer. I think that came out of that Bob Dylan thing. Are you a spokesman or are you just a dime singer? Are you the New Generation, or are you the old? And I think that resonated for a long time. But I can do a Donovan song, my song, Marvin Gaye, the Beatles, some obscure pop hit and end with "Coolsville," and somehow I can make that work, because, goddamn, I mean it. In my head, in my world, they all are one language, and they speak to me with joy and sorrow and hope, and these are the things that matter.

What happened with Ghostyhead?

[Original label] Reprise just wasn't interested in artist development, which I guess is the task they conjured when they thought about how to bring *Ghostyhead* out. They could not be bothered — if people thought they weren't gonna like it, why try to change their minds? So then it went to Mercury, where it was driven back like an angry dragon into the caves of paperwork and mean-spirited legal mindedness and kept for ransom in order for me to get out of my contract. Notice though, they did not put it out. It was the only record I have ever made that was unavailable — and it was my most recent. That was hard. So they kept it and did not release it as if to punish me for having been at that label when it was taken over by the organization that is taking over the world. They won't give it back. On the public level, I just don't know. It was not anti-music, it was quite musical, and every time I hear it I shake my head in appreciation.

What's next for you?

What's next is a lot of sleeping since my daughter just finished school and we don't have to get up at seven.

ROLLING STONE ONLINE, JUNE 25, 2000

Final Performance by Otis Spann Gets Belated Release

Thirty years after his death, blues legend Otis Spann's legacy is enhanced by a recently unearthed tape of his final performance. Titled *Otis Spann's Last Call (Live at the Boston Tea Party)*, the nine-song set was recorded just nine days before Spann died of liver cancer in April 1970.

Coming from the same Mississippi blues tradition as Muddy Waters (who may or may not have been his half-brother) Spann was a self-taught piano prodigy who worked as a member of the Chess Records house band before beginning a solo career in the 1960s. He died at forty, at what was called the height of his career.

The new disc is a labor of love for Peter Malick, a veteran eastern seaboard blues guitarist who played with Spann on those final nights. By that time, the then-eighteen-year-old Malick had played with Spann for more than a year, recording an album and becoming part of Spann's extended family.

"When I first played with Otis we had this instant rapport," Malick said. "We didn't have a lot to say each other verbally but had an instant musical connection. He wanted me to come play with him right away but I told him no, I had to finish high school first. But as soon as I graduated I went out to Chicago."

Malick, who never attended college, subsequently played with Boston's James Montgomery Band and as a solo artist before battling drug addiction in the Eighties. Throughout this time he believed the tape of Spann's final show was lost to the ages.

Two years ago Malick got a call from a friend in L.A. who "thought he had an Otis Spann tape of mine." Not only did it turn out to be the lost gig, but it was in excellent condition. So he edited the tape down from its two hours, then signed a contract with Spann's survivors to release the album later this month.

The performance is not at all typical for Spann. In the first place, he was unable to sing due to side effects from the cancer. (Vocals were handled by Luther Georgia Boy "Snake" Johnson and Lucille Spann, who told the crowd her husband could not sing because of laryngitis). The edited performance features only two originals, a couple of Muddy Waters tunes and a left-field selection, a subtle reworking of Lenny Welch's 1963 weeper, "Since I Fell For You."

That Malick's playing is more subdued than his current aggressive style isn't only because he was a shy kid. "We all knew what was happening, that it would be his last show," he recalls. "So I tried to rein myself in and give him more of a chance to play. Lucille was doing the same thing. She tended to oversing some-times but she restrained herself here. So this may be her best performance."

Lucille Spann died in 1993.

At a gravestone dedication last June in Chicago, Malick met a number of people who had been touched by Spann. Some will be providing unpublished photos which will either appear on the CD or the record company's web site, www.mrcatmusic.com. He hopes the real beneficiaries will be Spann's descen-dants, who "are struggling to make ends meet.

"They have received very little for Spann's body of work," Malick said. "I'm hoping that this CD will make some difference in their lives."

ROLLING STONE ONLINE, June 28, 2000

Experience Music Project Opens in Seattle

It wasn't your typical ribbon-cutting. Gazillionaire Paul Allen smashed a Stratocaster made of unflavored green rock candy, designed especially for the occasion by glass artist Dale Chihuly, into thousands of fragments. A wall of balloons popped at once. And the Experience Music Project was officially open.

This began a wide-ranging three-day rollout for the new museum. Friday's opening at the Seattle Center followed a party where Allen jammed with Herbie Hancock, Robbie Robertson and Dave Stewart. Three days of concerts opening today, including Metallica, Alanis Morissette, Taj Mahal, James Brown, Beck and the Kingsmen, just to name a few.

EMP reps bristle when someone calls it by its colloquial name, "the Hendrix Museum." It did have its beginning as a place for Microsoft cofounder Paul Allen to put his Hendrix stuff, but it has grown considerably — first into a commemo-ration of Pacific Northwest musicians, then into a celebration of popular music itself. Along the way, it evolved into a full-featured landscape-altering A-ticket 160,000-square-foot Rorschach inkblot of a building that is as permanently a part of the Seattle landscape as the neighboring Space Needle.

The building — designed by Frank Gehry — evokes different images for different people. From the air there is a smashed guitar, while the part that loomed over the opening ceremony looked like the back of Darth Vader's head. While some locals complain about the dissonance, it actually fits nicely in a neighborhood that contains the Space Needle and several out-to-lunch abstract sculptures. In fact, its shape is the biggest tribute to Hendrix himself and his in-your-face demeanor.

While the new facility will be compared with Cleveland's Rock 'n' Roll Hall of Fame, EMP-ers are quick to find differences. "The two follow different paths to the same destination," said EMP deputy director of public programming Robert Santelli. "The Rock Hall seeks to explain and pay tribute to icons, while this is more interactive and technology-driven. This is a more personal journey, where you have complete control." Adds senior curator Peter Blecha, "We love the Rock Hall but they are locked into telling the story of the greatest over-achievers. We want to tell the story of the underdogs." For that reason, he adds, there will be no EMP Beatles exhibit, and the 20 percent rotation of inventory will include something new.

So EMP isn't for rock snobs who already have their own ideas as to what is "important." Rather this is a democratization of the experience — that word again — of how the music feels and how you can participate.

Consider OnStage. Here you walk through a solid door and land onstage, where you grab a guitar, keyboard, drums or microphone and pantomime to a rowdy version of "Wild Thing." A TelePrompTer keeps you on the lyrical mark; otherwise you can indulge your rock-star fantasies (although there many be some problems with the management should you smash the guitar, or set it afire). You get a free set of souvenir tickets, while a commemorative photo costs $10.

How times have changed. In Hendrix's day, lip-synching was an affront to the music. Now it's an activity for the whole family.

Or Artist's Journey. On this ride, the only real motion comes from the seat assembly moving back and forth, the real action appears on a 28' x 70' wrap-around screen. Here the journey is a search for "funk," and the plot is hard to ex-plain, concerning a couple of aspiring musicians and an enhanced James Brown. But it's a blast, and resembles the best carnival rides in that you want to do it again as soon as it's over. Said Harry Lennix, an actor who appears in the film, "I can't tell you what 'funk' is, but I know it when I feel it." Of the museum, he adds, "The music is bigger than any shrine. This is just an introduction to the experience."

That word, again.

Parts look like a traditional museum, with artifacts and explanations. Early guitars from Bob Dylan and clothes worn by Janis Joplin and Heart. Clapton's "Brownie." Gold records and autographs. And, of course, the Hendrix collec-tion. Allen's original touchstones (the white Woodstock guitar and the felt hat) are enhanced by posters, films, albums and a digitization of a handwritten lyrics notebook. This part of the museum is necessarily non-interactive, although that doesn't decrease the desire to reach out and touch.

Visitors can go to the gift shop to complete the experience. Aside from the expected book/CD/souvenir offerings, you can buy a Squier Stratocaster for $149 — not all that more than in a regular discount music store and, as Blecha points out, the exact price of the original 1954 model.

For his part, Blecha doesn't really care whether people regard EMP as the Hendrix Museum "as long as it gets people to come and will piss the old fogies off that we're here. What's timeless about Jimi — aside from his music — was his excitement and his rebelliousness. He really couldn't be tamed. That really counts in a era where everything is so controlled."

ROLLING STONE ONLINE, June 24, 2000

Spirit of Hendrix Rises at Experience Music Project Celebration

Bo Diddley, Taj Mahal highlight legends lineup at weekend festival

Shortly before Bo Diddley began his set at the Experience Music Project celebration, Jimi Hendrix Experience bassist Noel Redding approached him with greetings from a mutual friend — and a request to sit in. Diddley agreed, and a throbbing "Mona" was the result. While he's lost the hair and now seems to be a shy natty type, Redding held his own against Diddley's blues wail. And those attending were treated to a brand new memorable experience.

The performers during these three days were extremely varied, ranging from modern rappers to geezer rockers. Redding, however, was the only full-time Hendrix band member to make an appearance. It was unannounced and extremely low-key. Following the brief onstage appearance he was to spend the evening jamming with Paul Allen and Dan Aykroyd in a Seattle club, and planned to be back in his home in Ireland "by tea time on Monday." While he says he has received no royalties for his recordings with Hendrix, he made the trip to honor his former bandmate. "I still miss him terribly," Redding said.

"This is all a great tribute. I find the gallery devoted to him to be very sad, and very beautiful."

There were several subtle and direct tributes to Hendrix throughout the weekend. Some were heartfelt, like Bo Diddley band member Jon Paris' gentle "Third Stone from the Sun" riffs during a curtain call. Others were tacky, like Paul Revere and the Raiders guitarist Doug Heath's Las Vegas-style behind-the-neck moves. But it became abundantly clear that only two people were essential to this gathering: Jimi Hendrix and Paul Allen. While Allen's reticence is well-known, shyness was also one of Hendrix's most endearing qualities. "He wasn't a madman, he was a very gentle guy," said Redding of Hendrix. Added Mike Finnegan, who played on *Electric Ladyland* and was here as part of Taj Mahal's band, "I think he would have been embarrassed by all of this."

At the same time as Metallica's set, Rickie Lee Jones was across the center performing in the theater usually occupied by the Seattle repertory company. Beginning with two songs from her upcoming covers album followed by another two from her experimental *Ghostyhead*, she peppered the evening with an assortment of some of her best (if not always best-known) songs. Backed occasionally by Joe Jackson, she stretched out every note, breaking out into a broad smile at the end of a song. Throughout, she was comfortable and cocky, seeming to truly enjoy herself on stage. In the recent past she's distanced herself from her older material, but this has changed. While she didn't quite get to "Chuck E.'s in Love," she played a career-spanning set with ebullience and affection.

Sister Nancy was at home with newborn twins, so Ann Wilson — the breath and soul of Heart — assembled a powerful band that played to her strengths even if they didn't play exactly what the crowd wanted to hear. With just four Heart songs, she filled out the set with some tunes from her side band, the Lovemongers, as well as covers of Joni Mitchell, Bacharach/Costello, Tina Turner and Paul McCartney. Set closer "State of Independence" was a magnificent full-length reading of a textured gem. The emotional, powerful song crashed to a sudden end, as much of the audience still bleated futile screams for "Barracuda."

A lot of Bo Diddley's set sounded the same — and that wasn't at all bad news. The thunka-thunka beat could be felt for miles, a spooky blend of blues and rock. But at the end he shifted gears and began a preachy-but-infectious rap that finished with the lines "Listen to Bo Diddley, stay in school and get your Ph.D." Just before Diddley was singing his rap, headliner Taj Mahal was in the workshop room in the museum underscoring the same message, singing the "Made Up on the Spot Stay in School Blues." While this presentation in front of a hundred or so folks resembled his popular acoustic sets in '70s arenas, when he finally hit the stage things were quite different. Fronting an eager six-piece band (bass, drums, guitar, keys and two horns), the subtle blues man transformed into a true soul king. Driven by Larry Fulcher's bone-crushing bass and Finnegan's buoyant piano, he reclaimed songs from Aretha, Otis and a bevy of lesser-knowns, turning them into his own.

Less impressive by far was the performance by Paul Revere and the Raiders. If the intention of EMP is to make rock 'n' roll a family attraction, these guys made it a bad ride. With only Revere remaining from the original band, everything that was once cool about the group has now become a sad parody. There were decent renditions of their best songs — "Hungry," "Good Thing," "Him or Me, What's it Gonna Be?" — but the time in between was punctuated by flat wisecracks and bad dancing. Revere would fiddle with the various props, blowing an American flag with a portable hair dryer. Appropriately enough, he positioned his organ behind a replica of the front of a Ford Edsel. Perhaps they should take up permanent residency in the museum, as an example of how a fresh sound can go sour.

ROLLING STONE ONLINE, June 26, 2000

Noel Redding Boxes His Own Experience

Interviewed in person, Seattle, WA

Ask Noel Redding what will be on the "new box set," and he won't offer any insight about the upcoming release that features dozens of unissued tracks of him playing with Jimi Hendrix. Rather, he will discuss *Thank You Very Much, Gud Luk, and Goodnight*, a just-completed anthology of his solo work from 1962 to the present.

Redding, fifty-four, played bass in the Experience from its formation in 1966 until he left in 1969. He was often frustrated by this partnership because he was a guitarist by trade and, according to some reports, was hired for the Experience as much for his look (a massive white-person's afro topped off by granny glasses) as his playing.

Redding now lives in County Cork, Ireland, in a house purchased from his Experience earnings. However, he said he has received no further payment for his time with the band. "I was forced to sign away my royalties in 1974," he says. "I even had to sell the bass I used during that time, for $16,000."

That particular bass was subsequently purchased by Paul Allen, and is now part of the Experience Music Project's Hendrix exhibit. "I never thought I'd see it again," Redding says, but he did during the museum's opening weekend. "I just stared at it for a long time. I was very moved."

While he admits that his relationship with the Hendrix estate is "pretty strange," he expects that he will receive some royalties from the upcoming Hendrix release. "I have it on paper that I will be paid," he says, although he's not sure how much.

Redding wrote two songs for the Experience, "She's So Fine" and "Little Miss Strange." These are included on his anthology, along with some tracks from two pre-Experience bands and Fat Mattress (Redding's band he led concurrent to his stint in the Experience). Additionally, there are tracks with Spirit guitarist Randy California and two members of the Spin Doctors.

Redding calls his 1996 jams with Spin Doctors' guitarist Anthony Krizan and drummer Frankie LaRocker "better than the Experience." Several tracks from that session are included here, as well as covers of songs by the Beatles, Bob Dylan and Blues Image.

There is nothing from the Experience aside from Redding's two solo tracks, although some existing tapes would be appropriate. According to Redding, Hendrix recorded a few of Redding's compositions with the Band of Gypsies, including one called "Dance." Redding says that Hendrix "basically lifted the song" but did so without malice. "I'm sure that he didn't remember it was mine." In any case, ownership of the song or its royalties are moot, as it remains un-issued.

A more interesting collaboration took place in 1986 when Redding and Experience drummer Mitch Mitchell (with whom Redding has since fallen out) traveled to former manager Chas Chandler's Newcastle home and recorded new tracks to at least four unreleased Hendrix demos. (In this they were pioneers, as this well preceded the Nineties trend of overdubbing incomplete tapes by famous dead people.) Redding could recall none of the titles of these songs aside from "Sunshine of Your Love." "There was a party thing, like a sing-along thing at a wedding, and another tune that had like a sitar in it," he says.

John McDermott, who assembled the upcoming Hendrix box set, confirmed the existence of these tracks but would not comment on their quality. Redding says that several British and American labels have shown interest in releasing his album, but there have been no solid commitments. Still, he's optimistic that it will see the light of day before the end of the year.

"With all the commotion about [the thirtieth anniversary of Hendrix's death] someone with any intelligence will put it out. It's all finished anyway."

ROLLING STONE ONLINE, July 2000

Hendrix Family Feud Continues

Leon Hendrix, Seattle 2002

The rights to Jimi Hendrix's music were returned to his family seven years ago, prompting fans to believe that the plundering of his recorded legacy would end and legendary unreleased tapes would finally see the light of day. Today, however, it is clear that the Hendrix family is not one that plays together.

Following the death of Al Hendrix (Jimi's father) in April, the survivors are playing out a battle scenario with million-dollar stakes. Brother Leon Hendrix, 54, sued the estate in August, claiming that he was denied his rightful inheritance and seeking to wrest control of the estate from Janie Hendrix, 41, who is president of Experience Hendrix, the company that owns and controls Jimi Hendrix's music and image.

Janie Hendrix, however, says she is only carrying out Al Hendrix's wishes. "It's too bad they couldn't have settled their differences," she told *Rolling Stone*. "Leon and Dad were very different people and, as Dad would say, they never saw eye to eye. I was surprised at Dad's will (where he only left Leon one gold record), but it was his money and he decided where it should go."

In preparation to strike a better royalty deal of his own, Al requested that Leon sign over his rights to the music in 1992, and Leon complied. However, according to Leon's attorneys, the document granting those rights — for which Leon was paid $1 million — was not a relinquishment of all of his rights.

On October 9, Leon slapped Janie with an additional defamation suit for her alleged claim that Leon and Jimi were only half-brothers. As refutation, Leon pulls out a copy of his birth certificate listing Al as his father. "He was my dad," Leon says. "And he never said or thought any different until Janie put that into his head." Experience Hendrix's The Jimi Hendrix Experience box set, released in 2000, fanned the flames, as the liner notes refer to Leon as Jimi's "troubled half-brother."

Even if the degree of Leon's relationship to Jimi can be argued, Janie's is clear: She is an adopted stepsister with no blood relationship to any member of the Hendrix family. "Janie is family in the legal sense," says attorney David Huber, who represents Leon. "But actual blood relatives deserve a share of this money."

Leon's latest suit also accuses Janie of defrauding the public by her claims that Experience Hendrix was a "family company" intent on winning rights back for musicians. "Leon and other family members were not allowed to participate in the company's function or operation, or to receive the benefits of those operations," the suit states.

Should the court rule in Leon's favor, he would be granted control over Jimi Hendrix's archival tapes and videos. Aside from allocating funds to the "real Hendrix" bloodline, he claims he would give back to the community and pay the musicians their due.

Experience Hendrix catalog manager John McDermott denies the latter claim: "We've never sent anything out C.O.D. Mr. Redding has received each release issued by Experience Hendrix at no charge to him."

Since 1997, Experience Hendrix has released a steady stream of CDs. Most are reissues or expanded versions of what was once available, aside from the four-disc *The Jimi Hendrix Experience*, which featured rare material. However, spurned on by talk of hundreds of lost tapes, many fans have expected more.

"[Janie has] promised a lot of things that haven't materialized," said Steven Roby, a former Experience Hendrix employee and author of *Black Gold: The Lost Archives of Jimi Hendrix*. "But the fans aren't too happy with her. Aside from putting out an occasional disc for collectors, we get things like golf balls, furniture, boxer shorts. It's pretty embarrassing." Adds filmmaker David Kramer, who is preparing a Beatles Anthology-style Jimi Hendrix documentary, "If Leon were in charge, he wouldn't put Jimi on a cushion so you could sit on his face."

It was the box set's release that fanned the flames of Leon's suit, as the liner notes refer to him as Jimi's "troubled half-brother. Should the court rule in Leon's favor, he would be granted control over the hundreds of hours of archival tape and videos. Aside from allocating funds to the "real Hendrix" bloodline, he claims he would give back to the community and pay the musicians their due (although it is unlikely Redding would end up with $20 or $30 million that he claims he is owed under the original contract).

Craig Dieffenbach, a 41-year-old Seattle real estate developer and Leon Hendrix's business manager, is footing the legal bills. Dieffenbach recently secured rights to the "PPX" tapes, sixty-six titles recorded between 1965 and 1967, featuring Curtis Knight on vocals, and Hendrix on guitar and vocals. "This is an impressive body of work that few people know about," Dieffenbach says. "The songs represent Hendrix's roots, and you can hear elements of the songs that made him famous."

There is also the part of the legacy that has nothing to do with music or money. Jimi's image — that of a free spirit who symbolized the drug use and casual sex of the times — has been actively suppressed and denied by Janie.

"The people who are running Experience Hendrix have no vision," Leon said. "They are just trying to whitewash history." Adds Kathy Etchingham, a former girlfriend of Jimi's who has allied herself with Redding and Leon, "Janie is a devout Christian, and is offended by Jimi's lifestyle. So she doesn't like Leon's lifestyle, and won't allow Hendrix music to be used in any context that suggests sex or drugs . . . Janie doesn't want people to see the truth about Jimi, and when someone says something about him that she doesn't like, she threatens them with legal action."

Janie Hendrix declined to comment for this story. This summer, an Experience Hendrix press release characterized Leon's complaint as part of "the sad story of a man who has made many bad choices in his life [and who] continues to lay the blame at the feet of others."

ROLLING STONE ONLINE October 25, 2002

Hendrix Celebrated in Seattle

Jimi Hendrix, had he not died in 1970 at age twenty-seven, would have celebrated his 60th birthday tomorrow. At Seattle's Experience Music Project Sunday night, family, friends, former mates in the Band of Gypsies and EMP founder Paul Allen got a jump on the occasion, coming together for a tribute to "the greatest guitarist that ever lived."

"Jimi will always be twenty-seven," said Gypsies bassist Billy Cox from the stage, capturing the prevailing mood in the colorful Sky Church. "But we are getting old."

Legendary bluesman Buddy Guy, whose guitar stylings Hendrix attempted to emulate when he was starting out, showed up to headline the event and honor a fellow guitar innovator. Former Earth, Wind and Fire guitarist Sheldon Reynolds (who is married to Janie Hendrix, Jimi's stepsister and president of Experience Hendrix, which controls his image and music) led a large ensemble through Hendrix classics like "Hey Joe," "Angel" and "If Six Was 9." The Band of Gypsies then ripped through "Freedom," "Power of Soul" and "Them Changes," and became truly inspired when joined by guitar virtuoso Eric Gales for "Foxy Lady." The various lineups then united for "Little Wing" and "Voodoo Child."

There were plenty of similarities to an actual Hendrix concert: a massive light show; the emcee imploring crowd members to introduce themselves to the person next to them; and an audience member losing consciousness. And, during the show, guitar manufacturer Fender presented Janie Hendrix with an exact copy of the white Stratocaster that Hendrix played at Woodstock in 1969 (the original is part of EMP's permanent collection).

While the focus was clearly on the music Jimi Hendrix did create, some couldn't help but speculate about what he would be doing today. "He would have expanded himself," Gypsies drummer Buddy Miles said. "He was like Beethoven. He could write for three pieces or for nine or ten . . . Whatever he'd be doing, it would be funky and greasy."

ROLLING STONE ONLINE, November 26, 2002

Control of Estate Remains With Guitarist's Stepsister

Leon Hendrix has abandoned his defamation suit against stepsister Janie Hendrix for her claim that Leon and late rocker Jimi Hendrix were only half-brothers. However, Leon will continue his fight to wrest control of Jimi's estate from Janie, who is no blood relation to Jimi but is the president of the estate's managing company Experience Hendrix.

Leon maintains that he is indeed the son of Jimi's father, Al Hendrix, but his unwillingness to take a DNA test has prompted Janie's camp to question whether Leon is sure that the test will come out in his favor.

"It's difficult to understand why he wouldn't be willing to provide a simple cheek swab of his DNA for genetic testing," says Janie's attorney, John Wilson. "That would prove conclusively whether or not he is Al's biological son. If it is established that Leon is not Al's biological son, that substantially undercuts Leon's claims to a portion of [Jimi's] estate."

Leon says he dropped the defamation suit because the costs would exceed any potential financial reward. He says that he still may take a DNA test but chooses not to do so now because "it clouds the issue. Janie is using all of this talk about DNA to distract from the real lawsuit."

The real lawsuit Leon refers to is his pursuit of total control of Jimi's estate. Leon claims that he was cheated out of his proper share of Al's inheritance and that Janie's various marketing strategies have damaged Jimi's legacy.

Janie contends that the family squabbling is doing the most harm. "It takes our focus away from the work we are doing here at Experience Hendrix," she says, "honoring and preserving Jimi's legacy."

ROLLING STONE ONLINE, March 20, 2003

Cyndi Lauper's Still Unusual

Cyndi Lauper, Seattle August 2002
Interviewed in person, Seattle, WA

On the surface, Cyndi Lauper hasn't changed that much since 1983, when her debut album catapulted her to fame next to other then-newbies Madonna and Prince: She still has a larger-than-life New York personality, a skewed fashion sense and a powerful operatic voice. Her old songs are still fresh, mostly because she has not lost enthusiasm for them. She is clearly having fun with her life and her music. Behind the gloss, however, the older (49) and wiser Lauper is poised to stay relevant, even if the general public views her as an amusing relic.

Heading this effort is *Shine*, a lively, independently produced EP that contains a microcosm of past Lauperisms. There is the ovaries-out title track — used as a set opener — that allows her to sing at the top of her lungs, tear around the stage and affirm life. The buoyant and punky "It's Hard to Be Me" fits neatly in a 1980s slipper, while the slinky "Madonna Whore" has a modern don't-fence-me-in theme. The ballad "Water's Edge" rounds out the set.

Currently Lauper is opening for Cher's "Farewell Tour" through December, playing most of *Shine* and a smattering of her best and best-known songs. *Shine* is available through retail and sold through her Web site (www.cyndilauper. com) is something less than what it once was. In a perfect world, it would have continued the creative arc of 1992's *Hat Full of Stars* and 1997's *Sisters of Avalon*. Both were skilled, experimental albums that pushed the limits of her talent, logical progressions from her chock-full-of-hits 1984 debut, *She's So Unusual*. But, according to Lauper, these later efforts were too, well, unusual, for her record company, Sony/Epic.

"I thought [*Sisters of Avalon*] was a great record, but my record company had issues," she says. "I was out there touring, pregnant, opening for Tina Turner. Tina was on Virgin at the time, and their people felt so sorry for me they helped with my promotion."

When the tour ended, Lauper asked to be released from her contract. Sony agreed, but only if she recorded a Christmas album. "I went along with that, because it was something I wanted to do anyway," she says. "And I did every-thing right. I opened the lighting of the tree at Rockefeller Center. I did *Rosie*, did *Letterman*, but people still couldn't get the records. They were promoting someone else that year. Maybe they didn't like the idea that I called it "Merry Christmas — Have a Nice Life!"

Lauper admits that some of her record company problems originate from her own lack of diplomacy. "Whenever I'm talking to someone important there's always a moment where the other people in the room choke on their food be-cause of something I said."

Released from Sony, she recorded the full-length *Shine*, which was set for release last year on Edel Records, but Edel went under before the album came out, and Lauper began looking for alternatives. Surprisingly, she'd play the new songs and audiences started singing along, prompting her to put something out for the fans.

"I didn't want to shoot my whole wad, but wanted to put something out and picked the ones that people were singing along with," she says. "Although I have no idea how they heard them in the first place."

While Lauper attempts to find the complete *Shine* a home, she admits it's somewhat outdated. Written and recorded before last September's terrorist attacks, the album is "very 2001, which is not where I am anymore." As a result, there is an entire second album in the can, but there are no concrete plans for its release.

But in the battle of Lauper versus the suits, the odds are good. "The gatekeepers will come and go," she says. "But I'll always be here. I know how to sing. I know how to write. When I was a little kid I could always win anybody over by singing. When I thought my house was haunted I figured that if I could sing a song and charm the ghosts they wouldn't kill me. And it must have worked . . . I'm still here."

ROLLING STONE ONLINE, August 2002

Heart Pump Out New Beats

Nancy Wilson, Ann Wilson, Seattle, WA May 2003
Interviewed in person

For the second year in a row, Ann and Nancy Wilson have taken the resuscitated Heart out on tour. While last year's jaunt yielded a career-spanning live album, the newly released *Alive in Seattle*, the current tour serves as a warm-up for the recording of their first new album in ten years. The sisters took some time to chat after a recent in-store appearance.

What's the new album like?

Nancy: It's still a little "ballad light." We need a couple of aching love songs, we already have the hard-rocking stuff. Right now the demos are like poetry, or hard rock Philosophy 101. It's all in our own words.

Ann: It has to be age-appropriate. How can a 55-year-old possibly find sincere interest into the same concerns as a 19-year-old? Unless you are talking down to them and trying to make a record that young people would buy. In those cases it's not real, it's strained.

Nancy: This will not be a strained album.

Will you use the touring band (that includes Guns N' Roses' Gilbey Clarke and Alice in Chains' Mike Inez) on the record?

Nancy: We'll be coming off the road rehearsed and we'll be ready to go. Either that, or we'll never want to see them again.

Do you have a label?

Ann: We're hoping that Sony will consider us, as they've helped us on the live album.

Why did it take so long to assert yourselves?

Ann: Before I was more inclined to say, "Let's just get this album out and go have some more fun." Nowadays we're stronger. I mean, we've seen the strings.

Nancy: Yes, we've been to the puppet show, and we've seen the strings.

Ann: So we're not going through that kind of shit anymore.

What was so painful?

Ann: Accepting other people's music. As a singer, if someone else's words are coming out of my mouth that takes half of my soul away from the song. So I was making a devil's bargain.

A lot of those songs did very well.

Ann: That's why we always sound so whiney when we talk about the '80s because we are totally biting the hand that feeds us. "Oh my God! We had to have all of those number ones!"

How has your working relationship evolved?

Ann: Now, Nancy has something going with her husband, doing scores and helping with the scripts. She has another artistic collaborator. So Cameron and I have to take turns.

Someone gave you a script today to take to your husband. Does that happen a lot?

Nancy: No, that was actually very flattering. Scripts are hard to write, so I respect anyone who has written one.

Will you pass this on?

Nancy: I'll look it over. If it doesn't suck I might show it to him. But he's pretty busy.

What did you get from John Entwistle (on the Beatles tribute tour "A Walk Down Abbey Road")?

Ann: He was one of the funniest old guys that I've ever worked with in my life. We did one gig where we flew from Boston to the big island of Hawaii for one night, and then flew back the next day. So they sat me next to Entwistle for both flights and the first thing he does is turn to me and say "Do you snore?" and I said "No, do you?" So he says "I've always been asleep so I never could tell." The whole time. over and back, all he'd do is read these naval adventure novels and then he just went to sleep.

Nancy: Did he snore?

Ann: No.

Nancy: So you really lucked out.

ALTERNATE VERSION OF ROLLING STONE ONLINE PIECE, MAY 2003

5

2006-2012

*A*t some point entertainment writing became less entertaining. I stopped trying to discover new bands because it was clear I liked the old ones better. The good news was that many of these artists continued to tour and get up close to the audience, while the bad news was the fact they really didn't have much more to say.

Publishing also changed. All my freelance clients disappeared and it became too difficult to sell original pieces. I still thought that a perspective of the past was worth explaining, especially when those times were so potent and become more so with all the looking back.

In the 1960s, no one in my circle listed to anything from long ago (which meant 20 years before) although there was an entity known as the Catskills where all the bygone performers went to rehash a no longer relevant time, and then die off. Or that was the impression. What was happening now was most important, and anything old was best left behind.

Today, audiences still mine the 1960s for lost sounds and sights. We are celebrating the 50th anniversaries of certain performers' careers; while this seems tiresome to many of us there are still enough people interested to make it worthwhile. Money enters into it, people like Bob Dylan, The Beach Boys and The Rolling Stones will do it big or not at all. For *others, seeing John Sebastian, Taj Mahal or Tom Rush is the real reward, and a lot easier to accomplish.*

This was the period where I hooked up with Sonicboomers and Rock's Back Pages, both organized efforts to keep the music and the message alive. Many pieces from these sources are displayed in previous sections but they fit here chronologically. The inability to sell pieces to major outlets was frustrating, because I knew these were good stories worth telling and I could tell them well, but even that didn't matter so much anymore. I began participating in the modern practice known as blogging. This wasn't quite the same as writing for Rolling Stone, *but provided enough of a readership to make the effort worthwhile.*

This was also the time when a lot of performers began dying off of natural causes. In some ways this is more of a shock than death by misadventure. When a performer overdoses or runs his car into a wall it's from a distance. You don't do a lot of drugs or drive like an idiot, so it can't happen to you. Or you do partake in these activities and can use the unfortunate event as a wake up call.

Davy Jones and Levon Helm are the most recent examples of this. The mass grief following Jones' death was unexpected, since he was hardly in the public eye and his accomplishments were so long ago. Additionally, rock snobs like myself acknowledged his contributions but hardly put him in the top tier. But that didn't matter here. Jones was a big part of the musical past, so his death shuts the door on those times.

Old age doesn't give you the opportunity for such distance. It happens to all of us sooner or later. Davy Jones was a teen idol, which meant that most of his fans were a bit younger than he. His death at what was once seen as an old age means that it comes sooner now, for us.

And if you are alive long enough cancer will get you, as Helm and many others are proving as true.

This loops around to the reason for this volume. I've been writing for years, but was never motivated to pull it all together since I wasn't sure that I had done anything really special and there were hundreds of others better suited to tell the tale. I changed my mind, realizing that many of those formerly wise souls had died off, or lost their memories. At least I had written it all down and published it somewhere.

These are all chronological, aside from the Tom Rush piece that was written and published in 2009. I put it at the end because it corresponds with the first story in the book and in a representation of the whole "what comes around" theme that keeps recurring.

Wheelchair Legends: How Some Rockers Grow Old Gracefully and Others Do Not

Micky Dolenz, Puyallup WA September 2006

PUYALLUP, WASHINGTON — Are there gatherings like this anywhere outside of the modern American West? A million people come to a converted dusty field over a period of two weeks, to jump on wild rides, stuff themselves with trans-fats and get up close and personal with various combinations of livestock. They walk away with cheap souvenirs, from promotional backpacks that smell like diesel to magnets that look like metal testicles and whirr like crickets as you throw them in the air.

Additionally, audiences can get up close to the formerly famous, those who once required a long wait and big bucks in order to be part of their scene. Every evening there is a fairground musical attraction, someone either on their way up or down. Carrie Underwood, the current American Idol, is the biggest name, while the Beach Boys (or more precisely, the Beach Boy) will play here next week. Tonight we have come to see the Rock N' Roll Legends, remnants of four 1960s bands (Herman's Hermits, The Monkees, The Turtles and the Grass Roots).

We get the real Peter Noone, not the embarrassing mess of a revival band that features the original drummer and three substitutes. And you can't beat the price or the wait. Anyone who pays regular fair admission can witness competent versions of songs they once loved, sung with a moderate amount of authenticity by the original voices. For $15 more they can get a seat up close.

"It's great to be out here in the open air," said Turtles lead singer Howard Kaylan, with a dig at the alternate venue for this type of show. "It sure beats singing at one of those Indian casinos."

I Was So Much Older Then

"Authenticity" is the most important word tonight, along with "ambivalence." In their heyday, these bands lived or died by the authenticity sword. They all strived to be different and original. Derivativeness was the kiss of death. Remember the outcry when we heard that the Monkees didn't play their own instruments. At the time, the Turtles, Beach Boys and even the Beatles didn't exactly raise their hands and admit they were guilty of the same crime.

Today, absolute authenticity is not an option. Almost every 1960s band has at least one dead member. You then eliminate those who hate each other's guts, or those who once played their own instruments but can't anymore.

On this tour we have the original voices, with pretty much the same guitar-bass-keyboard-drums accompaniment. Since there are no absolute rules — or they change with each listener — these performers can get away with anything that sounds good. Some audience members won't even require that much.

Ambivalence comes from the fact that we don't really care if these guys are the originals or not. These songs evoked a feeling; a place and time. And those in the audience who weren't there the first time aren't likely to complain — or even notice — how it doesn't match the originals.

The best example of this authenticity slide is, again, the Beach Boys. Mike Love is the only original member, and still sings lead on many recognizable hits. But ringers perform the Wilson brothers' parts well enough. Noone, who is himself in constant argument with a former band member who co-opts the Hermits' name, says the Beach Boys have never sounded better live.

So what happens when Love, 65, no longer wants to tour? Four original members are already missing, with no apparent protest aside from critics and snobs. Soon enough, Love will be replaced by someone who sings in his general register and the band will continue. This is not without precedence; jazz bands often tour for decades under the names of their dead founders.

Grass Rudeness

I spent much of the mid-1960s listening to the Monkees and Herman's Hermits. I bought their albums, bestowing them with the same intensity and dedication as my just-olders were devoting to The Who and the Kinks. I thought the Monkees' *Headquarters* was actually superior to its two predecessors. And while I still have never had any opportunity to view a movie called *Hold On* I can attest that the Hermits' soundtrack was definitely keen.

But I would feel a lot better today had I followed the trajectory of The Grass Roots. At the time I thought they were pretty lame, compared to what else was going on. Their singles were good enough, but not so much that I would ever buy one. I was, after all, twelve. There was a lot of really great music coming out every week, and it was another two years before I could afford *Buffalo Springfield Again*.

Upon hearing of this traveling show with Noone, Micky Dolenz, Turtle principals Mark Volman and Kaylan and Grass Root Rob Grill, I set out to tell the story to those who may still care. But my interview request was a bit too honest, asking to talk to all but adding, "I can do without Grill, given a choice." Tactless and rude perhaps, but I felt talking with him would waste everyone's time. After all, both Rob and I are over 50, where the time supply isn't infinite.

The note is distributed to all the artists. Noone and Dolenz respond immediately, with the Turtles' Mark Volman coming in a few hours later. Then a phone message:

"Hello, I represent Rob Grill and we got a letter here, and it says 'I can do without talking to Rob Grill, given the choice.' So we'll just take that choice out of your hands. I want to thank you for your interest, or lack thereof. You can call this number if you want to talk to me, or if you want to talk to Mr. Grill. Who is me."

He is still pissed when I return the call. I apologize, but he is unmoved. I had no class, he said. He hangs up. I dial again. He will not relent. He says no one will let me into the show. No one will talk to me. And I shouldn't bother him again.

Noone and Volman stay true to their word, each chatting on the phone for more than an hour. But Dolenz backs out. His representative writes, saying "his schedule does not allow." When I push, he admits "that whole mess with Rob Grill kind of screwed it up."

When *Sgt. Pepper* emerged in June 1967 I tucked away the newly released *Headquarters* pretty much forever. These past few weeks would have been a lot more stress-free if I had then sacrificed The Grass Roots' *Let's Live for Today.*

You Really Like Me

The musicians' view of themselves is alternately profound and humorous.

"These four acts are some of the strongest visual acts you will see," Volman said. "They are survivors. They have been able to, year after year, make a good living. They have put their children through college. They have owned homes. They are strong businessmen. They are real professionals."

"You can always tell the guys who were in the original band," Noone said. "Because they can't read the setlist."

Noone's setlist has some heft. He had a long string of hits with the Hermits, some stand the test of time and some don't. Somewhere along the line he fell out of the spotlight, losing the general public focus while hanging on to a core of fans that insist he far surpasses any of his contemporaries. This, like his continuous performance of old hits is not unique — although his enthusiasm is.

While we may not think of Noone in the same breath as John, Paul, Mick or Pete, he once breathed the same air. And they all keep in touch.

"It's a survival thing," he said. "Like an old regiment, or a platoon. But we aren't all like Fabian, where we look at each other and say 'you look marvelous.' You can't look at Keith Richards and say that he looks great. But it's great that we are still here."

Most Hermits-era bands borrowed blues idioms and fed it back to the Americans whose countrymen invented it in the first place. But there was nothing bluesy about the Hermits. Their music was evenly divided between American "oldies," English music hall tunes (or imitations thereof), and new songs by composers like Graham Gouldman and Goffin-King.

"We wanted to do songs that were different," Noone said. "We couldn't do 'Roll Over Beethoven' because the Beatles did it, and they did it better than us. We couldn't do 'Love Potion #9' because the Searchers did it. So we took some English music hall songs, and some that sounded like English music hall, like 'Mrs. Brown'."

Like the folk era that immediately preceded, bands often did the same songs. Both the Hermits and Freddie and the Dreamers did "I Understand." The Hermits shared "Where Were You When I Needed You" with the Grass Roots. Hit singles were a crapshoot. Gouldman's "Bus Stop" was a hit for the Hollies instead of the Hermits, even as their versions sounded about the same through a transistor radio. And the Hermits sweetened up the Kinks' "Dandy" and Donovan's "Museum," which were basically rescued album tracks.

Noone's real cultural contribution didn't occur until the late 1990s, when he invented blogging. While all the former rock stars were fiddle-farting with the Internet and punching out identical promotional web pages, Noone was writing down his every thought for public consumption. He peppered the site with reminisces, which in every other decade would have turned into a forgettable book. He added a healthy dose of fantasy: his "Club Me" shows him taking on personas like "Peteloaf" and "The Very Reverend Sun Lung Noone."

When I first visited www.peternoone.com in 1999 I was struck by the whimsical detail. A lot of these remembrances wouldn't work in a book, as they were mostly charming lies. We got a trip into Noone's imagination, which may be a little more fertile than your own. Besides, he met John Lennon. And Stevie Wonder, when he was Little.

Consider this entry, about his visit to Detroit's Motown studio in 1965:

"I was sort of nonplussed that (Wonder) actually 'knew' my songs, and was so comfortable with himself, but off he went singing 'Mrs. Brown You've Got a Lovely Daughter' with the most perfect impersonation of me I have ever heard. Being a quick-witted sort of chap, I told him that I was a huge fan of his work, but hadn't got my harmonica with me but, that by an incredible quirk of circumstance I had just purchased his latest album and that I had it with me right there under my arm.

"He was duly impressed and signed it and it is in my personal hall of shame and funny things I have done. I would have told him the truth eventually but my Mum told me it was all right to be funny if it didn't hurt anyone's feelings and I never got another opportunity to tell Marvin Gaye that Little Stevie Wonder had signed all over his face."

True? Maybe. Worth reading? Absolutely. We don't need another rock star bio that provides a different viewpoint of something we already know. Noone's writing is much like he talks eyes wide and free of guile. He isn't really name-dropping, because he's still jazzed about these stories.

How John Lennon once told him that fans are great, if they don't breathe on you. How Jimmy Page asked to play on the Hermits' records and can be heard on "Silhouettes" and "Wonderful World." How David Bowie played what was to become *Hunky Dory*, and Noone thought he "had discovered the new Paul McCartney, by accident." Of these, "Oh, You Pretty Things," was one of the last Hermits singles. Bowie was on the session, Noone recalls that "he was a fantastic pianist, but could only play on the black keys." And every time Noone sees Bowie, he again offers his keyboard services.

I tell Noone that I've never heard his version of "Pretty Things" and he erupts. "It's a great record!" he says as he asks for my e-mail. A moment later an MP3 arrives in my inbox. It's a worthy curiosity, but also quite clear why this wasn't a hit. It lacks both the reedy appeal of Hermits' records and the plaintive menace of Bowie's own version.

Hot for Teacher

Aware of the available options, Mark Volman earned a master's degree in his forties and is now a college professor, teaching history and music business theory at Belmont University in Nashville. Classes are Tuesday and Thursday; he takes the Turtles out on the weekends.

"When we were 17 years old we weren't really thinking about the business," Volman said. "We were doing this to make records, tour and meet girls. We wanted to do something that our parents didn't think we could do.

"There is not a big future for someone with a music degree. If you play the French horn there aren't a lot of symphonies where you can work. In my class I teach kids about surviving in the business, in case their own music doesn't pan out."

Volman must be a blast in the classroom, but few of us will have the privilege firsthand. There is, of course, a website (www.askprofessorflo.com) that contains a portion of the syllabus and where you can (presumably) get your music business questions answered.

The Turtles perfect single, "Happy Together," hasn't lost its luster. The band knew the song was great, but had no idea it would be so huge. While they would never complain, it's clear that it messed them up. The record company pushed for another song just like it, and withheld funds when it didn't come. They gave in once or twice ("Elenore," "You Showed Me") but their singles-band status eclipsed two wonderful albums, *The Turtles Present the Battle of the Bands* and the Ray Davies-produced *Turtle Soup*. At the time, the Kinks' latest was *Village Green Preservation Society*.

"I always thought we were pretty close to the Kinks," Volman said. "We didn't have the same edge, but we had the same songwriting philosophy." Davies didn't leave too obvious a mark on the album, although parts of 'How You Loved Me' tells us what Dave Davies would have sounded like back then if he sang on pitch.

They still perform "Happy Together" enthusiastically, but its transformation into a sing-along takes away its menacing overtones. Listen to the words; it seems to be less of a love song than a stalker's hymn.

"The words conjured up a lot of emotion for people who could not be where they wanted to be or with who they wanted to be with," Volman said. "People who were in Vietnam told me how that song brought them so close to feeling like they were home."

When I ask whether he would like to correct any mistakes he laughs and says, "That is the first good question you've asked me." But he goes on to say he wouldn't change a thing, aside from the producer's credit.

Today's Turtles are as much about comedy as music. Volman — rotund, with a wave of curls and a beatific, confused expression — always made us laugh. Kaylan, who has looked like an old guy for some time, spends his onstage time looking befuddled, especially during a routine where he proclaims "all of those bands in the '60s and '70s who had a few hits and you never knew who they were and then went away were us."

He rattles off several names, up to and including Nirvana and Britney Spears, until Volman stages an intervention and a more subdued Kaylan announced "apparently there has been some confusion. We were not the O'Jays."

From the opening "You Baby" to "Happy Together," they roll good-naturedly through their best-known hits. The renditions are faithful and competent, and they enjoy themselves immensely. There are a few odd spots, such as a version of "Gimme Some Lovin" sung by the bass player. This is confusing, as the song had nothing to do with the Turtles. And a long buildup to what they call "our new record" ("This is an experiment. It could really suck. But we feel really at home here and hope you will enjoy this") turns out to be a version of Neil Young's "Cinnamon Girl."

"Really suck" becomes the evening's grand understatement. Saying this is a new song is a classic case of bait-and-switch. The audience applauds, but we already know it is peppered with a bunch of unparticular yahoos.

After "Happy Together," Volman and Kaylan walk through the crowd toward the merchandising station (everyone signs autographs after the show, another reason it is not like the old days). The first synthesized bits of *Who's Next* filters through the PA as the crowd offers roaming standing ovation. It's a poetic moment, right out of a hero movie. It's a bit hokey but only a real mope wouldn't cheer along.

Dolenz arrives to an instrumental version of the Monkees' theme song, then bounces straight into "Last Train to Clarksville. The sound is clear and his voice sounds great. He's covering the entire Monkees catalogue and not just what he sang. We get "A Little Bit Me, A Little Bit You," and an embarrassing version of Mike Nesmith's "Different Drum" sung by Micky's sister, Coco. She redeems herself with some deft vocal counterpoints on "Daydream Believer."

Dolenz is also the only one on the bill who looks appreciably different than the old days. With a beard, suit and hat, all black, he could be a rabbi or a salesman. While his vocal clarity is the best part of his set, he sings as well at 61 as 21. He still isn't much of a drummer, but his 4/4 pounding is just right for "Mary Mary." The set list, however, disappoints. A lot of their songs — those performed by Dolenz — hold up well. But tonight, we don't get to hear "Saturday's Child," "For Pete's Sake" or "Porpoise Song" — the one Monkees track that qualifies as brilliant.

There are always unplayed songs that someone in the audience wants to hear, and package shows necessarily aim for the lowest common denominator. Still, they are onstage for 35 minutes or so, and it would be nice if they could play their best songs instead of falling back on perceived crowd-pleasers. Every piece of shtick squanders their time onstage. Dolenz gives his sister the chance to sing a song Mike Nesmith wrote for Linda Ronstadt, and even those who don't hate the performance will wonder how it fits in. And the Turtles' version of a Spencer Davis song sacrifices second-string hits or outstanding album tracks.

Enjoyment here requires you too adjust your expectations. This ranges from the willingness to accept ingratiating need of some of the acts to read off their resume, or the general tackiness that goes beyond finding gobs of ketchup on your chair. I may be a snob, but I dropped Dolenz' live CD like a hot coal when I noticed the cover misspelled one of his songs as "Plesent Valley Sunday." And even as these guys brag about their own history, they still get it wrong. After "It Ain't Me, Babe" Volman announces "that is a song that Bob Dylan wrote for us." He was being facetious, but the audience didn't know the difference. This is how myths get started.

The rock star manual says nothing about competing with carnival lights for the audiences' attention and submitting to hours of signing autographs on vinyl records that are older than many people there — although Noone makes the best of it. One t-shirt is an old-style shot of the Hermits, but with his face super-imposed on all five players. As he signs a pile of shirts backstage he refers to the image as "five ten-inch Peters."

Noone also does the onstage shtick, tossing off irreverent imitations of Johnny Cash and Tom Jones. Still, he is the only one tonight who seems genuine, who really connects with and actually enjoys the music. Volman and Kaylan make it clear they are goofing around, and Dolenz, while he sounds great, is a little aloof.

Perhaps this is a mathematical drawback. You would be hard-pressed to name Hermits other than Noone or those who backed Volman and Kaylan in the Turtles (OK, I can, but I'm not like everybody else). Dolenz, as one-fourth of a well-known group, inevitably calls attention to those who aren't there.

Noone is always laughing and running around, at one point he grabs a stack of CDs and gives them to several kids (that is to say, those under 15) who are sitting near the front. This is a generous act, and some audience members think that the lady who is walking through the crowd selling the discs is giving them away.

Monkee Si, Monkee Deux

Volman attributes the failure to produce new music to closed-minded radio programmers. All the available outlets — pop radio, classic rock, satellite, would all show a lack of interest in a new Turtles or Hermits album. So many of them don't even try. If people want to hear the old stuff, that's what they'll get. Every ten years or so they may do a new live album of the old songs, just to be producing something.

Some have produced new music and placed clips on cookie-cutter web pages. Here, you learn that Peter Tork has chosen a form of acoustic blues that is almost immediately annoying. But there are few exceptions. Eric Burdon has re-leased an album a year for three years, a live one with just two crowd-pleasers and two new blues rock masterpieces. *Soul of A Man* is especially pure; he seems to work the same mine as always. Except today he is a lot more consistent and in control. This album strikes the balance between who he is and who we want him to be. So Burdon actually recreates that part of the 1960s, when you would go to a concert to hear the new songs and they are as compelling as the old ones.

Noone, it turns out, often scolds Burdon for his onstage indulgences; saying that audiences want to hear the old songs as they remember them. Noone follows his own advice, mostly, until he stretches "I'm Henry the Eighth, I Am" into a punky ten-minute sing-along jam.

Dolenz's former band mate, the perpetually cantankerous Mike Nesmith, isn't stuck in the past. The first thing you notice about his new album, *Rays*, is that it has nothing to do with that guy in the Monkees who played country for a while and had something to do with the beginnings of MTV. The vocals, when he decides to sing, sound a little like the Wool Hat guy but the rest of it is just too wild. It's cinematic, but too irritating to be ambient. It's a good choice for your iTunes, though; when it pops up there is an immediate, gleeful "what the hell is that?"

Right after Volman says how no one is interested in new Turtles music, he lets slip that his partner has released a new album earlier this year. Kaylan's *Dust Bunnies* is an odd affair; he's half screaming the words against an abrasive background, although it's not quite metal. Three quarters in I recognize one song, a slowed-down version of the Honeycombs' "Have I The Right." Further research (this is the disadvantage of downloading) finds that only one is an original, the rest are covers of the most obscure songs from people like Tim Buckley, John Miles and Charles Aznavour. Some of it works, while others are so annoying that you can't get to the skip button fast enough.

These selections are, as it turns out, Kaylan's personal favorites from his songwriter buddies. That they aren't real "originals" actually makes it worse.

Five days later I stumble into a club date featuring P.F. Sloan, who wrote at least five of the songs played at the fair. It is quite a different scene; instead of a suntanned, middle-aged mob we get a handful of graying hippies entertained in a small dark room by a 60-year-old greaser. He opens with "Secret Agent Man" and plays it as if Dylan was having a go — in this case, dragging it out into several verses and blowing the harmonica between each one. He follows the opener with a few alternately boring and irritating new songs.

It gets better when he unleashes a quiet version of "You Baby," the buoyant opener to the Turtles' set days before. Even as the unplugged trend has lost its luster, this is a perfect balance: A familiar song stripped down to its essence; familiar yet new. He follows this with a subtle version of "Where Were You When

I Needed You," far superior to the overwrought original Grass Roots version (on which, it is said, he sang lead).

If some old guy in dark glasses were to show up at any club and play "Eve of Destruction" and "Let's Live for Today," you would think it was a joke. Sloan gets away with this because he wrote the songs, and (on paper, at least) gets to take any liberties he wants. If you like these new versions you can take them home, on a cheaply produced CD for sale in the back. In this respect, the Sloan event is identical to the fair.

It is a continuous privilege how we can see the past greats in a small club, an open amphitheater or a casino playing songs from the old days. But it's also a mixed blessing, as sooner or later we dovetail back to the ideas of authenticity and quality — remembering when they were actually the same.

ROCK'S BACKPAGES, October 2006

Arlo Guthrie: 'Alice' is Back on the Menu

Arlo Guthrie, Bremerton, WA April 2007
Interviewed by phone, Bainbridge Island, WA to Key West, FL

"ALICE'S RESTAURANT" is back on the menu. First released in 1967 as the
title track of Arlo Guthrie's debut album, the 18-minute talking blues narrative
became a counterculture touchstone, and along with "In-a-Gadda-Da-Vida,"
redefined what was played on radio. Guthrie, then 20, took audiences by surprise
with his sly, sarcastic delivery of a tale concerning Thanksgiving, garbage and
draft boards.

The song was decidedly of its time, and has a definite "you had to be there"
feel. It is now quaint to imagine high school kids sitting around in circles playing the full version of the song to each other, forming clubs called "The Group
W Bench" to celebrate their rebellion. Unlike the aggressive nature of modern
social commentary, "Alice" made listeners simultaneously laugh and think. And
to this day, there are still people who take time out of their Thanksgiving to play
the song in full as if it were part of their family history.

Arlo is headlining the Guthrie Family Legacy tour. He is the linchpin between his father, (folksinger Woody Guthrie, who wrote "This Land is Your Land"
and characterized his guitar as a machine that fights fascism) and his children.
Son Abe is the band's musical director. Daughter Sarah Lee, along with husband
Johnny Irion, filters Woody through Arlo to come up with her own brand of
socially compelling roots rock.

As part of a tour that began last July, the Guthrie clan touches down at the
Admiral Theater April 12. At press time there were only about 100 tickets remaining, with circles, arrows and a paragraph on the back of every one.

Key West Inn, this is Tammy. Can I help you?

Arlo Guthrie, please.

Arlo Guthrie? The musician? Is he staying here?

I was given this number.

I'll check. Hang on.

Thank you.

Hello?

*Mr. Guthrie? This is Charlie Bermant, from What's Up Magazine, Kitsap County,
Washington.*

Hi. Where's that?

Bremerton. You are playing the Admiral Theater on April 12.

Oh yeah. I love the Admiral. It's a great place.

What should we expect to hear?

We are on the last six weeks of the Guthrie Family Legacy Tour. It's a way to
have fun with my family, singing some of my dad's old songs and some of his new

songs. Some of my old songs and some of my new songs. And some spontaneous songs. And "Alice" is back on the menu.

Your dad died in 1967. How can there be new songs?

He left about 3,500 handwritten poems with no tune. My sister took some of them to different musicians and it resulted in several albums by Billy Bragg, Wilco and some other people. I've worked on some of the songs too, but we are all family so there is no copyright.

Why 'Alice' now?

These times are looking eerily familiar. Right now, you never know where the next group of soldiers are going to come from. So the song has some legs. The song originally took me about a year to write, from 1965 to 1966. So we are celebrating its 40th anniversary. I never thought I'd be singing it for that long. I'd never thought I'd be performing for this long. We did it for the 15th anniversary in 1983, and re-recorded the whole Alice's Restaurant album in 1996 in the same church where it all happened. Now it is closer to the way we did it originally. We took some of the material out. A lot of people today don't know who Nixon was, and don't know anything about the 18-minute gap.

What did your father think of "Alice"?

We like to say that we played it for him and he passed away. It was way before CDs so we had an acetate, a test pressing, that we played for him. By that time he was pretty gone. He smiled.

Did you play it for him as a work in progress?

No.

How does it feel to turn 60?

I haven't really thought about that yet. I don't ever know what's going to happen. I started playing at the beginning of the "Folk Scare," and was six to ten years younger than most of the people that were playing, like Bob Dylan and Phil Ochs. I was always one of the young kids showing up at the festivals. Now I'm one of the older ones playing. There are not many of us around. But right now there are some great new pickers.

How do the stories fit in?

When I started performing and included stories the audience would tell me to shut up and sing. After I had played "Alice" for a while and then stopped the audience wanted me to stop singing and talk. But I am not out to please everybody. I'm not a pop star that just repeats himself. If I take a loss in the audience because I don't play the same thing over and over that's fine. There are other places that people can go to see that kind of stuff.

How do you keep things fresh?

If I get to the point where I can do a song in my sleep it becomes like a trained-seal act. If I ever find myself drifting while playing a song I will just take it off the show. But It's a two-way street. You have to train the audience to accept the new stuff and they have to train you to know what is working. But you want to be creative. Some of the songs that you play over and over again you add new elements. Like "Coming into Los Angeles" or "City of New Orleans." Some parts are exactly the same.

We can always do a good show. But we can never do a great show unless we are willing to risk doing a bad one. We take that risk, and it pays off about one in a hundred times. To do a great show where everything works and everyone plays right doesn't happen too often. I've done it three or four times throughout the years. Fortunately I've gotten them on tape and released them as albums.

What's the secret to doing a great show?

If I knew that, I'd do one every night.

How are you feeling now?

I feel great. Never felt better. There was a test that I could have taken for the (hereditary) disease (Huntington's Chorea) but it would only tell me if I had it. There was nothing I could do about it. Who the hell wants to know?

Your kids feel the same way?

Yeah.

Thanks for talking to me. I may come to one of the shows, and promise that I won't disrupt things by yelling for "Guabi Guabi" (from 1977's Amigos).

Well, just call out for it. If we are relaxed enough and in the mood we just might try it.

Thanks, Arlo.

WHAT'S UP, March 23, 2007

Bee Gees' Generations

PORTLAND, OREGON — Last year, self-proclaimed pop music geek Ellen Osborn was tooling around town when she got an idea: "There should be an all-female group that exclusively performs Bee Gees songs," she said to the person who was driving. "They should be called the Shee Bee Gees. Someone needs to do this."

Realizing soon enough that "someone will have to be me," she learned to play bass and recruited three acquaintances. By then, the idea evolved to only include the early chapter of the Bee Gees story, when the brothers Barry, Robin and Maurice were left-field melodists instead of dance music icons.

Anyone who has heard the early Bee Gees will love the Shee Bee Gees concept; how well they play is beside the point. Even so, they are supposedly quite good. A family member who overheard a rehearsal characterized them as "pigeons cooing at each other." They can play just 15 songs and have only performed a handful of times, but have already attracted early Bee Gees fans who never thought they would hear any of this rare, precious and beautiful music onstage.

In addition to Osborn, the Shee Bee Gees are drummer Heather Larimer, guitarist Anna Shelton and vocalist Alex Valdivieso. Their repertoire contains some you would expect; "Lonely Days," "Melody Fair" and "Run to Me." At the same time, they dip into fan-only treasures like "Birdie Told Me," "Kitty Can" and "You'll Never See My Face Again." Said Larimer: "We've turned that one into a girl-group number. It's nothing like the Bee Gees; it sounds more like the Shangri-Las."

The Gibb brothers' three-part harmony is revised and rewritten, with the fourth voice filling in for the keyboards or orchestra. You can guess how this might sound from an alternate version of "Turn of the Century" from *The Studio Albums 1967-1968* box set, where Maurice scat-sings the guide vocal for the orchestra. Or the mouth-percussion background on "Kitty Can."

Osborne speaks of true Bee Gees fans as if they were a persecuted minority. "People come up to us and say 'Which one are you?' or 'Which one is Andy?'" Osborn said. "That is not us. We are not a normal tribute band." Adds Larimer: "The reason to do a cover is to show people what a great song it is. If you are completely true to the original, then what's the point?"

Maurice Code

The new box set documents the Bee Gees first extraordinary creative spurt. Each of the original LPs – *1st*, *Horizontal* and *Idea* – appears in mono and stereo mixes with an extra disc featuring singles, outtakes and alternate versions. Some of these tracks have a convoluted history, appearing first on B-sides and then showing up on poorly executed budget albums. A box set in the early 1990s contained several songs on CD for the first time, but that release sought to present the band's entire history on four discs.

While there are at least four Bee Gees-hits CDs with generally the same track lists, the bulk of their 40-year run is pretty much unavailable. This box set — which will fragment into three separate releases after the initial 10,000 copies sell out — starts the process that will eventually set things right. It places the music in its original context, so you can see what worked and what didn't. There are some great tracks on these albums, and some real stinkers. Trouble is, people can never agree on which is which. When we have the original albums we can make our own decisions.

In 1967, I bought *Bee Gees 1st* at its release, on the strength of "New York Mining Disaster" and a slam-bang video of "In My Own Time" that was shown on *Laugh-In*. That day I was involved in what passed for *Saturday Night Fever* as a 13-year-old, babysitting. After the kids were asleep and there was nothing on TV I played the album on my own portable mono phonograph. In the middle of the third song, "Red Chair Fade Away," I heard a baby cry. I checked on the kids. Nothing. I played the album again. Same thing happened. By the third time I realized the child's cry was part of the song.

Barry the Hatchet

At that time, I didn't know from Barry, Robin or Maurice. I now recognize their vocal switch-offs, back then it all sounded like one particularly versatile voice. None of the songs were yet hits, but this was the smoothest, most compelling pop music I had heard in some time, satisfying the thirst for something that first sounded a little like the Beatles but then took a sharp left turn.

While these albums are still fresh and interesting the bonus tracks are inconsistent. Some have historical interest — the aforementioned "Turn of the Century." Only a few, like "Chocolate Symphony," are extraordinary. With most of the outtakes it appears that whoever made the decision to leave them off of the album in the first place made the right call. While not worth hearing more than once, these extras paint what must have been an accurate portrayal of the band at the time: Adorable, immensely talented teenagers armed with a tape deck singing the first thing that came to their minds.

The first three albums (along with 1969's *Odessa*) are butterflies in amber. The imperfections are clear but the music is creative, compelling and, often enough, brilliant. It's as if they got up every day and decided to record a new song. What may sound dated today was fresh and interesting when the combinations were still new.

As spectacular as these first four albums may be, expectations for entire reissue series prompts a raging ambivalence. Despite overwhelming commercial success, they were never as good as they were here. After the end of this creative spurt it always seemed like they were trying too hard. For this reason, expanded versions of their middle-period albums don't exactly set your hair afire. Let's hope the reissue deal includes an online option, for those who really don't get some of the stranger stuff. (And with all the posh packaging, the set is historically inaccurate: Bee Gees records were never released by Reprise in those days, least of all with the steamboat label of the pre-RCA American Kinks albums.)

Rhino hasn't yet decided reissue dates or details. They will either unleash one group of reissues at a time (like the Beatles) or dump them all at once (like the Rolling Stones). In either case, they will eventually get around to refurbishing their 2001's *This is Where I Came In*. It was a fitting enough swan song, even if the group's own comparisons to Bee Gees *1st* didn't ring true. It was more like the Bee Gees' *White Album*, with the three members bringing their individual efforts to the table. Most of it worked very well. Barry's buoyant "Sacred Trust" was supposedly pitched to and rejected by the Backstreet Boys, while Robin's "Embrace" shows how, as Osborn says, "no one can sing like him."

As for Maurice, whose unexpected death ensured this would be the last Bee Gees album (no calling on Kenney Jones this time) his two numbers showed that as a lead vocalist he was still one of the best harmony singers around. Casual Bee Gees fans never noticed Maurice, but he provided a demonstration of how the absence of a key member changes everything.

For now, Barry and Robin have no plans to record together, although they occasionally perform a public duet. Robin has already released an unspeakably bad live album/DVD of Bee Gees hits and a solo album. Barry has bought Johnny Cash's old house and plans to release a country album. This may not be good news, as he is more likely to make the equivalent of a bad Kenny Rogers album then match any of the Bee Gees' periodic country gems like "South Dakota Morning" or "Come on Over."

Robin the Cradle

Osborn traveled to the Bee Gees through neither their early hits nor the disco era. She chose 1970's Cucumber Castle, made by Barry and Maurice without Robin, as an entry point. At the time she felt Robin's reedy vocals and bizarre phrasing were a little hard to take. Bee Gees fans throughout history have had the same reaction but they all come around. "I love his voice now," Osborn said. "He has so much control."

Barry, she said, is the master of profound simplicity.

"Some of their songs are so simple and passionate," Osborn said, pounding the table for emphasis. "On 'To Love Somebody', Barry sings it twice. He goes 'you don't know what it's like.' Then he repeats it. 'You DON'T KNOW what it's like...'.'" "These songs are enormously satisfying," Larimer added. "It feels like they should be sung in church."

The Shee Bee Gees don't have a set course and aren't really sailing their own ship. They depend on the kindness of others for studio time and publicity. Plans to record in December fell through; their only outlet aside from infrequent live shows is three songs on a MySpace page. Appropriately, they are aiming to release a single, perhaps a ballad ("Melody Fair") backed by a rocker ("The Earnest of Being George"). "Each step is a surprise," Larimer said. "When we first met it was, 'Hey, we can play.' Wow. Then it was, 'Hey do you want to play a show?' Then it was, 'Hey, do you want to record?' Wow. And 'Do we want to be interviewed?' Wow."

Which is sort of how it happened, for those He Bee Gees.

ROCK'S BACKPAGES, November 2007

Eric Burdon, Snoqualmie WA July 2011

Burdon, Deconstructed

Interviews by email and phone from Bainbridge Island, WA

"I was such a rotten little bastard when I was young."

In 1970, a teenager named Terry Wilson slipped into a Pasadena, Texas club to check out a local band called T.H.E. and "was blown away by this tall skinny kid with buck teeth, who had a Farfisa organ set on top of his piano. He had to reach up to play the organ, and he sang a great version of 'Funny How Time Slips Away.' It was amazing."

There were quite a few young kids out that night, and most of them eventually segued into live normal lives. But this pair moved around and kept in touch, recording and performing with all stripes. This month, they performed separately with musicians who were then playing on large stages halfway across the world. Wilson propelled Eric Burdon's latest litter of Animals through an energized set in a Tacoma casino, while Rabbit Bundrick pounded keys for The Who during the Super Bowl halftime show.

Wilson and Bundrick belong to an ever-expanding circle of "ringers," musicians who hook up with veteran performers to present stage versions of songs that were popular long ago. Ringers are a necessary part of the ecosystem, since the surviving original members of any group can't play together, if they can play at all. And Burdon, who is not one to provide plasticized versions of his hits, benefits from Wilson's drive.

"Eric hasn't gotten his due," Wilson said. "He deserves to be as appreciated as Paul McCartney and Mick Jagger. He has always known how to find the best songs and how to sing him. And what he and Jagger brought to the table, putting American blues into rock 'n' roll, was astounding.

"But he still amazes me," Wilson said of Burdon. "He has this anarchist glint in his eye. And he knows how to have fun."

"Because my best ain't good enough."

This night in Tacoma, the most common question asked is whether these are the "original" Animals, even as it is pretty clear the singer is the same. But everything else has changed. This particular lineup — Wilson, keyboardist Red Young, guitarist Billy Watts and drummer Branden Temple—have only been together a few months, even though Wilson and Young played with Burdon in a previous life.

They play nine "hits," two from the latest album, two blues classics and a Hendrix song, along with an ironic version of "Nobody Loves You When You Are Down and Out." The songs start out familiar, before taking left turns down the improvisation avenue. "When I Was Young" adds a scat vocal, and "House of the Rising Sun" doesn't even use the famous guitar arpeggio that every kid my age needed to learn so he didn't get the crap kicked out of him. "It's My Life," never the best Animals single, just wants to explode. It seems that after years of playing this one he's finally learned how to turn it up to full strength.

Of his contemporaries still performing, Burdon falls somewhere in between the letter-perfect but soulless recreations of the Beach Boys and Bob Dylan's complete deconstruction of his own catalog.

"There are people who want to hear a song performed a certain way." Wilson said. "We are true to the originals, but Eric has moved forward, and broadened. He encourages us to go anywhere we want, to improvise. He doesn't want to play the songs the exact same way all the time. We have fun with it, and Eric has a passion that comes across live."

"You could hear 'We Gotta Get Out Of This Place' five nights in a row and they all will be different depending on the mood, the audience and how we feel," Young said. "It's a five-way conversation on stage. We never know what will happen next — even if we start into the wrong song or if Eric goes into a rap — whatever — we're all there together. To me, this is the band I've always wanted to be in and I'm sure that shows in performance."

Young said the band has about a five-hour repertoire, which it selects and refines at the beginning of each tour. The individual members (two in Texas; two and Burdon in California) learn songs on their own and "rehearse" for about a day before pulling together a set list. Things change. "Don't Bring Me Down" was the default opener for a time, but was replaced this year by "When I Was Young." This is an apt choice as it sets the stage for a voyage into the past.

"It's my life, and I'll do what I want."

Politicians, popes and even poets have attempted to control their media image, but they could all take lessons from Burdon. His contemporaries are eager to reflect about their golden years and do what it takes to keep their legend alive. Even Roger Daltrey participated in promotional efforts for his recent solo tour.

Burdon, who is far less recognizable than Daltrey, doesn't play the game at all. You would think that he would be eager to reflect about his life, to establish his nook in the rock statuary, but he's not interested in talking. He does not grant personal interviews, neither indulging a fan writer's scrutiny nor stooping to promote a particular show. If a publication wants to write a piece about Burdon it must submit the questions to his manager/wife/gatekeeper through e-mail, and wait for the answers.

"It is the best format for me," he writes, about two weeks after I sent him a list of ten questions. "I get to keep a record of what my thoughts are plus I can answer only the questions I choose to address. I have been doing interviews for over forty years now and I have been misquoted on numerous occasions."

You wouldn't tolerate this from a politician or public figure. But no one elected Burdon to anything, and he has no obligation to do anything but show up, play for 75 minutes and include a healthy slice of the hits that people want to hear. He has no obligation to perform them as we knew them, or to even play particularly well — although this night in the Tacoma casino, he kicks ass.

Many veteran performers just go through the motions and hope the familiar songs will provoke warm nostalgia. Burdon, like John Fogerty, truly loves the music he has been "forced" to play for more than 40 years. He is one of the few in the Class of '64 who still gets audiences really excited, showing a passion for the music that shakes the walls of the sterile casinos where he spends much of his performing time.

What do "British Invasion" veterans who are still working have in common?

I would say the common denominator is most of the original British invasion bands were squabbling amongst themselves, as to who owns what and who should be performing under their original band names that is, including myself.

Of the music from those days what holds up the best, and what doesn't?

Beatles, Stones, Kinks, Pretty Things, Gary Brooker, Gino Washington, John Fogerty and John Cale.

How do you structure your business? Has the economy forced you to sacrifice anything?

! was really fortunate when it came to the economic crisis, as it didn't seem to affect me. My manager had already booked me lightly for 2009 and 2010, allowing me free time to write and prepare for my next album. As for the shows I don't count them I just enjoy them, it's traveling that kills me.

What is your best album? (you can break this up into best solo and best Animals)

The next one!

What was your proudest moment?

Pride rarely figures in my life, when the feeling comes over me I dismiss it like a blink of an eye.

What are your most important relationships?

Every face out there in front of me when I'm on stage.

"When I think of all the good times that I've wasted, having good times."

While there is a certain amount of luck involved, Burdon did not take a career path that would have landed him the Super Bowl gig. While you could argue the relative quality of the Who vs. Burdon, the Townshend/Daltrey gang is in a different league. Burdon's made a few good records, but never released an album that has taken the world's breath away like *Who's Next* or *Tommy*. Burdon's rep comes from a handful of hits which he plays every night, with most of the audience unaware of their context outside of the transistor radio.

As Burdon is introduced onstage, the announcer crows, "In 1964 three bands mattered, the Beatles, the Rolling Stones and the Animals." Of those today, the Stones still draw a crowd in concert, although the new records are unconvincing. The Beatles — now known as McCartney, Inc. — sells out shows with a great band and a rich repertoire. As for "originals," Paul and Eric's band have an equal number.

Circumstantially, Burdon most resembles Peter Noone, who led Herman's Hermits parallel to Burdon's Animals. They had the same management, and both released albums titled *On Tour* that were not recorded live. They are old friends, dating back to the early tours when 22-year-old Eric sheltered 16-year-old Peter from the wages of sin. Noone plays energetic shows, dragging "I'm Henry VII I Am" to ungodly lengths, in the same way Burdon stretches his old stuff. The two old pals also bear a similar cross; the drummer from each original band leads a group of ringers around England with a challenge to the name.

While not a part of the British Invasion set, the closest musical connection is with Bob Dylan. Both take liberties with the music, though Dylan's re-imagining of old tunes is more dramatic than Burdon's. Their bands are both loud and precise, although Burdon does a bit more improvising. Dylan has transformed himself into the electric bluesman where Burdon has always been, but it goes both ways. It is impossible to listen to "Don't Ever Let Nobody Drag Your Spirit Down" from *Soul of a Man* without conjuring *Love and Theft*.

The biggest difference is aural. Dylan's voice has been to the gravel mine and back since the 1960s heyday, while Burdon hasn't lost any steam. Wilson's assessment: "Bob's a mumbler. Eric's a singer's singer. But they both have bands from Texas. You can tell the difference with a Texas band, no one else plays like that. "

"I want someone to tell me, just what is the soul of a man?"

Wilson and Young were in Burdon's band in the early 1980s and working on their new album when they were pushed aside in favor of a reunion of the original Animals. Their work provides the template for a new album, the still remarkable *Ark*. The three haven't yet recorded together, but are preparing to record new material this year. This will represent the final part of a trilogy of new albums, beginning with 2004's *A Secret Life* followed two years later by *Soul of a Man*. The former had a plurality of Burdon originals, while the latter was an assemblage of blues covers that sounded like Burdon originals.

The direction of the new record is undetermined, aside from a commitment from Tony Braunagel, another Texan who is a longtime colleague of Wilson and Young who drummed in Burdon's band for a while. "We don't know what it will sound like yet," Wilson said of the project. "Eric will come in with a lot of ideas, thoughts on scraps of paper, pieces of poetry, that gets assembled together. He puts things on the table, and then we'll massage it all into a record."

Burdon has written some very good songs, but his best work results from his ability to recognize great songs and make them his musical property. "House of the Rising Sun" was a folk song. While he can pick winners, the song's originators haven't always shown the proper thanks. Nina Simone gave Burdon grief for adding too much punch to her torchy "Don't Let Me Be Misunderstood." while Barry Mann's preferred reading of his "We Gotta Get Outta This Place" is as a slow, folky blues. If Mann had his way, we'd remember this rave-up as fondly as "Eve of Destruction." Which means not much.

What else do you have left to do musically, that you haven't done before? Is there more to say about your life that is unsaid?

It's a mistake to stray too far from your roots. You must know how far you can venture with audiences. I have for a long time thought about doing a spoken-word concept disc. With so many wonderful new programs available on digital format it could be fun. To answer the second part of your question, I would say that the life I live is complex in many formats. That although I try to pin it down, I left so many parts of it out. I try to live my life listening to music, writing lyrics and concepts, living as privately as possible, staying healthy, growing old gracefully and trying to understand my wife.

"Go to San Francisco, If not for the sake of this song for the sake of your own peace of mind."

You hear this a lot: "I wish we had seen him, when we had the chance," pertaining to the lost opportunity to see one of the greats. Many times these chances are cut short by death, but in many cases the obstacles are, lives, wives or schedules. Eric Burdon, or somebody, plays the casino or the state fair nearby, and you never make the extra effort. Sooner or later, the opportunity's lost.

It will be a cool thing to see the Who play the Super Bowl, with a hyperactive medley of their hits and TV themes, as it proves to those who were there at the beginning that they were right all along, Even as many of our former concert buddies limit their live music to small doses at halftime, it's never hurts to recall why you got out of the house in the first place. And Burdon has enough passion, commitment and authenticity to get you off the couch, today.

Burdon won't ever play the Super Bowl, but he is still the real deal-- with enough passion, commitment and authenticity to lift us off any couch in the country. Right now, I'm committed to seeing him the next time he plays around here, but I'll still have to check the date and get back to you.

Set List, Tacoma, WA 1/23/2010: *When I Was Young/ Don't Bring Me Down / San Franciscan Nights /Don't Let Me Be Misunderstood/ Devil Run/ I'm Crying/ I Believe to My Soul/ Boom Boom/ It's My Life/ Red Cross Store/ House of the Rising Sun/ You Got Me Floatin'/ We Gotta Get Out of This Place/ Nobody Knows You When You're Down and Out/ Shame Shame Shame*

SONICBOOMERS, February 2010

John Sebastian's Spoonful of Magic

Interview by phone, Issaquah, WA to Woodstock, NY

The best 1960s bands always sounded so original, when in fact they filtered existing musical idioms such as folk and blues to gain a unique sound. While the Lovin' Spoonful made some great pop singles ("Rain on the Roof" and "She is Still a Mystery" immediately come to mind), they used an infusion of acoustic blues known as "jug band music" as its calling card.

After the Spoonful, principal member John Sebastian parlayed a last-minute appearance at the Woodstock Festival into an active solo career. When the Woodstock buzz had worn down he scored again with "Welcome Back," a catchy tune written especially for the TV show that gave another New York John — Travolta — his first break.

After slipping out of the public eye, Sebastian has moved back toward his roots through an excursion with the J-Band in the 1990s and a recent partnership with mandolin player David Grisman. His solo act has some unique qualities, since he faces the audience armed with an electric guitar and a small amp, rather than the acoustic setup that everyone else uses. His act is a little like Roger McGuinn where he mixes up performances and stories that, taken together, are a bit of a history lesson. Perhaps that's why they both play in a lot of high school auditoriums.

He plays a baritone guitar to accommodate a lower vocal range, and mixes it up between old blues songs and Lovin' Spoonful staples. The former are well-served by his vocal growl, while the latter becomes a bit of a shock. You hear the familiar intro, but the voice doesn't come in at the same pitch. It's similar to the adjustment of Bob Dylan's voice over the same period, but not quite as drastic.

Sebastian shared some of his recollections in a call from his home in (where else?) Woodstock, N.Y.

Who comes to see you these days?

I get people in their sixties, my contemporaries, who want to hear as many Spoonful songs as possible. There are a lot of people who came to me as a result of the album I made with David, and want to hear a lot of acoustic guitars. In the Northwest there is another faction, fans of jug band music. I discovered that audience in the 1990s, while I was playing with the J-Band. These people would come to the shows, to hear whatever renditions we would do of the songs they loved.

I provide a pen-and-ink approach to the songs, providing a guitar-only version of what was on the record. I give a pretty close approximation even with one guitar. I know all of the layers, and what licks are needed. When I play electric I use a baritone guitar, which has a lower pitch and a larger sound.

How did the Spoonful sound develop?

Adding elements of jug band music to the Spoonful came out of the need to fill stage time, when we were playing eight sets a night. So we'd do whatever we knew, which were electric versions of songs that we knew from before the band got started. These songs started as filler on the albums, and then became the best parts of the albums. We had a silent mission statement: we did so many singles that we tried to make the next single sound completely different from the last one. Although there was some continuity. "Do You Believe in Magic" and "You Didn't Have to Be So Nice" were both shuffles and both used the autoharp. But the songs themselves were very different.

We realized that albums deserved more thought, so we decided to make sure that everything we put on the albums was worthwhile, and different from what we had done. We would do our best to introduce new musical styles whenever possible. (Guitarist) Zal Yanovsky was a wonderful mimic and could play all kinds of things. He would suddenly say, "Hey, I want to play like (C&W pianist) Floyd Cramer," and come up with a solo that sounded just like him. We spent a lot of time trying to do different styles of American music.

Are there unresolved issues with the Spoonful?

The Spoonful had a fun reunion when Paul Simon asked us to be in his movie *One Trick Pony*. I couldn't turn that down, but after it was done a door was closed. At one time the other guys offered Zally a chance to join without me and he turned them down. Then they asked me to join without Zally and I turned them down. It seemed like they were trying to cut Zally out, which was unfortunate.

About twice a year I get calls from places like casinos, where they offer to pay three times the normal fee if I bring in a band. For a while I got the guys from NRBQ. They're wonderful, but they are dispersed through different bands. The three members of the Spoonful are playing together, and I don't have problem with that. They do the material well, with the right energy. The fact that they are playing the old songs has freed me to do what I want.

You can tell that a lot of the Spoonful clips are lip-synced. What was going through your head at the time?

By the time the Spoonful went on these shows to lip-sync we had seen enough other groups do it, so we knew what we needed do to perform the songs without actually singing. When we did the high-visibility shows, like *Ed Sullivan*, we did what we were supposed to do. Even on those shows the camera would move by Zally, and you could see him mouthing, "I'm not really singing."

Sometimes we would do local TV shows where the DJ didn't know anything about us, and was just trying to get another group to fill up air time. For those shows we would come up with stuff to do, like we would change instruments, and just pantomime. This was kind of a wink to the real fans, who knew how it was supposed to be. It became a way for us to differentiate ourselves from the Serendipity Singers, or whoever came next.

You are famous for tripping while onstage at Woodstock. How important were the drugs, really?

We were all smoking pot. After a while Zally became more of a drinker, because he was Canadian. When he and (bassist) Steven (Boone) got busted and were forced to name their source it ruined the whole mood of the Spoonful. Which was ironic, because I was the big pot smoker. By the time I got to Woodstock I remained a pot smoker, but there was a natural high there. In an interview it is the easy thing to say, "Yeah, I was really high," but it was actually a very small part of the event. In fact, I had a small part of some pill that someone gave me before I went onstage, but it wasn't a real acid feeling.

What is harder to explain is the experience of being uplifted by the audience. So if someone says, "You must have been really high" I say, "Yeah, but I was high because a million people were watching me."

You've done a few instructional tapes for Homespun, which is run by Happy Traum. Is this a way to keep the folk tradition going in the digital age?

I used to think instructional tapes were kind of corny, so the first few times that Happy asked me to do one I turned him down. But after a while I gave in. Happy has a real understanding of the information that we are passing along. It has to do with both our backgrounds, when we started out we were idolizing those 70-year-old guys from the south who played the blues. It can be very hard to understand these guitar parts. So I decided to give something back while my knuckles are still working, so people can see the mysteries of some of these guitar techniques.

"Younger Generation" contained some real wisdom that fit any time. Did writing that song give you an edge in your own child-rearing experience?

I don't think that it made it any easier for me. I didn't have any articulate insights. It was the same road traveled by many of my contemporaries who were having children at the same time, where we were finding out that the fun and laughter is usually in retrospect, especially if you are raising a pair of intelligent, inquisitive boys.

SONICBOOMERS, APRIL 2, 2010

Baby boomers Applaud 1960s Icon Country Joe in Port Townsend

PORT TOWNSEND, WASH. —The 1960s musicians who still are touring often present nostalgia acts, playing a familiar selection of their hits that is designed to make the audience open its wallets.

Country Joe McDonald, who performed in Port Townsend on Thursday night to a crowd of about 100 people at the Upstage Theatre and Restaurant, follows a different path.

Instead of a strict recreation of the familiar, he provides a capsulated look of his career, incorporating satire, politics and history.

He does play the big hits from Country Joe and Fish at the end of the show, leading the crowd in a perfunctory version of "Gimme an F!" followed by the Vietnam-era anti-war anthem "I Feel Like I'm Fixin' to Die Rag."

The crowd participated enthusiastically, especially in "Fixin' to Die," when McDonald stopped singing and let the crowd take over for the complete "one, two, three what are we fighting for" chorus.

McDonald, 68, looks different from his famous poses at the Woodstock Festival in 1969.

Instead of tie-dye and long hair, he wore comfortable grandpa shoes, rolled-up khakis and a plaid shirt as he sat atop a stool to perform.

McDonald, born Joseph Allen, now is clean-shaven and short-haired.

But when he is singing an edgy political song or providing a wry comment, the glint in his eye tells you that it is the same guy from the history books, who helped redefine obscenity and continued a tradition blending of politics and music.

"We have all aged," said a fan who identified herself only as Eliska. "But not really."

Another difference between McDonald and a nostalgia act is its variety.

He launched into a long story about the rumored hallucinogenic properties of banana peels, when he was told that drying them yielded a substance as potent as marijuana.

"At the time we were eating nothing but peanut butter and banana sandwiches," he said. "We were throwing the peels away and wasting our money on weed."

The notion snowballed, resulting in newspaper headlines and rumors.

After a few months the Drug Enforcement Agency conducted a test and found the peels were benign, as far as getting high goes.

In the meantime, the media had reported the rumor and you couldn't find any bananas in Berkeley, McDonald said.

McDonald shifted gears, playing a song from the first-person viewpoint of an army nurse.

This was followed by a segment from a musical project he has worked on for several years, examining the life of nursing pioneer Florence Nightingale.

For those in attendance who remember the 1960s this was a more potent reminder of the era than any hit song.

Instead of today's carefully choreographed presentations, concerts were often ragged affairs that embraced a variety of styles and ideas.

And the audience pretty much went along with it.

McDonald also drew from his next project, a 13-CD box set that features music from the Vietnam era.

The set, titled *Next Stop, Vietnam*, features well-known tunes from Bob Dylan and the Doors, as well as songs written and recorded by the soldiers themselves.

Those attending Thursday's show, especially those who stayed for the second set, felt a personal connection with McDonald.

"Country Joe was a major part of my life," said Aaron Von Awe of Port Townsend. "His music meant a lot at the time. He was a major spokesman in the 1960s."

Von Awe brought along a worn copy of Country Joe and the Fish's fourth album, 1969's *Here We Are Again*, to get signed.

Von Awe saw McDonald perform several times in the 1960s along with people like Jimi Hendrix and Janis Joplin.

He was excited to see that McDonald play, but admitted that he hasn't played the Fish record for some time.

"My taste now runs to Miles Davis and other kinds of jazz," Von Awe said. "I remember the music well, but don't listen to it much anymore,"

The signed record, he said, would be a gift for his 10-year-old grandson.

"This is a historical relic," Von Awe said. "Maybe my grandson will listen to it someday and get a sense of what it was like back then."

Von Awe had the album signed and chatted with McDonald, after the singer's invitation that closed the first set, a merchandising pitch with a twist.

"If anyone wants to come up and tell me some stupid stories about the 1960s that you think actually happened, come on up and I'll listen," he said. "We are also selling CDs and posters."

McDonald began the first set with a loud "gimme an F," and the crowd responded. He didn't get to the "U" until the end of the second set.

"I usually dedicate this song to the commander in chief but haven't yet dedicated it to President Obama," he said. "We all still love him."

The crowd reaction to this was tepid.

"We still want to love him."

The reaction was only slightly more enthusiastic.

"We don't hate him as much as George Bush."

The crowd then came alive, and McDonald again shouted for an "F."

PENINSULA DAILY NEWS, May 30, 2010

Taj Mahal Highlight of Centrum Blues Fest

Taj Mahal, Port Townsend WA August 2011

PORT TOWNSEND, WASH. — Centrum's yearly Acoustic Blues Festival, always a special event for aspiring and accomplished blues musicians, was kicked into another realm this year with a whirlwind visit from Taj Mahal, the veteran singer of the blues world.

Mahal, 69, played a sold-out show Wednesday night in McCurdy Pavilion, leading a trio through an overview of his 40-year recording and performing career.

While the festival always gets a high-class headliner, Mahal's appearance was an extra treat made even more unusual with a one-hour "workshop" where he sat onstage in the 200-seat Wheeler Theater in front of a few hundred people and chatted about music, life and philosophy as if he were sitting on the back porch.

The other guy on this particular porch was Corey Harris, Centrum's artistic director for blues, who pointed Mahal toward topics and let it rip.

"It is important that musicians engage themselves in their community," Mahal said. "We need to see ourselves as part of the world and not think that the world revolves around us."

Mahal defies categorization. He is usually presented as a blues artist but regularly injects other stylistic elements into his recordings and performances.

He said musicians need to stay connected with all the sounds happening around them.

For this, he provided two polar examples:

Blues legend Robert Johnson, who died in 1938 at the age of 27 — his centenary is being observed this year — was plugged into all the contemporary sources of the 1920s, which he used as influences on his music.

And Mahal was probably the only Lady Gaga fan in the room.

"She can play piano," he said. "And she's figured out how to make money in a recession."

Mahal began recording in the 1960s when he played a lot of electric guitar but now presents a more organic sound using acoustic guitars and various instruments from around the world.

"The 1960s was good to me because it was when what I wanted to do and what was going on sort of collided," he said.

At the time, he got to meet a lot of his idols, sharing stages and stories in much the same way that budding blues musicians may one day recall Wednesday's workshop.

His music is nearly technology-free, but he has an appreciation for how the online world can spread musical ideas.

"We do need to put some energy into making sure that music is available," he said.

"The Internet has done a wonderful job in making people aware of what is out there, but it needs a conductor so people know where to go."

Technology has decreased the attention span of listeners and the time they spend with specific pieces of music.

"In the old days, people would live with a record for years until the grooves were worn off," he said. "Ask Keith Richards, he and Mick would listen to the same records over and over and learn everything on there."

Mahal said people shouldn't believe the stereotype that blues musicians are unintelligent because of the music's simplicity.

"A lot of times, musicians are playing for a lot of people who aren't highly educated, so they can't give them a 90-dollar word every time you turn around.

"But when they come forward and talk to you, you'd be surprised about all the things they know."

Mahal performed a number of solo shows at Centrum in the 1990s, but this was his first appearance at the Blues Festival, which began Sunday and extends through next Sunday.

In the past, the festival headliner has played Saturday night, but Mahal's schedule necessitated a midweek performance.

His appearance signals the midpoint of the festival, between the workshops and learning sessions attended only by the festival participants and the more public, open weekend fare.

This includes two nights of "Blues in the Clubs" on Friday and Saturday in which performers will fill seven locations in downtown Port Townsend, providing a varied lineup of one-of-a-kind jams.

For $25 a night, people can wander in and out of The Undertown, The Upstage, the Boiler Room, The Public House, Sirens, Key City Public Theatre and the Cotton Club to hear the music.

All of these venues except the Cotton Club will be familiar to Port Townsend natives and visitors. The new venue is the Cotton Building, 607 Water St., which is one of the highlights of the new Civic District renovation.

PENINSULA DAILY NEWS, August 4, 2011

Too Much, The Magic Boat

After forty years or so, the concert experience gets a little old even though some of the people who have playing through the ages still can put on a pretty good show. Even so, too many of us have lost interest in the endless hassles of scoring good seats, waiting on long lines and fighting the crowds. In the past we'd be herded through the turnstiles and start mooing, these days the crowds aren't worth it. Most nights, you'd rather stay home and watch a concert video than drive downtown to see the band play live, especially if you've seen them play a few times before.

Which is why music cruises, like the fifth annual Cayamo Cruise which ended on Sunday, represents the future of concert going, for people who are too old to deal with these indignities and still young enough to enjoy the music.

There are some perceptual obstacles. Those of us who fight the idea of getting old and falling into age stereotypes still hang on to a generalization of our own; that ocean cruises are excruciating events full of bad food and whining geezers. But Cayamo, as well as several events hosted by Sixthman and other companies, is not your grandmother's cruise. You might not go on a cruise anymore than you would go to Las Vegas or Branson, but as soon as you embark the excuses disappear. People go from "I can't believe you dragged me here" to "Can we book next year?" in seconds flat.

There are 30 or so artists, ranging from those of the highest visibility to people you have never heard of, performing in a variety of venues throughout the week. This less resembles a traditional cruise than the multistage festival except that waiting for a band while sunning yourself on deck is way better than waiting outside until the gates open.

The stats: The sold-out ship was carrying 2,383 passengers and 1,078 crew, with 938 of the guests onboard for the first time. There were a lot of repeaters, 544 in their second year, 389 in their third, 201 in their fourth and 145 who have attended all five times.

The most interesting numbers won't ever be compiled, like how many people who haven't seen each other for 40 years meet up, how many friendships begin there and how many lives intersect. I enjoyed some remarkable coincidences, meeting people who knew old friends of mine that I'd not seen in years. And I even met someone who was at the same Red Sox-Mariners game that I attended in 2006 (although he had better seats).

And since everyone on the boat is there for the same reason, it's easy to talk to anyone. You could meet someone from New Mexico and ask them if they knew an old friend and you didn't feel stupid for asking — maybe because in enough cases they had met who you were talking about. You need to adjust going home, where you aren't supposed to talk to strangers.

On Thursday night Buddy Miller took the stage with a rousing "Worry Too Much," which pretty much short circuited everything. After the music, his humility is the second-best part, after backing up everyone from Emmylou Harris to Robert Plant, he didn't quite believe that we were there to listen to his ownself. Words can't do it justice, so the best I can do here is to dub it as incendiary gospel rock.

Richard Thompson also reached the stratosphere with a late night trio performance, which he characterized as "a folk rock power trio, somewhere between Cream and the Kingston Trio," riffing a version of "Sunshine of Your Love" that borrows lyrics from "Tom Dooley" (at a previous performance he made the same joke, substituting the Jimi Hendrix Experience and Peter, Paul and Mary).

During this set he pretty much set the guitar on fire, appending familiar songs with long solos that spoke with volume. Comparing one musician to another is always a cop-out, but Richard and Jimi definitely overlapped. I saw Hendrix once and it took months to recover, Thompson is the only time since that I've seen a guitarist with such fluidity and imagination.

On the way out of the show I ran into Nancy Covey (Mrs. Thompson) who wryly said something like, "That wasn't too bad."

"That was hot," said I, saying the first word that popped into my head. But she had seen it before.

"Just doing his job," she said.

It was no surprise that these guys blew me away, I've been a Buddy fan since forever and a Thompson worshipper for 25 years before that. But while you may need a headliner to justify the cost and convenience of a cruise, the new discoveries are what make the trip special.

Thanks here to Shawn Mullins. I'd never heard him (so shoot me), but his warm enthusiasm made my unfamiliarity irrelevant. During "Lullaby," the Sixthman crew joined him onstage, dressed in white bathrobes. Everyone who saw this wanted to hug someone, cry or both.

Enter the Haggis was another find. These guys are having too much fun turning everyone they meet first into a fan and then a friend. It turns out the cruise was only the first step in fan interaction; the band is sponsoring an excursion where the fans get to ride around Ireland on a bus with the band.

Overall the cafeteria food was pretty good, although there were times where we filled a plate with what appeared to be appetizing food and threw it away before taking a second bite. This happened with the music too, where we left the table three times. One was Greg Brown, who just seemed abrasive.

Loudon Wainwright III opened with a song about fan obsession and dedicated it "to the guy who I just met in the elevator," a comment that seemed snarky and mean, especially since the satire didn't come across. And if we wanted to see endless tongue-flicking we would have taken the KISS cruise instead.

Lucinda Williams was never my favorite, and her show did nothing to change this. Her vocals were muddled, the band was too loud and she had no stage presence. She gave a more compelling performance later that night in an elevator, rambling about the cruise, her insomniac husband and that she didn't want to leave the boat. She was pretty looped, but unlike her show, you could figure out what she was saying.

I can hear the Lucinda brigade call for blood, but there are no accountants for taste. I came to hear Richard and Buddy and the rest was just frosting. While watching the aforementioned transcendent Thompson performance I saw people covering their ears and walking out. They may have been Lucinda's fans looking to open their minds, or maybe they'd had enough that day.

No matter, there was room on the boat for everyone-even those who didn't glom onto a particular artist. Many of the repeaters didn't really care who was on the bill; they trusted Sixthman's choices. As a first timer I'd never give anyone that much power, especially when thousands of dollars are involved. Next year I will be a bit more relaxed, lacking a compelling headliner I'll gamble there will be enough new things to make it worthwhile.

People used to love going to the Catskills, where they could catch vintage entertainers on their way down or new folks on their way up. Cruising is the new Catskills, with improvements: The food is better, the music more vital, clothes more comfortable and everything is in living color.

NO DEPRESSION, February 13, 2012

Hanging with Richard Thompson

Richard Thompson, Cayamo Cruise February 2012
Interviewed by phone, Port Townsend, WA to somewhere in California

Richard Thompson is messing with the standard performer/audience equation in two ways this year. There was his participation in the Cayamo Songwriters' cruise in February, and then there'll be his acting as an instructor at the first "Frets and Refrains" guitar camp. It takes place in July in a bucolic Catskill Mountain setting.

While Thompson has received steady accolades for ages, he is still the best guitarist that you have never heard of. This allows him to participate in these ventures, since the participants are more earnest admirers than dangerous wack jobs. While his fans will talk incessantly about his special talents, he is still faced with the same dilemma as all the musicians of his generation: How to keep audiences engaged and interested. Fans who meet him say he is a bit reserved but unerringly polite; he may not invite you to sit at his table but he is generous enough with his time to answer your questions and acknowledge your compliments.

Frets and Refrains takes place from July 16 to July 20 at the Full Moon Resort in Big Indian, NY, and isn't a cheap ticket. Combined lodging packages are available from other local hotels, but the only on-site rooms now available are upwards of $2,100, unless you are willing to pay $1,000 for a campsite. Thompson will teach an acoustic guitar master class every morning. About 30 slots are left at this writing.

Many amateur guitarists will jump at the chance to jam with Richard but I'll be sitting this one out. I'm a dedicated fan but don't play very well, and even if I did I'd find the format a bit intimidating. Thompson says he'll be welcoming of all skill levels, but I'd rather get my RT fix at Cayamo, where nothing is expected of me aside from getting to the show on time.

Thompson also released a special 45 rpm single in honor of Record Store Day on April 21, containing new versions of "Haul Me Up" and "1952 Vincent Black Lightning," along with a download code for a recent take of "Night Comes In."

How did it happen that you are teaching at a guitar camp?

I was approached. They run a series of camps that have Todd Rundgren and Dweezil Zappa, and some other people. They asked me to be part of the series, I thought it would be an interesting challenge so I said yes.

What's the curriculum?

My son Teddy will be teaching. Martin Simpson will be teaching fingerpicking styles, and there will be a couple of other people I can't mention yet. There will be various approaches; the class I am teaching will have its own angle on guitar playing and songwriting.

My main ambition with the camp is to get people to think in a different way about the guitar, to think out of the box and change their perceptions about guitar playing.

Who's coming so far?

There are a lot of different people in the 40-50-60 age group although there are some younger people as well. There are some people who are experts, which is kind of scary. I'll have to take a few lessons from them. I think the target is singer-songwriters who accompany themselves on the guitar, people who want to open up their brains a bit.

What if someone comes and asks you to teach them "Beeswing," or another one of your songs specifically?

I would give them the tools to play that song or play something like it. There are some people who will come because they like the music I play, or they like my guitar playing or my songwriting. That's understandable. I'd be happy to develop those people as much as we can, but we are hoping for 100, 110 people. There will be no time for a one-on-one; I won't be able to spend an hour a day with each person at the camp. But I can give them the tools that will set them on the road to play things like "Beeswing."

But a well-to-do person who is a pretty poor guitarist might decide that it was worth the money to hang out with you for a week.

I think that's just fine. When you go to a camp like this there is a kind of immersion aspect to it; you are rooming with guitarists, you are eating with guitarists, so there is a lot that is being passed around and filtered down. If you are a beginner the people that are on a higher level and pass it down to you. There will be be a bit of musical osmosis happening and being there will be an extraordinary experience. It will be a 24-hour musical immersion.

What do you expect to learn?

I expect to learn about my own playing and my style of music. Because I am self-taught I play in an unorthodox way. I don't do a lot of self-examination so it will be interesting for me to be more reflective about what I am doing. You always learn from other musicians; there are always musicians who have skill sets that you don't have. I'll be picking up a few tips from the students, some of whom may be more advanced than I am.

That would be hard to fathom.

Not really. There could be someone who has a great skill in bluegrass or flat-picking, things that I am not very good at that I can learn.

The camp is only for acoustic guitarists?

It will be an acoustic guitar camp. In the future we may do an electric guitar camp, but this is just for acoustic guitar.

You have a duality of skill with both acoustic and electric. What are the differences in your approach?

They are different instruments, although there are overlapping skills you can take from one to the other, both with the left hand and the right hand. Most electric guitar is played with lighter strings and there is a lot more string bending and solo playing.

With the acoustic guitar, you end up being more orchestral. You are trying to make the guitar sound as big as you can. There are more open strings and drones; you want to make more noise. If you are playing a solo, you are trying to self-accompany that solo at the same time.

When you are wrapped up in a particularly inspiring solo onstage, what is going through your head?

When you are really into it you are in a different state, there is almost nothing passing through your head. It's a little like an out-of-body experience. People sometimes describe it as the music playing itself. I think you go into a trance state. Another cliche is that the music plays you. I think these are all reasonable descriptions of something that's not really describable.

How did you get involved with Record Store Day?

I was asked to participate; it really wasn't my idea. If I were on my own I wouldn't know how to approach it. I was happy to be involved but I didn't have any songs chosen and we didn't have time to go into the studio and record anything. We had a 10-day turnaround from having the idea to having to have something pressed. We were looking for content and were lucky to find some live tracks that were available.

These were takes of songs that were already available. Why do people like hearing different versions?

I wish I knew the answer to that, but I'm glad they do. When you play live it's different every night, it's boring to always do the same thing. You play in a larger room, there is a different vibe, and that's why a different version might be better than the original. You go back several eras, where Louis Armstrong did many versions of the same song over a 20-year period, all recorded in the studio. And people do like to collect different versions; if you are a Grateful Dead fan you want to have every solo that Jerry Garcia recorded. Ever.

There are about 30 versions of Jimi Hendrix's "Red House."

Only 30? There is an unevenness to output, even in the case of Hendrix. There could be a version of "Red House" that isn't quite as scintillating as the others. With myself, on some nights I try very hard but nothing is going to happen. On the other hand there could be a live version that far outstrips the studio version. A collector is looking for different performances.

With your participation in the guitar camp and Cayamo are you trying to connect with your audience in a different way?

The audiences are changing. The record business is changing. Artists are looking for different things to do. As the record market has shrunk, artists are looking for alternate ways to reach their audience, and the audience isn't as predictable as it used to be. They don't just buy records and go to concerts; they are looking for different experiences.

There is a huge boom in musical cruises, which reflects a big lifestyle shift. With the music camp, it provides a different way to hang out with the artists that you admire and hear the music that you like.

Will you do Cayamo next year?

I've been asked and I think I will say yes. It really is quite fun. The audience loved it, and the fact that it sells out in hours is a testament to how much people enjoy that particular cruise.

For some people, one concert a month is enough, for others going to three, for or five concerts a day is just fine. They are very happy to spend a week listening to all kinds of music.

NO DEPRESSION, APRIL 6, 2012

Rodney Crowell's Melodic Literacy

Rodney Crowell, who turns 62 on August 7, has been on our radar since the 1970s, when he was the freshest horse in Emmylou Harris' songwriting stable. Since then he's been a left-of-center presence, a master of diverse categories but a prisoner of none.

He's always been a words guy, and his latest project, *Kin*, is a joint effort with writer Mary Karr that features Harris, Norah Jones, Vince Gill, Rosanne Cash and a great LeAnn Womack rave-up, "Momma's On A Roll." It's all about family and relationships; quirky folk and home cooked meals.

Adding to his lit cred he wrote a memoir, *Chinaberry Sidewalks*, which talked about his hardscrabble childhood and painted a remarkable portrait of his parents and their influence on his life and music. A lot of musicians are writing books to tell stories we already know in greater detail, but you can be halfway through Crowell's character-driven tale before realizing that he's not feeding us the true dope about Emmylou or Johnny Cash or life on the road. And that's a good thing.

This winter Crowell will appear on the Cayamo Cruise, joining Richard Thompson, Buddy Miller, Brandi Carlile and others to create a floating songwriter's paradise. This will be followed by *One Yellow Moon*, a duets album he recorded with Harris that has been in the works for a while.

So for Crowell, 62 looks as exciting as 26.

How did 'Kin' begin?

I sat down with Mary Karr, she's a great poet and a writer and was real supportive when I was writing the book, so we fell into writing songs. I wasn't thinking about making a record of any kind. I was just saying to her "you're brilliant, you're a language scholar, let's see what we can do. " It just caught fire.

After five or six songs I knew these weren't songs that I was going to put on one of my albums, this is a collection of paintings that we need to put on a wall somewhere.

We didn't set out to get a lot of people on the album on purpose. As we wrote the songs we realized that a lot of the songs had a female narrative and since Mary doesn't sing we needed a female voice. We thought we'd get one female voice to sing those songs and I'd sing the male parts.

Norah Jones was a big fan of Mary's and has recorded a couple of my songs, but she could only do one. Emmy hears about it, and it started to grow. It kind of made itself. A lot of my best albums kind of make themselves. There is a kind of art or music or storytelling that comes from a place where there is no design for a marketplace. These kinds of things have worked out better for me than when I was trying to anticipate what somebody wanted to hear.

I had a big success a few years back and didn't recover fully when it was time to move away from that, I tried to reclaim it and I failed. Somebody gave me too much money, more money than I could handle, so I tried to oblige them with something that wasn't true to my heart. Now no one's waving a lot of money at me so I just do what I want to do.

What worked, and didn't?

I made a few records, *Let the Picture Paint Itself* and *Jewel of the South,* if you put them both together you could get three quarters of a pretty good record. But I wouldn't buy those albums. *Sex and Gasoline* has some of my best work, that one was overlooked. It happens. There is a natural flow in an artist's career when things are happening in other corners of the room. You might have a really good piece of work that doesn't get noticed. It's not anyone's fault, it's not that people don't care, it just means that the universe is elsewhere.

And you can't force it.

I can't. Back at the Brill Building they certainly could do it but it was a different time. The language hadn't been poured over the coals. They were coming up with an interesting and compelling new language, and it is a lot harder to do that in 2012 than it was in 1967.

I work better when my intuition is leading the charge, if I follow my intuition and my heart chances are it will be more timeless. If my brain gets involved in trying to run the show chances are I'm going to come up short.

How did you end up on Cayamo?

I don't really know, someone suggested me. I'm a decent songwriter so there was a movement that said "you've never had this guy on the boat." I've gone on a boat before, Delbert McClinton has a blues cruise, I loved the music and the playing but the boats get a little queasy sometimes.

Will you bring a band?

I haven't made up my mind, when I get some more information I'll see what works best. Since it's a songwriter cruise it might be better to be more acoustic. I attach a lot of importance to language, and I want people to hear the words. You want to move people and get people to move, that's the balance we need to strike.

Sometimes when I play with a drummer and electric guitars I can't hear anything. The other night my band was playing and they were really blowing, then I came out for the encore and sang with Emmylou. Her band was so quiet and I could hear every note I was singing. So I was thinking "why can't my guys behave?"

What's next for you?

There is the duets record with Emmy, we just finished mastering it today and it will be out early next year. With Emmy and I, our paths have crossed, we came up around the same time in the 1970s, and we always talked about making a record of songs that we liked and both wanted to sing. There are old Roger Miller and Kris Kristofferson songs, we thought that we don't have to write these songs so we might as well just have fun.

I also have another solo album that's almost done. So I have some stuff in the pipeline.

If you were building the Mt. Rushmore of American music which four artists would you include?

Hank Williams, Howling Wolf, Ray Charles and Bob Dylan. I'd also have to add Merle Haggard and Johnny Cash. I'm going to need six.

NO DEPRESSION, AUGUST 5, 2012

Ian Hunter's Campaign Swing

SEATTLE— Ian Hunter has drawn the same fans for ages and they are all here tonight, but this is more than just All the Old Dudes. A new album, a crack band and perfect weather prove that people who've followed Hunter for all this time were right in the first place.

When I'm President, released Sept. 4, is comfort music for classic rock refugees who crave new combinations and will feel just fine if they never hear "Won't Get Fooled Again" again. It's typical as Hunter albums go, with odes to rock and roll mixed with bombastic power ballads and a few surprises. One is "Fatally Flawed," which starts out gentle and then explodes; two or three times.

"I love the bombast, and how that song goes from naught to ten." Hunter said.

"I love it when the high drama kicks in."

Another surprise is the title track, a literate rant about the elections and the political system. It's easy to scorn artists who babble on about politics as they are often stupid, disagree with what we know is the truth or both.

"When I'm President" just clicks. The tune a direct descendent of the buoyant rock and roll that has been Hunter's calling card from the beginning. And at the break he hits the nail on the head, politically speaking.

"You come in with the best intent when you become president.....but something happens to you up on the hill, it's business as usual. So you want to buck the system? Welcome to the pit and the pendulum."

"I'm pretty down the middle. But I don't like the Republican people, it's a great idea but some of the people who've got a hold of it are out of control," Hunter said.

"It seems like everyone is angry at everyone else and that needs to change. But I don't really want to be president, it's a horrible job. The very last line in the song is 'when I'm president pigs are gonna fly so it can be taken as a guy spouting off in a bar. Which is sort of what I'm doing." This particular night Hunter and band whip through an hour set of career high points. Four of them were album openers, so it feels like a hit parade. As he's winding up "Sweet Jane" he says "that's it" and walks off the stage. The crowd knows there is more to come as "All the Young Dudes" is yet unplayed.

He returns with "Roll Away the Stone," "Saturday Gigs" and "Dudes," which he's played thousands of times but still keeps fresh. The song goes on forever and the crowd does the back and forth wave that started when the song was a hit. Some of the people who waved back then are probably here tonight.

"The audiences haven't really changed, they're still crazy, but we are seeing a few more younger people because the older ones have all tottered off," he said.

"But they act the same. When we had the (2009 Mott the Hoople) reunion in London they were standing up like they always did. I'd say 'sit down, there's a seat right behind you' but they never did."

A lot of Hunter's contemporaries won't play anything more recent than their old hits, but he mixes in some new stuff.

"Portland isn't one of my strongholds but last night we played six new songs, I thought it was a bit too many but the band had rehearsed them and they sounded great," Hunter said.

"We surrounded it with stuff they knew but it didn't seem to matter, they accepted it like anything else."

Hunter said he tries for a balance of one third new, one third solo hits and one third Mott "but it doesn't always happen that way."

Hunter, 73, faces the same challenges as all his contemporaries, how to keep and satisfy the audiences who showed past passion for his music. He doesn't seem to have a plan, aside from writing an interactive Q&A on his web site every month. This shuttles between the informative and the obscure, he sometimes provides details but often the notations are clipped: "Irena, Sorry, I don't."

But "Horse's Mouth," as the column is known, can be a lot of fun; especially for fans who get a personal nod from Hunter that no one else can share.

"I do my best to answer people and just go on from there," he said.

"They've all been very nice to me and I feel that I owe it to them to answer their questions because they've looked after me for all these years.

"But before the Web there were pockets of fans everywhere, we've given them a way to talk to each other. And we get a lot of travelers at our gigs, which is something that never happened before."

Even has Hunter releases compelling new music he will always be tied to his past. Strolling around the festival grounds today I'm telling people I am going to see Ian Hunter. They say "who's that?" and when I mention Mott the Hoople they go "oh, yeah."

Hunter's fame heading Mott was an aberration, it was preceded by years of sweaty gigs in small places and followed by years of "Who's that? Oh, yeah."

According to the documentary "Ballad of Mott the Hoople" these early gigs were full of people who saw the band as their own and were left behind when they became glam rock kings. Those of us who were not early fans then picked up the torch, making it bigger although not always better.

The circle is complete. Hunter is now greeted by an enthusiastic cadre who claim him as their own. There may be other artists following a similar path and generating a replica of the same excitement, but right now this is the center of the world for us.

He didn't plan this, or any other phase of his career.

"I don't have any ambition, I never did," he said.

"I sort of do what I want to do and the next thing comes along, although right now there are 40 gigs I have to play."

ROCK'S BACKPAGES, SEPT. 4, 2012

Tom Rush: No Regrets

Interviewed in person, Kent, WA

Tom Rush is telling a story about writing "No Regrets," the potent end-of-relationship ballad for which he is best known. It was, he said, written for a woman he had not yet won, and figured that it would help his chances. It worked, as she was then pictured on the cover of *The Circle Game*, his breakthrough 1968 album.

The story continues, about how the song becomes a self-fulfilling prophecy. The relationship ends, and the woman departs. To Venice. Where she drowns. Rush sobs. The audience laughs. And the story continues, adding to an evening that combines tall tales about modern life and songs about what it takes to live it. Folksingers have offered combinations of stories, songs and miscellaneous observations forever, and it still works when done right.

"Did I mention that I have a kid in college? he says before the intermission, prime time for merchandising. "If everyone buys a CD, then he can go to college. And if everyone buys three CDs then he won't need to go to college. He'd like that."

Rush recorded nine studio albums between 1963 and 1974, and just released a tenth, *What I Know*, earlier this year. He says it is "maybe the best thing I've done." Great records are more than just music and lyrics; their effect also depends on where you were when you first heard them. So even if *What I Know* doesn't whack you upside the head today, it could achieve future greatness.

During his touring years he was all about telephones and managers and where he had to be at noon. Today, he takes short mini-tours, traveling solo with suitcase and guitars in hand, handling all the merchandising and performing all the roadie's duties on his own. He spends ten minutes in the lobby prior to the show, demonstrating how to run the credit cards. He isn't often recognized on planes, except for some security personnel who have left little fan notes in his guitar case.

The venues have also changed, since the glory days of Carnegie Hall and the Kennedy Center. Tonight, he is scheduled in the performing arts center at the Kent-Meridian High School in Kent, Washington. It's quite an ordeal getting in, through miles of suburban clutter that leads to a labyrinthine palace devoted to secondary education. After asking directions from a series of clueless joggers we finally find the right door, which leads into a school lunchroom.

The "hidden" auditorium is posh and comfortable with a great line of sight. If nothing else in today's world is certain it is clear that kids these days have a nice place to practice.

It turns out that the school setting is appropriate, as tonight's audience is the senior class. This same group could have gathered in 1970. Recognizing this, my 53-year-old companion notes that she is the youngest person in the room.

Rush not only plays a healthy two sets, but spends the intermission and post-concert period in the lobby signing autographs and hearing how much these songs meant once upon a time ago. He's heard it all before, but still listens politely. "I don't mind the personal contact," he said. "I answer the e-mails folks send me and go out and chat with them at halftime and after the show. These people have paid my rent for 50 years so the least I can do is go out and say hello."

Rush is best known as a "folksinger," which has several definitions. One of the most widely held is someone who travels from town to town, learning a song in one place and teaching it in another. Modern times have complicated things, but in some ways it has stayed the same. An illustration comes later during the protracted "No Regrets" intro, when Rush tells of how a few lines from the song "magically appeared" into the head of a singer, who added it to what he was singing at the time.

This would be only flattering, except the singer was that guy in U2, and his memory twitch found life on TV, on a DVD and in live performances. Pretty soon Rush paid them a cordial visit, but reminded them after all this re-use "there were royalties involved."

We don't have the documents, but Rush doesn't seem especially upset about the situation. "No Regrets" was a hit for the Walker Brothers, which Bono probably heard growing up. Perhaps he in fact spontaneously recalled the song and thought he'd give them a plug.

Except for the fact that good folk singing is a little like good journalism: You should always attribute your sources. And if there are two types of musicians, Rush belongs to the category that is scrupulous about acknowledging song's origins.

For this year's senior class, there are three killer songs. These are predictable: The aforementioned "No Regrets," Joni Mitchell's "Urge for Going" and "Child's Song." Tonight's audience most likely first heard this powerfully affecting song about leaving home in proximity to their own experience, now they hear it from the opposite side. Rush himself is visibly moved at the song's close, choking back his own emotions before swinging into "Who Do You Love." He asks our permission to play one more song because he does not want to leave us with a sad one.

Yes, he's done this before. But it is still authentic. Much like a good folk song.

Rush talks about following the old blues guys around Boston, acting like a star-struck geek. Now, he is the old guy. And we hope that somebody is following Rush around and learning his tricks, because even in these new media days there are some things you need to learn on your own. Rush has a few contemporaries left, still making new music and avoiding the indignity of playing a string of hits to people in casinos.

"Sometimes we sit around and tell war stories," he said of his old fraternity. "But most of us focus on what is going on now, not what happened before. The road behind us is less interesting than what's coming up."

SONICBOOMERS, JULY 31, 2009

A Fan's Notes

Once you've been writing for a while you instinctively know what to include and what to leave out. There are things that you would never bring up because it would cast the subjects (who you wanted to impress) in an unfair or negative light. Or you left stuff out because it wasn't relevant to the story or might harm your own reputation. For obvious reasons, you can't talk about how you smoked pot with Barry Gibb because it would mean admitting that you smoked in the first place, especially if you want to use the published clip to help get your first job.

But you ended up telling stories about details that no one would care about, other than another fan.

You tell these stories for a while and then forget about them. Years later you are stringing together a selection of published pieces when you are asked to frame the collection with some remembrances and "where are they now?" section.

Some of these vignettes are longer than the others, and there are some artists where there is no more to say aside from what is included in the original articles.

Everything else here is 100 percent true, to the best of my recollection. Some of these have been told many times, while there are others I've kept to myself because they make me look like a bit of a jerk. When you are somebody's fan you end up saying and doing dumb things that you kick yourself about right after saying them. But when 60 fast approaches it becomes time to come clean.

Ellen 'Tori' Amos is an internationally known singer-songwriter and chanteuse. Most recent new album: 2011's *Night of the Hunters.*

I first met Ellen in a posh Washington, D.C. hotel in 1980 where she was a 17-year-old cocktail pianist. I made her the focus of an article about piano bars, and I'd go to see her every few months at Georgetown's Marbury House. Once she asked me what song I wanted to hear, I answered with "Silver Springs," a then-obscure Stevie Nicks song. She played it well, but on the record Stevie sings two voices and fades, while Ellen had to sing all the verses twice. She could do that with any song, play it off the top of her head. The last time I saw her she was moving to California and asked me if she should change her name to Tori. "I don't know," I said. "I kind of like Ellen."

Journalism rules dictated that little Ellen couldn't get her own piece, so I included a couple of other pianists in the article. One was so dreadfully boring that I excised her from this version of the piece; I just didn't have the energy to retype her quotes. The second, Michael Moore-Kelley, is still doing the cocktail piano thing in Florida. After I retyped the piece I sent him a copy but he didn't respond.

The Beach Boys are currently touring with Brian Wilson. Most recent new album: 2012's *That's Why God Made the Radio.*

The Beach Boys were the subject of my first published pieces, a pair of reviews for my high school paper (not included). Also left out was a screed written for the *Washington City Paper* in 1983 covering the band's White House appearance, which was less an account of the event than an angry, poorly written essay about how the band peaked in the early 1970s and went downhill after they changed their repertoire to include a majority of surf and car songs. This was my premise, which I swore to repeat until things changed, or someone listened.

I talked to band members Mike Love and Bruce Johnston for a 1998 piece in *USA Today,* after which time Johnston told me the band had fired founding member Alan Jardine because he was so difficult. Johnston warned me to stay away from Jardine, calling him "litigious." I ignored the warning, since it was my opinion that Love and Johnston were the ones who were mismanaging the Beach Boys by playing all the surf crap and staying clear of the more artsy stuff.

I covered Jardine the following year, driving to a southern Oregon casino to see his band perform. The review was my first piece for *Rolling Stone Online*. The repertoire was still mostly surf but Jardine pushed the right buttons with me by pledging allegiance to their better stuff and saying that he wanted to play more of those songs onstage.

Music coverage needs news to become a beat. In this case I glommed on to Jardine's legal fights with the rest of the band, in which he wanted to use a portion of the Beach Boys name for his band and the management refused. This culminated in a lengthy phone discussion with Jardine on Thanksgiving Day 1999, where he explained his case and I resolved to bring it to the public. This was heady stuff, spending turkey day on the phone with a Beach Boy, who seemed generally interested in my opinion about his place in the musical strata.

The resulting piece, "Beach Boy vs. Beach Boy," began as an advocacy piece for Jardine but found balance as soon as I talked to Beach Boys management. It's possible the management sensed my bias, but journalists have slagged Mike Love for years and they were willing to offer responses to Jardine's charges. The published piece was pretty evenhanded, even with my "bias" I had managed to portray both sides.

As the months proceeded the courts handed Jardine one defeat after another, for which I faithfully covered both sides. Jardine got crankier each time, until during one conversation he hinted legal action if the story didn't come out the way he wanted. I reacted like any other reporter who gets a legal threat, veiled or otherwise: I ended the conversation and resolved to never talk to Jardine without my attorney present. Which is a promise that I have managed to keep for ten years now.

The Bee Gees became inactive after the 2003 death of Maurice Gibb. Robin Gibb's 2012 passing ended the possibility of any partial reunion. Last album: 2001's *This is Where I Came In*.

I bought *BeeGees First* when it came out in 1967, and was always fascinated by their sound, how it seemed that one voice was actually three, and how colossally geeky Robin Gibb appeared. If someone who looks like that can make it, maybe I had a chance. I saw them twice in the early 1970s, once with an orchestra, and when they became available for interviews I drove to Philadelphia and did my best. Which wasn't all that bad, considering how green I was. I came up with relatively intelligent questions, and was able to spend two weeks that summer polishing it. We even went into their dressing room "for a minute" which turned into an hour. After a while Barry Gibb took out a joint, and I said "Oh, no, let me do the honors," and brought out one of mine which we smoked (Maurice and Robin abstained, with dirty looks). As a trade Barry gave me his joint, which I kept in a drawer before finally lighting it up months later, at which time I found it was hash and tobacco. It wasn't very powerful. So that probably means that Barry was more stoned that night onstage that he wanted to be.

During the interview the band told me about a movie they were planning called "The Bull on the Barroom Floor," which I mentioned prominently in my article. Months later, probably around the same time I smoked that joint, I met another kid at school who had interviewed the Bee Gees that summer, in Pittsburgh. He told me how they all went to a bar and decided to make something up for the next interview. They came up with a movie, called "The Bull on the Barroom Floor." They never made the movie or even brought it up in any other interview I read, although a biographer mentioned it in a book about the band.

Buffalo Springfield broke up in 1968 and reunited for performances in 2010 and 2011. They are currently on hiatus, again.

Most Buffalo Springfield fans never got to see them live, although by all accounts they were something to behold. For us, seeing Crosby, Stills, Nash and Young would have to do.

It was backstage at a CSN&Y show in 2000 where I heard the Buffalo Springfield box set (named, appropriately, *Box Set*) was nearing release. With Rolling Stone Online backing me up I did a little digging and tracked down a release date and ended up with phone interviews with three members of the band. Unfortunately none of them were Stephen Stills or Neil Young.

Bassist Bruce Palmer sounded pretty out of it, although it could have been the time zone. I managed to pull a few quotes out of him that were remotely useful. Drummer Dewey Martin was the opposite, I couldn't get him to stop talking. He was still miffed that Stills and Young wouldn't let Martin use the Buffalo Springfield name, and was especially mad at Young for holding up the release of *Box Set* and his expected royalties.

Guitarist Richie Furay was more helpful and objective. He also wasn't angry or invested in the idea of a reunion. He had quit the music business to become a minister in Colorado and was removed from the whole scene. He said he didn't go see CSN&Y when they were in town, due to a previously scheduled bible study class, but said he'd participate in a reunion if Steve and Neil put it together. Mindful of the illwill coming from Palmer and Martin, I asked if Buffalo Springfield would tour with a different bassist and drummer and he pointed out that "it wouldn't be a Buffalo Springfield reunion then, would it?"

During a trip to L,A., I was assigned to cover a Doors event at the Whisky a Go Go and made plans to meet Martin for dinner beforehand. He didn't show. I went back to the club when he came barreling in, apologetic and flushed. He was all ready to go 90 minutes before, but couldn't find his other shoe. It had finally turned up, as he proudly stuck out his foot.

After the show he drove me downtown to my hotel, telling me the same stories I'd heard a few times before. He suggested an early breakfast, or coffee. I demurred; after all I was in town to cover a computer convention. There was a time where I'd give up anything to hang out with a member of a great '60s band, even the drummer, but that ship had sunk.

Eric Burdon tours incessantly, mostly appearing in casinos. Most recent album: 2012' *Til Your River Runs Dry*.

I've wanted to talk to Burdon since I first saw him perform in 1983 with the original Animals. Once he started touring casinos I made an effort to write something several times, but I couldn't sell the idea. That changed in 2010 when I was working with Sonicboomers.com, and approached Burdon for an interview. I wrote his manager and she informed me that Burdon would not be interviewed in person or over the phone but would respond to questions by email. This was a bit off-putting, because I knew that I couldn't write an in-depth profile without some back and forth.

I pushed a little, with no luck. It puzzled me that Burdon would not want to talk to me and get his story out. Who did he think he was to miss this opportunity? After a while it evolved more into who do I think I am, to conclude that he would actually spend his valuable time going over the same old shit? He still talks to some publications when it suits him, but obviously shut down his interaction with the press some time ago. If I want to know about Burdon, I was told, just read his books.

After I saw him live I came up with another angle, to talk to his band. They may not have been the "originals" but they were a blast and provided some needed perspective and compelling stories. This led to a book idea, Ringers, where I sought to interview musicians who have taken the place of original band members; who make a good living and can hold their heads high. Maybe Ringers will happen, someday.

I later learned that Burdon's manager is also his wife. Not that I would have acted any differently, but it would have been nice to know.

T-Bone Burnett is best known as a producer of soundtracks and is credited with reviving the careers of many vintage musicians. Most recent album: 2008's *Tooth of Crime*. The first time I saw Burnett play he had a full band and opened for Richard Thompson, that night I liked T-Bone better than Richard. The last time I saw him it was in 2005, but he had changed. Before, he let us know he was way cooler than we were, but was still involved and engaged with the audience. Now, he was clearly playing for himself and his buddies, daring us to not understand. We really didn't. The wordy songs were dry and dead. On the way we coined a term for musicians and artists who don't really care what the audience thinks and commits especially grievous forms of musical masturbation; dubbing them as "sticky."

Crosby, Stills, Nash and (occasionally) Young tour the sheds and fairs every year with the same steadfast show, and when Young joins in, the show is elevated into the stratosphere. That is due to happen any year now. Most recent albums: 2004's *Crosby and Nash*, 2009's *Live at Shepherd's Bush* (Stills) and 2012's *Americana* (Young).

Graham Nash was part of the cadre of musicians involved in the convergence of music and technology in the early 1990s, during which time I made his acquaintance. I interviewed him several times about this blend, and he was always helpful and open. I never had any illusions that he knew who I was, since I didn't actually interview him in person until 2000.

That Portland show which was on Nash's 58th birthday ended up as an example of freelancer multitasking. I reviewed the show for *Rolling Stone.com* and did an interview with Crosby and Nash for a boomer web site called *MyPrimetime.com*. On the side I gathered the material for the aforementioned Buffalo Springfield piece. I was brought backstage and sat in the canteen, and my instructions were unexpected. I thought they'd tell me to stay away from the food. Instead, I was told in no uncertain terms that I wasn't to talk to Young or even look at him for too long.

After dinner I was led to Crosby's dressing room. Here was a guy I've wanted to meet and interview for years. I figured that he had much to say about a variety of topics and I wanted to mine that knowledge.

But he wasn't cooperating. He reminded me of a politician who answers the questions that he wants to, regardless of what you ask. He didn't really volunteer anything, and managed to weave in a reference to the kid who stood in front of a tank in China's Tiananmen Square the year before; the subject of a song on the new LP.

Nash came in late, and we started joking around about his tardiness, and why Crosby always had to do all the work. Crosby said something about having written all of Nash's songs.

"Both of them?" I said.

Oops.

We were all professionals, and the interview limped to its inevitable conclusion. I've talked to Nash a few times since then and I'm sure he doesn't remember any of this. From then on I instituted a new rule: If I feel like saying something wise or sarcastic in a celebrity interview, I should just hold my tongue.

Come to think of it, that's a pretty good rule even when you're not talking to a celebrity.

Roger Daltrey is still lead singer for The Who. Most recent new album: 2006's *Endless Wire*.

I got lucky with this one. He was touring solo at the same time I was writing for Sonicboomers.com and set up a phone chat. It was pretty nerve-wracking, talking over Transatlantic lines while trying to suss out the next question and hoping the tape recorder was working. At the show I saw quite a few people with the Backstage Package, who had paid $300 above the ticket price for the privilege of a handshake and a picture. As a fan I wouldn't like that much, and suspected that Daltrey didn't either.

I've only collected autographs twice, from Tom Rush and Diana Rigg, because I didn't know better. If I'd kept it up I'd have quite a collection by now, but I think that I got a better deal. Having talked to someone and published a piece is a more valuable souvenir than an autograph or a picture.

Joe Ely continues to perform and record. Most recent new album: 2011's *Satisfied at Last*.

Music lovers are an odd bunch and you make friends you never forget. When I lived in Albuquerque I hung around with a guy named Bill Simoneau who got me jobs on stage crews and selling t-shirts. Bill was a one-of-a-kind oddball with perfect pitch, and a few years later he got a job as Joe Ely's guitar tech. I was then living in California, and was there the night that Ely's equipment van was broken into and he lost all his gear which was never recovered.

The next year the band returned and I toured around with him, going to the Apple Company picnic south of San Jose. The band was on a huge stage surrounded by bales of hay, and they had room to stretch. This was in contrast to the next night when they played the small Cotati Cabaret north of San Francisco, where people were packed in like sardines. Joe seemed like a nice enough guy, and Bill set up an interview where Joe talked about his new album, as well as his project of writing a new national anthem.

The anthem project never happened. I heard later that Joe traveled to D.C. with co-authors Terry Allen, Jimmie Dale Gilmore and Butch Hancock, and performed 13 proposed songs at the Smithsonian. The tape was lost in a fire a few months later, and was never recreated.

The Go-Go's broke up in 1986 and have toured sporadically since. Most recent new album: 2001's *God Bless the Go-Gos's*.

My interaction with Go-Go's was an unpleasant experience, both for me and them. They made it clear they really didn't want to be interviewed and provided perfunctory answers, which made my lame questions sound even worse. I managed to pull out a decent profile piece, but am grateful this opportunity occurred before Q&A opportunities were the norm and the quotes needed to stand on their own. Still, I was doing my best to make an impression, asking why "Go-Go's" was possessive instead of plural. Belinda Carlisle either didn't know what I was talking about or pretended to be stupid. I told this story for about a year until a colleague came up with a reason that made sense: "If it was written as a plural you would pronounce it go-goss.'"Too bad Belinda didn't come up with that explanation on her own.

You expect spin in any interview, but outright lies are still disturbing. In this case I ended up repeating the explanation that Charlotte Caffey couldn't play her guitar parts on the new album because of carpal tunnel syndrome, which no one had heard about at the time. It turned out she was addicted to heroin. You wouldn't expect the truth in this case, but still feel stupid for spreading the untruth.

Arlo Guthrie is still an activist, heads the Guthrie Center in Great Barrington, MA. Most recent album: 2007's *In Times Like These*.

I first heard "Alice's Restaurant" in 1968 on a college radio station. My parents had gone out and I was glad to be free of them for the evening. We did speak occasionally, and the next day I told them about "Alice" since my appreciation of folk music had come from them. The Weavers, Joan Baez and Peter, Paul and Mary were played constantly in our house and we used to all gather around the TV to watch "Hootenanny."

My mother then told me they had seen Arlo play "Alice" the night before, at the same time I was listening to him on the radio. I was pretty mad then, years later I realized they were probably glad to be free of me for the evening.

George Harrison died in 2001.

Getting into see George Harrison was a harrowing ordeal. I sold the idea to the *Toronto Globe and Mail* and lined up a phone interview, until a Globe editor questioned why a Canadian paper was paying a guy in San Francisco to talk to someone in Los Angeles. So I drove straight to L.A. to do the interview in person. I waited in a room for hours not knowing whether it was going to happen or not, with nothing but an advance cassette of his new album (*Cloud Nine*) for company.

I knew he was in the next room, riding the interview mill, but the first time I saw him was in the men's room at the next urinal. I resisted the urge to say anything, knowing that I would get my chance.

I wasn't really paying attention, letting the tape recorder do its thing and trying to phrase the next question.

Afterwards I got into the car and drove north after popping the cassette into the car stereo. It was then I realized two things: I could have asked him anything, he seemed so willing to chat. And the results were, as interviews go, pretty lame. While I self-syndicated the piece to several papers across the country, I realize that it lacked substance.

This section opens with the original Globe and Mail piece followed by a complete transcript of the conversation. This interview was conducted prior to the prevalence of Q&A format interviews, so the contrast is worth noting. The transcript has some bonus material, such as Harrison asking me if I wanted him to relate something that no one else knew about The Beatles and I said no. I had then what was a fatal flaw in an interviewer: a respect for the subject's privacy.

In 2008 I received an email from Martin Scorcese's "people" asking if I still had the audio from my interview with George, to be used in a documentary then being prepared. I used to tape all my interviews but they had degenerated a long time ago and had been tossed away, so I missed the chance to be part of the movie that was released on the tenth anniversary of Harrison's death.

There was some regret about this missed opportunity, but mostly it felt like I dodged a bullet. I wasn't especially bummed about losing the tapes, because I had never listened to any of them after completing the transcription. I may have evolved into a decent writer, but my interview voice isn't ready for the radio. I take too long to get to the question, and can't hide my nerves. So even if I ended up getting some pretty good answers, I'd cringe if anyone heard my end of the conversation. Especially with George Harrison.

Garth Hudson lives in Woodstock and tours occasionally. Most recent album: 2010's *Garth Hudson Presents: A Canadian Celebration of The Band*.

My visit with the Hudsons is best described in *The World According to Garth* contained here. His three nights in my hometown (Port Townsend, WA) was pretty challenging, especially for those who wanted him to follow any kind of program. Some of this was basic, like trying to get him onstage at a time approximating showtime. Other goals were unrealistic, like my desire to get him to a church with a huge antique pipe organ and make a video of the event.

At first I was willing to give up quite a bit for the privilege of standing next to the flame. Whatever money I "invested" would be paid back in some ephemeral way. But a line was crossed a few days in when it felt like they were taking advantage. Like when I'm standing off to the side of the club and Maud catches my eye and gives me what I thought was a warm smile. She followed that up with a request/demand for something. It strikes me that Garth and Maud (and other formerly famous to some degree) coast through life while people offer help, buy them meals and generally take care of their needs. It is still a thrill to meet someone from the golden age, buy them a steak or a beer, and hang out for a bit. But sometimes when you get too close it ruins the illusion.

It took a few months to gain some perspective and retroactively adjust my expectations. I was approaching the Hudsons' visit as a journalist, intent on capturing and interpreting the moment to provide a different aspect on a time and place that is too closely examined. If I had approached it as a fan I may have enjoyed myself a bit more.

Garth is not like you or me. Geniuses operate on a different level than the rest of us, so we can't really expect them to get to the church on time or to agree that something that seems obvious to you as good idea is worth pursuing.

I've spent much of my life listening to music and then trying to go deeper; getting to know the people who make the music. This time I questioned the need to peek behind the curtain.

Rickie Lee Jones continues to tour and record sporadically. Most recent album: 2009's *Balm in Gilead*.

Up until 2007 when I first interviewed Jones I'd either talk to subjects on the phone or in person. Jones, or her management, suggested that I send her questions through e-mail. I'd only been on the Internet about two years at that point and was a bit skeptical, the new media offered no opportunity for interaction and allowed the subject complete control over what was answered. But a chance to write about Jones and an assignment from *USA Today* convinced me to play along.

The good news was that I didn't have to transcribe any tape or rely on inaccurate notes; the quotes were presented in easily editable form to be woven into the story. The results were pretty good, and the next time I interviewed Jones for *Rolling Stone.com* I didn't even ask to talk to her on the phone. The e-mail format suited Jones well, and also removed the possibility of any nervousness or disconnect on my part.

The Kinks. On hiatus. Last new album: 1992's *Phobia*.

The Kinks are one of the most examined and discussed bands, their twisted history often channelled into tales of underappreciation and the unfairness of the world. Which reflects the lives of the (predominantly male) fans who have chosen them as an avatar.

I was one of those fans. Maybe I still am. But there are mitigating factors. When I started writing my mission was to convince people to listen to the music I knew was great, and I unleashed a half-dozen persuasive essays that appeared in college papers and other minor publications throughout the country. No matter they were all based on John Mendelsohn's literate liner notes for *The Kink Kronikles,* these early pieces taught me the value of originality and objectivity. Which my own efforts generally lacked. I learned that people didn't need to hear about every album or local show by the Kinks, or anybody else.

I also saw The Kinks perform about a dozen times between 1972 and 1984. Most of these shows fell short of expectations, and a few were downright dreadful. I loved them just the same. We can borrow the shopworn sports metaphor, I was professing loyalty to the underdog home team, who will do so much better the next time.

I interviewed Ray Davies over the phone in 1986 and had a short backstage chat with Dave Davies in 2002. Both are included here. I nearly landed another interview with Ray in 2012 as this book was going to press, and would have held things up for its inclusion. I wasn't overly upset when the interview fell through. It's not that I'm that much less of a fan, I've only managed expectations. If you tell people that a certain band is great for 30 years and they don't listen you stop trying. It's the classic definition of insanity. And I wasn't sure what I could ask Ray a question that he hadn't heard and answered before many times.

The regret kicked in a few weeks later when Ray closed the Olympics. If I had landed that interview the topic would have come up and I would have added something to the conversation. Which is always the point.

Cyndi Lauper has evolved into a GLBT pioneer and Celebrity Apprentice contestant. Most recent album: 2010's *Memphis Blues.*

Hooking up with Rolling Stone.com gave me a bit more respect but not a lot more room, I still had to keep it to seven hundred words. That didn't bother Cyndi, she was making darn sure that she got her message across.

I spent about eight hours with her. I attended an afternoon performance at the local Borders, then got in the tour bus and rode to the venue. We talked for a while before the show, and afterwards when Cher was onstage. I missed all of Cher's show, aside from the beginning when she came down from the rafters in a feathery outfit singing "I Still Haven't Found What I'm Looking For."

I told Cyndi how much I liked her swamp version of Joni Mitchell's "Carey" from a TV special, and she related a long, detailed story about how she had a vision of the song, to do it slow, but the band wouldn't co-operate in rehearsals. She rehearsed the way the band wanted it but in performance counted off a slow tempo so they had no choice but to follow. The video of this remarkable performance has never been officially released although you can find it on YouTube.

It echoed what Rickie Lee Jones had said a few years ago, that a lot of musicians didn't take direction from women. I found this hard to believe. I mean, if Cyndi or Rickie Lee told you to do something a certain way, why wouldn't you?

We talked in the bus back to the hotel and out in the street for a while. I was losing interest, and had run out of tape. It was 10:45, and the last ferry home was 11:15. Ten minutes, fifteen, twenty. I didn't have the ability to shut her up so just let her wind down. I ran like hell and just made the boat.

Nils Lofgren is now guitarist for Bruce Springsteen's E Street Band. Most recent new album: 2011's *Old School.*

What does Nils have in common with Tori Amos? They are both from the D.C. area and I first met them when they were 17. Nils was a year ahead of me at Walter Johnson High School, but had dropped out before I got there. He was the local hero, and I was excited to interview him in 1983. We met at my parents' house, which was just down the street from his parents. I wrote the interview and set out to sell it but found no interest so I went to Plan B, a local arts paper called the Unicorn Times. They didn't pay, but let me do what I wanted.

A year later Nils joined the E Street Band, at which time it would have presumably been easier to sell the story, but by that time it would have been a different one.

Roger McGuinn tours small halls with an autobiographical show. Most recent album: 2012's *CCD*.

McGuinn's been around a long time, and has perfected the art of managing a dual private and public persona. He answers questions from reporters, signs autographs after a show and participates in the "meet and greet" ritual when asked. But there are lines you can't cross. He won't talk about David Crosby, not actually refusing to answer but deflecting the query in a way that makes follow-up impossible. The best word to describe him is "gentleman;" he is polite and refined, helpful, but is not too forthcoming with his private thoughts.

I interviewed him over the phone prior to his appearance at a small theater in Bremerton, Wash. His show consists of stories and songs, including some of the hits while providing a historical background about the 1960s Folk Boom. I wasn't the market for this because I lived through that era and knew pretty much everything about it. Except there were a few nuggets I had not heard before.

One of my favorite McGuinn tracks was 1976's "Dreamland," a Joni Mitchell song which he lifted into another realm with the help of Mick Ronson. Mitchell eventually recorded the song as a jungle chant, which wasn't nearly as good. For me, McGuinn's version was one of the greatest songs from a great decade.

At the Bremerton show I mentioned to McGuinn's wife that I loved the song and regretted that I had never seen him perform it onstage with Ronson, and guessed that it was a song he wouldn't play onstage any more. But in the middle of his seemingly structured historical show, he played the multiversed song. It turned out that Camille McGuinn had phoned him backstage and made the request on my behalf.

He messed up some of the verses and played the Joni Mitchell version, but it was still a great moment.

Keb' Mo.' Most recent album: 2011's *The Reflection*.

I was on a promo list for any CDs with added content for inclusion in a *Washington Post* column "CD+ What." One day I received Keb Mo's *Just Like You*. I have no recollection of the digital content, but it turned out that he was appearing in my town that week. It was a magical time, an era when writers were revered and outlets were plentiful and I was able to quickly sell the piece to the *Mr. Showbiz* web site.

I met Mo,' whose real name is Kevin Moore, in the lobby of his downtown Portland hotel. After the interview he asked if I knew about any local music stores because he needed some effects pedals. I took him to Apple Music downtown where he tried out the gear. The obsequious sales dude asked Moore what he was doing in Portland, the reply was "I'm doing something at The Zoo." Which was actually headlining a show for its summer concert series. We left the store and the clerk was no wiser.

Ronnie Lane died of complications surrounding MS in 1997.

When I met Lane in San Francisco he had already been sick for years. It was the only interview I ever conducted where the subject was lying down, and the setting--a threadbare hotel room with barely enough room to sneeze-added to the melancholy. He spoke in a weak voice and I had to move the tape recorder onto his pillow. Interviews are by nature an invasion, but this was the first time I actually felt guilty about doing my job.

While he didn't make any records after that time he hung on for longer than expected; living on for ten years after my interview. I'd been a fan of Lane and the Small Faces since the early 1970s and was gratified that he was getting some respect even as his health declined.

Respect doesn't matter if you don't have health care, and Lane struggled to the end. Two years later Rod Stewart released a tribute to Lane, a recording of "Ooh La La," the title track from the Faces' fourth album. The story is that Stewart skipped the original session because he was losing interest in the Faces, forcing Ron Wood to sing lead.

It's a good thing that Stewart was absent from the original since Wood's version was a great record that has become a pub rock classic. Stewart did the song justice, but you wonder why he didn't record it five years earlier when the royalties would have increased Lane's quality of life.

Noel Redding, Jimi Hendrix' bassist, died in 2003. I met Noel Redding at the opening of the Seattle's Experience Music Project in 2000. He didn't have a very high profile and acted like an uninvited guest, although once people knew who he was they were awed. He seemed to have made peace with Janie Hendrix, who controls the Hendrix purse strings, and said that he "had it on paper that I will be paid," but didn't know how much. A few years later I heard that he wanted to talk again, that he had some things to say about the estate. He couldn't come to the phone or write out the answers, but offered to take written questions which would be read to him and recorded. This was a most unsatisfactory interview since I wasn't in the room. There was no way to interact, sense an answer's nuance or follow up. With all that, he didn't say anything that I could use in a published piece. But it would be cool if I could dig up that tape.

Diana Rigg was once a sex symbol, now a Dame who plays a lot of really intense older women on PBS and elsewhere. Rigg was in D.C. for more than a month acting in *The Misanthrope* at the Kennedy Center. I hadn't a clue as to what the play was about but was dazzled by her performance. A few days later I caught her on the way into the theater and gave her a fan letter, she then left a message with my roommate that I was to appear in the same spot at 6 p.m. Friday, and I would get 30 minutes.

It was the worst kind of interview, in which you don't really listen to the answers because you are thinking about the next question. On one level it doesn't matter since it's all on tape and you can sort it out later as long as you get all the questions asked. The drawback is that you don't really engage in the conversation.

(The version presented here was created in 2009 from the original transcript, which I found in a musty box, editing in the best quotes and making it seem like a single, intelligent conversation between a sharp interviewer and a literate subject).

I wrote it up for the school paper, must have been about 2,000 words. I didn't leave anything out. I don't know if anyone ever read the whole thing. I wrote another version of the piece, took the train up to New York and took it to *Ms.*, which unsurprisingly passed.

Coincidentally or not, Rigg was then in New York for the play's Broadway run. I packaged a copy of the article and a short note and took it to her at the theater. This time the stage door guy let me right in, and I surprised her while she was wearing a nightgown and a stocking cap. I got out of there fast. A few months later I was in London where the play had traveled and left her another note.

At the time I called it devotion and admiration. These days such behavior is known as stalking. I was certainly born at the right time; if I acted like this today I'd be arrested.

Mick Ronson died in 1991.

Getting a record review published in the *Washington Post* was a pretty heady accomplishment for a 20-year-old. I had written a review of Dylan's *Blood on the Tracks* the month before and had taken it down to the Post. There was no security, so I was able to go right to the arts editor's office. He read the piece on the spot, said it was good but they had already assigned someone to review the album, and that I should try with someone who wasn't so well-known. I picked Ronson, who had just released a passable album, and exaggerated its importance. The piece was accepted by the *Post*, which probably had something to do with getting me into journalism school.

I booked an interview with Ian Hunter and Ronson a few months later, which was to take place after a concert. Except the concert fell apart musically and they cancelled the interview. I got another chance in 1988 in Portland, Ore, but the questions were labored and the answers mundane. Hunter babbled on while Ronson lay on the couch. The conversation was so dismal that I didn't even transcribe the tape. In Sept. 2012 I again attempted a Hunter interview, but it was plagued by a poor phone connection that made it impossible for him to hear my questions. I salvaged this version and included it here as an example as to how success can be elusive in spite of your best efforts.

Todd Rundgren used to live in Woodstock. Moved to Sausalito first and then Hawaii. Tours regularly, often recreating his classic albums in complete shows. Most recent album: 2011's *Todd Rundgren's Johnson*.

While any decision has many antecedents, Rundgren was the catalyst for my career. Before I had claimed a major in life I met Rundgren on the street twice and struck up a conversation. He seemed annoyed and anxious to move on. I then wondered how I could carry on a conversation with him, and other musicians I met on the street, where he'd actually want to participate. I hit on the idea of becoming a journalist, where an interview would be something they would sit still for. It didn't occur to me to just leave them alone.

Rundgren represents many firsts for me. A review of his concert was the first piece I wrote for my college paper because I wanted to prove that I was as good as any other rock journalist. I was of course wrong, And he was the first prominent musician that I built a relationship with, interviewing him multiple times over a period of years.

I first interviewed him in 1985, in Woodstock's Bear Cafe. He perked up when I told him that I worked for PC Magazine, and said that he wished he could get his hands on some of the new PC graphics programs. A week later he was in the magazine's office, and we had recruited him to participate in a graphics project. The magazine would supply him with the necessary hardware and software to create. And all he had to do was create.

At that point someone told me that Rundgren had the habit of using people for what they could do for him and moving on when they couldn't offer anything else. In a cycle that undoubtedly occurred before and since, I didn't care because it meant that I got to hang out with him.

The project never came to fruition. He lugged a PC supplied by the magazine on the *Acapella* tour, but as far as I know never even opened the case. The roadies must have been thrilled.

I moved to San Francisco in late 1985; he moved there six months later. I went to a few parties at his house, but the meaningful part came with my use of him as a frequent news source. Art and technology was cross-pollinating, and he was in the middle of the convergence.

I saw him live several times, most interestingly at a Sunnyvale, Calif. show where he played solo aided only by a PC loaded with Roger Powell's *Texture*. That show was memorable because his six-year-old son Randy, now a professional baseball player, was sleeping onstage.

In the late 1990s, one of his people called me to ask if I'd write a piece about interfaces for *Windows* magazine that would go out under his name and in his voice. How much does it pay? I asked. Nothing, I was told. I remembered the wisdom from years before, that he used people to do things for him and expected them to agree because it was cool to hang out with him. I didn't do anything to break that chain.

Tom Rush continues to tour, playing small clubs and high schools. Most recent album: 2009's *What I Know.*

Tom Rush was the first person I ever interviewed. Most budding journalists start with the mailman or a guy down the street who does something interesting; I went straight to what I thought was the top at the time.

I called up Rush at a radio station and asked if I could interview him for my college paper. He told me to come down to the club the next night between shows. I arrived, we talked, I left. I didn't ask for a ticket to the show and he didn't offer to put me on the guest list.

I interviewed Rush twice more. In 1983 he had re-emerged with a live album on his own label, beginning the now-popular trend of artists taking control of their own marketing and distribution. Rush needed to do this because he couldn't get a record deal.

The last time was in 2009 in a high school auditorium in Kent, Wash., when he again had a new album to promote. I was a huge Tom Rush fan during the 1960s and 1970s, seeing him perform about six times during that era. It tapered off, with two shows in the '80s and nothing until 2009. He made some very powerful music in the early days but he didn't sustain my interest or enthusiasm. The concert highlights in 2009 were the same as in 1971 and the interpretations weren't any better. I guess the good news is they weren't any worse.

These interviews, also, weren't particularly enlightening. He was polite, co-operative and helpful but seemed to lack warmth. He was submitting to an interview because it was required, a payback to the fans that had paid his way for the last forty years.

I skipped the 1983 Rush interview for this volume because it seemed like overkill, especially considering that he's one of those artists who have lost luster since the time we first heard him. But the two pieces provided here, at the beginning and the end, provide a historical arc representing both the state of the music business and my own writing. An unskilled beginning, full of hope and an ending; a comfortable settling into maturity and a sense of reflection.

And after all, "Urge for Going" still sounds great.

Starland Vocal Band is now a musical footnote. After winning the Best New Artist Grammy in 1977 the lite-rock band never met its potential. The band, which was made up of two married couples, broke up in 1981. The couples both split shortly after.

I arrived at my first-ever journalism job for the *Pampa Daily News* on the Texas Panhandle on September 19, 1977. While the editor was determining what I should do on my first day I mentioned that the Grammy-winning Starland were playing the fair that weekend and I joked that I could always drive to Amarillo for an interview because I already knew them peripherally (singer Margot Chapman had played at a friend's wedding with her previous band, Breakfast Again).

Starland and I were both young and full of promise, except things didn't look good for either of us on that particular day. They were playing in a half-empty rodeo arena with terrible acoustics, and I was beginning a job that I knew I would hate before too long. I was involuntarily relocated; after two weeks the editor said that I wasn't going to work out and let me go. Luckily enough, I found a more hospitable home in Northern New Mexico.

I had forgotten about meeting Starland until I found the clip in 2012. I recalled that it was a dull interview of uninterested subjects by a green reporter. Reading it over today it doesn't suck that much, especially when you consider how I was able to pound it out in a few hours with a minimum of fuss for that day's paper.

Richard Thompson continues to solidify his reputation as the best unknown guitarist in the world, even as he becomes better known. Most recent new album, 2012's *Dream Attic*.

It may now seem like I'm stuck in the past and not open to new bands, but there was a time where I welcomed the discovery of new music. There was a catch. The 1960s was such a fertile source of music that it was hard to take it in when it happened, especially at my young age and allowance-based income bracket. Time was spent excavating the recent past. I wasn't a Beach Boys fan until 1971 and caught onto the Kinks a year later.

I didn't know much about Richard Thompson in 1982 when I went to see him perform on a school night with his soon-to-be-ex-wife Linda. They were astounding, even though they had broken up as a couple and the anger was visible onstage. I've seen Thompson quite a few times since then. He is a masterful guitarist and a terrific songwriter and his shows are always surprising. But nothing matched the first time.

Three years later the Thompsons released simultaneous albums and I interviewed both. I met Richard in Polygram's New York office where he was participating in the interview mill. He was polite and helpful, but I perceived a lack of enthusiasm. You'd be unenthusiastic too, if you had to spend the day talking to journalists in half-hour increments.

I interviewed Thompson again in 2012, this time over the phone and about a single topic. Things had changed since the last time when I tried to cram as much as possible into a half-hour interview and a 1,200-word piece. This time I was more relaxed and relied on the modern media's shortcut, the Q&A.

I used to hate Q&A interviews; I thought they were lazy. They take control out of the hands of the writer because you can only use authentic dialogue, in context. Two things have changed my mind: my increased skill and comfort as an interviewer and the corresponding decrease in reader attention span. So I have decided it's better to do one thing well than to attempt to cover every base.

The Tubes still tour small clubs and casinos, with many of the same members and a lot of the same songs. Fee Waybill still does his "Quay Lewd" bit, although now he's making fun of something that most people in the audience haven't ever heard or heard about.

The piece included here doesn't contain any actual interview material, the band quotes originate from a press conference that invited college journalists. It was during Bruce Springsteen's upward trajectory, and a few weeks after he was featured on simultaneous Time and Newsweek covers. I was suffering a bit of a backlash, I wasn't nuts about Springsteen at the time and all the hype made me less so. I took the opportunity to create a scenario in the story, where one person claims that Springsteen was a fake and the Tubes were the real thing.

This was of course a weak argument. The Tubes were fun, but I had no doubt they would be another in a long line of bands that I favored that were ignored by the rest of the world. I liked it that way, because I had them to myself. It gave me the opportunity to feel superior and I didn't have to fight the entire civilized world for concert tickets.

Thirty seven years on Springsteen is a national monument although he has done so without my help. I recognize his talent and staying power, I just don't like him all that much. This could change if I saw him perform, but that's not likely to happen. There is the aforementioned ticket competition problem, and large crowds are hard to take. Especially a Springsteen crowd, which for me would resemble a revival meeting at a church where I am not a member.

It's easier to see the Tubes, and I took that opportunity in 2011 to catch one of their shows. It was on a whim, we found out about the performance in a small Seattle club that afternoon, calling the box office with some apprehension. Are there tickets available? Of course, we were told. And they were weren't prohibitively expensive.

The members of music's greatest generation fall into three categories. Many are inactive due to the inevitables of aging; retirement or death. Those in the latter group are rapidly increasing, each year we lose a few more great ones. Others are still performing actively, still with relevance. Springsteen, Neil Young, Bob Dylan, Richard Thompson, Paul Simon and others still have much to say. There are fewer of these as time goes on.

My sweet spot is occupied by performers like The Tubes, Eric Burdon, and Arlo Guthrie. Your list may differ. The best of these still believe in the music and pump passion into their performance. And the really good news is that you can often see them up close, and talk to them later.

PHILADELPHIA, Feb. 19, 1973. I snuck my camera in to a concert by David Bowie and the Spiders where I had a front row seat and got a few decent shots until Bowie took a costume change. His return coincided with a tough guy arriving telling me to stop or they'd take my camera away.

SEATTLE, WA, Nov. 5, 2005—Paul McCartney took time out during his tour for an author appearance at a bookstore, where he read portions of his children's book to a bunch of kids who really weren't sure who he was, then signing autographs for some of the miles of fans who had turned up to get a closer look at the former Beatle than they would in any concert hall.

COPY EDITING: Laura Bell, Jim Thomsen

We all have our stories. I hope you have enjoyed mine, maybe one day you can tell me yours. I'd like to hear from my readers, if you get a chance please write me at aserioushobby@gmail.com and tell me who you are. I'll answer any mail with a free PDF of "Imagine There's No Beatles," a short story that was included in beta versions of this project but was removed when I decided to stick to the facts.

Charlie Bermant

Made in the USA
Columbia, SC
28 July 2017